D1069271

Distance Learning in Higher Education

Distance Learning in Higher Education

A PROGRAMMATIC APPROACH
TO PLANNING, DESIGN, INSTRUCTION,
EVALUATION, AND ACCREDITATION

Alfred P. Rovai
Michael K. Ponton
Jason D. Baker

TEACHERS
COLLEGE
PRESS

Teachers College
Columbia University
New York and London

Published by Teachers College Press, 1234 Amsterdam Avenue, New York, NY 10027

Library of Congress Cataloging-in-Publication Data

Rovai, Alfred P.
    Distance learning in higher education : a programmatic approach to planning, design, instruction, evaluation, and accreditation / Alfred P. Rovai, Michael K. Ponton, Jason D. Baker.
        p. cm.
    Includes bibliographical references and index.
    ISBN 978-0-8077-4878-7 (hardcover : alk. paper)
    1. Distance education—United States.   2. Education, Higher—Computer-assisted instruction—United States.   I. Ponton, Michael K.   II. Baker, Jason D.   III. Title.
    LC5805.R68 2008
    378.1'758—dc22

                                                                    2008007766

ISBN: 978-0-8077-4878-7 (hardcover)

Printed on acid-free paper
Manufactured in the United States of America

15 14 13 12 11 10 09 08   8 7 6 5 4 3 2 1

Contents

Preface

> John Dewey worked to restore education to its primitive, pre-print phase. He wanted to get the student out of the passive role of consumer of uniformly packaged learning. In fact, Dewey in reacting against passive print culture was surf-boarding along on the new electronic wave. (McLuhan, 1962, p. 144)

As Marshall McLuhan suggests, over the ages the introduction of new media has transformed culture and society, from the introduction of handwriting, through the invention of the printing press, to the widespread availability of home computers and the Internet. Technology and the connective power of the Internet have made distance education a growth industry that enables schools to reach wider, more diverse audiences and change the very nature of teaching and learning.

Web-based or online learning is expected to be the fastest-growing method for delivering education and training. Arguably the biggest benefit of this type of learning is that it eliminates the expense and inconvenience of getting the instructor and students in the same place. Moreover, asynchronous online programs provide the added convenience of not having to meet at specified times. Thus, the "anywhere, anytime" nature of many distance education programs is a big draw for individuals who have family and work responsibilities that can interfere with participation in traditional, on-campus programs or who live in isolated communities.

The focus of this book is on postsecondary distance education using online technologies. The principles and strategies discussed herein apply to corporate online learning as well as to formal college and university programs. The term *online learning* is used synonymously with *Web-based learning* and *Internet-based learning*. The term does not suggest that the entire learning experience must be online. Blended or hybrid programs that utilize a mix of traditional and new media, such as the Internet, to distribute learning modes are becoming increasingly popular. Thus, the amount of teaching and learning using online technologies can vary within any program and course.

The content of books on distance education can be described as falling somewhere along a continuum anchored at one end by a strong research orientation with little, if any, practical advice. At the other end, the continuum is anchored by a strong practical orientation with few links to the theoretical and research-based underpinnings of the teaching and learning strategies presented. Moreover, research-oriented books are often difficult for practitioners to understand and apply, while practitioner-oriented books may be inconsequential. Without a theoretical basis, the practical advice lacks a conceptual framework for planning and implementing an effective teaching and learning strategy.

The purpose of this book is to focus on the middle space between these two extremes by balancing theory and research with practical advice so that readers are well prepared for the excitement and the opportunities of designing and implementing distance education programs and courses in an adult learning environment. Various aspects of distance education, together with a discussion of challenges and solutions, are presented.

This book is based on the following research-based suppositions:

- How technology is used is more important than which technology is used.
- Learning environments should make appropriate use of a variety of media and communication tools.
- Effective program design is more than a collection of individual course designs.
- Effective learning strategies include problem-based as well as knowledge-based approaches.
- Student support services are especially important for distance education programs.
- All individuals do not learn in the same way.
- Adults are not monolithic regarding their personal characteristics and preferences, although they do share many learning characteristics.
- Cooperation and collaboration are important elements of distance learning.
- The cross-cultural implications of educational activities that cross national or cultural boundaries must be integrated in the planning, designing, and teaching of distance education programs.
- Learners are more interested in communicating and learning with each other than with databases.
- Communities of inquiry require careful nurturing.
- There are important differences in effective teaching principles between face-to-face and online courses.

PURPOSE AND ORGANIZATION

Although there are many volumes written on distance education, this book takes a fresh look at recent distance education research and goes beyond examining course design and online instruction by addressing programmatic issues. It is divided into 11 chapters that:

- Lay a theoretical and research foundation for distance education
- Identify gender and cross-cultural challenges to distance learning and strategies that respond to these challenges

- Describe the strategic planning process relevant to distance education programs
- Translate theory and research into practice by describing how to design and implement online programs and courses
- Describe cooperative and collaborative group activities that are suitable for synchronous and/or asynchronous learning environments
- Explain how to facilitate and moderate interactions effectively using a constructivist epistemology within an adult education context
- Present a model for evaluation of distance education programs
- Discuss institution and distance education program accreditation issues by providing evidence of quality and identifying red flags
- Examine course evaluation in terms of strategies that promote valid and reliable evaluations.

Various chapters also include resources such as course designs, online course materials, grading rubrics, and assessment tasks that are culturally responsive and implement the strategies promoted in this book. Accordingly, the book can be used as a core text or as a supplemental volume for postsecondary courses as well as professional development certificate programs in distance education. It can also serve as a useful reference text for distance education instructors, program and course designers, instructional designers, educational administrators, researchers, strategic planners, and program evaluators.

ACKNOWLEDGMENTS

And certainly there were many others . . . from whom I had assimilated a word, a glance, but of whom as individual beings I remembered nothing; a book is a great cemetery in which, for the most part, the names upon the tombs are effaced. (Proust, 1927/1960, p. 256)

Preparation of this book was a labor of love aided by the collected wisdom of the many educational researchers and practitioners whose words or writings influenced us. We extend our gratitude to the many individuals who provided suggestions and comments regarding this book or who influenced us in our professional readings. In particular, we extend thanks to the professional staff at Teachers College Press and their reviewers for their encouragement, constructive feedback, and support.

CHAPTER 1

Concepts of Distance Learning

Distance learning is any type of learning in which the components of a structured learning activity (i.e., learners, instructor, and learning resources) are separated by time and/or geography. The National Center for Educational Statistics (2006) reports 32% of U.S. adults who participated in educational activities during 2004–2005 used distance education. The varied forms of distance education include "video tapes, CDs, DVDs, television, radio, the Internet, computer or video conferencing, mail, telephone or voicemail, or other types of remote instruction technology" (Table note, ¶ 1). Thus, the electronic tools used for distance learning are numerous, and participation is pervasive among adults. Additionally, distance learning is frequently used to promote *open learning*, a term that implies a greater openness for learning that is frequently missing from traditional education programs. Open learning reduces constraints and removes barriers for learners by promoting qualities such as greater learner autonomy, independence, and flexibility.

The purpose of this chapter is to introduce salient theories that are foundational to many of the concepts, perspectives, and guidelines presented throughout this book. The theories presented provide a teaching and learning philosophy that helps the reader understand the aims of distance learning, thereby informing instructional design via the intelligent determination of appropriate tools. Subsequent chapters draw on these theories and provide more specialized theories and concepts as appropriate.

BACKGROUND

The role of the Internet in adult learning is growing as the result of advances in throughput (i.e., data transfer speed), Web authoring tools, search engines, and the widespread availability of home computers and Internet access. According to Pew Internet and American Life Project (2006a, p. 3), 73% of all American adults (about 147 million), up from 66% in 2005, use the Internet for reasons that include improving their ability to perform their jobs, gathering health-care information, and pursuing hobbies and interests.

During the fall 2005 semester, approximately 3.2 million college students took at least one online course, an increase from 2.3 million one year earlier (Allen & Seaman, 2006). With the advent of numerous Internet-based learning management systems, distance education delivered mostly asynchronously via the Internet is the most popular distance learning mode used in higher education today.

Stansfield, McLellan, and Connolly (2004) maintain that online learning provides:

- Increased opportunities for reflecting on and refining ideas
- A greater degree of learner control over instructional materials
- Flexibility permitted by unrestricted access to course materials
- Richer levels of interaction, both in relation to the materials and in the opportunities presented for active learning by means of conferencing and collaborative learning activities.

The ideal online learning environment, as depicted in Figure 1.1, is interactive and places the learner at the center of many remote resources by way of both asynchronous and synchronous communication tools. It provides learners with sufficient resources to take charge of their own learning. Included is the learning management system itself, such as Blackboard or WebCT, which provides many of the teaching and learning tools and instructional content required by the learner. To be successful, distant learners must also have remote access to library services, such as online reference services, document delivery, and so forth, and to student support services, such as registration, advising, counseling, tutoring, bookstore services, technical help, and so on. Consistent with social learning theories and the constructivist philosophy of learning, distance students must be able to interact with their professors, tutors, mentors, teaching assistants, and administrative staff, as well as with other students.

FIGURE 1.1. Online Learning Environment

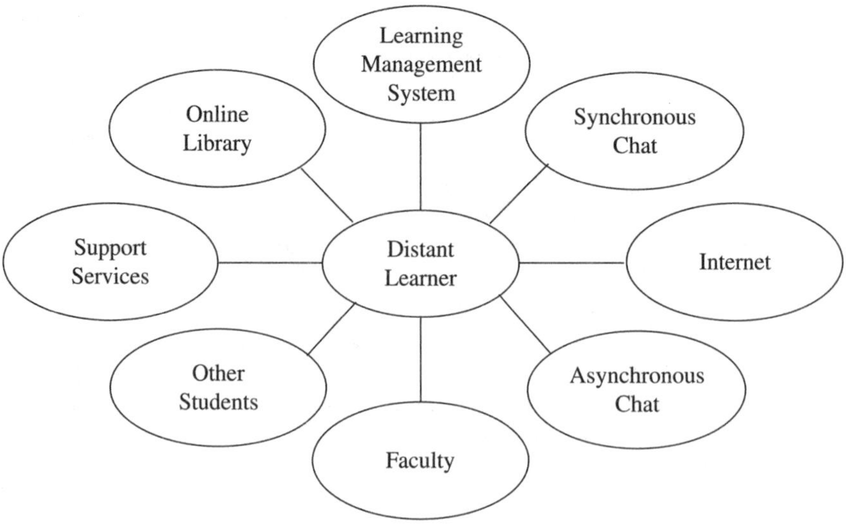

Successful distance education programs provide ample opportunities for dynamic exchange that add meaning and value to course content. Although much of this interaction takes place within the learning management system by means of discussion forums, complementary forms of communication are also desirable, such as e-mail and synchronous chats using the telephone, instant messaging (IM), and even face-to-face discussions. Naturally, to allow the system to work efficiently, learners require convenient access to fast and reliable Internet service.

As noted above, there are numerous modes of distance learning; however, the focus of this book is the planning, design, delivery, and evaluation of online programs and courses for adult learners *that optimize learning*. While many instructional design considerations are common between online and face-to-face teaching, many of the tools used are decidedly different.

Use of Internet-based tools alone does not expand students' knowledge. Dede (1996) maintains that students need to see the connections between what they are learning, the rest of their lives, and the mental models that they already use. He therefore suggests that the role of the distance education teacher is to structure learning experiences that move students from their assimilation of facts to generation of mental models that depict new ways of thinking about key issues and relationships. Designers of online instruction must therefore understand related philosophies and theories of learning and the characteristics of adult learners to guide them in the creation of environments that use technologies to facilitate learning.

THEORETICAL FOUNDATIONS

Volumes have been written with regard to each of the topics in this section. Therefore, the purpose is not to provide an exhaustive review, but rather to highlight important considerations that will inform the chapters to follow. Although cursory connections may be made to online learning in some instances, substantive implications of greater complexity should be expected in later chapters. However, common threads of perspective will be apparent, thereby facilitating the formulation of a philosophical foundation for online learning with concomitant implications for instructional systems design.

Constructivism

Early distance education courses, such as correspondence courses, were based on an instructivist approach to teaching. Using this approach, teachers deliver content to mostly passive students. Limited opportunities for student-initiated questions, independent thought, or interpersonal interaction occur in this environment. However, during the past few decades, there has been a shift away from this approach toward one that is learner-centered and collaborative, and that uses a constructivist philosophy.

Constructivism recognizes that students are at different levels of understanding and have different life experiences. The individuality of perspective, due to unique life experiences, creates subjective sense-making of sensory inputs. Thus, the basic premise of constructivism is that each individual *constructs* his or her own meanings. However, within this broad perspective, constructivism comes in several varieties, including cognitive constructivism, social constructivism, and radical constructivism.

Cognitive constructivism, based largely on the work of Jean Piaget, holds that knowledge is the result of the processes of accommodation and assimilation as the learner constructs knowledge that accurately corresponds to reality as it exists in the real world. The focus is on internal sense-making.

Social constructivism is the philosophy used in this book. It is closely associated with the work of both Jean Piaget and Lev Vygotsky, and assumes that both individual sense-making and social processes are central and essential to the learning process. Thus, learning is a shared, rather than an individual, experience. Like cognitive constructivism, it assumes that objective reality is knowable to the individual.

Radical constructivism is based on the view that knowledge is constructed from individual experience and is not an accurate representation of external reality. Both cognitive constructivism and radical constructivism fail to account adequately for the language and the social dimensions of learning; radical constructivism also does not recognize the existence of objective truth. Without objective truth, radical constructivists criticize assessment of student learning based on the teacher's view of truth.

Constructivism influences our conceptualization of learning. Experience is not the mere description of our lived events but rather the cognitive interpretations and affective reactions to them. Analogously, teachers can create events that objectively exist (i.e., truly occur) and may be labeled by an observer as "good teaching" without any control over what, if anything, is actually learned.

However, concepts of learning do inform instruction. As Resnick and Klopfer (1989) contend, for many years, "theories of classroom management, textbook design, and organization of [educational] practice all flowed from . . . [the] assumption" that learning is "an accumulation of pieces of knowledge and bits of skill" (p. 2). In contrast, modern notions of constructivism assert that learners are thinkers who build knowledge upon a foundation of experience and are not mere repositories of information (Resnick & Klopfer, 1989).

The social constructivist philosophy suggests that instructors create educational events that catalyze active learning, thereby integrating course content into students' extant knowledge. Instructional techniques that can support this outcome include:

- Cognitive scaffolding: Instructors assist students by providing suggestions, comments, and feedback to help bridge the gap between present student abilities and mastery of instructional objectives.

- Fading: Instructors gradually remove learning supports as the students gain mastery.
- Cognitive apprenticeship: Students learn by engaging in authentic activities with experts in the field.
- Collaborative learning: Students construct knowledge by interacting with others in learning groups.

Adult Teaching and Learning

Knowles created a model of adult teaching, which he called andragogy, based on six assumptions that differentiate the teaching of adults from the teaching of children: need to know, self-concept, experience, readiness, orientation to learn, and motivation (Knowles, Holton, & Swanson, 2005). Although the term *adult* can be used to categorize a person of a given age, legal, or social status, Knowles, Holton, and Swanson (2005) emphasize the importance of the "psychological definition" (p. 64) of an adult as an individual who has reached a realization of personal responsibility for his/her life that is manifest in self-directedness.

Adults need to know the potential benefits associated with accomplishing instructional outcomes. To increase learner engagement, instructors should explain the benefits of learning specific content and accurately assess the discrepancy between current and desired future states, thereby guiding appropriate instructional design. It is very difficult for an adult learner to get the most out of instruction if the reason for participating is unclear or if the instruction seems mismatched to deficiencies in knowledge or skills.

Knowles, Holton, and Swanson (2005) suggest that adults have a self-concept of personal responsibility for their individual agency to direct their life trajectories. This self-characterization results in "a deep psychological need to be seen by others and treated by others as being capable of self-direction" (p. 65). Thus, awareness that the instructor sees and treats adult learners as self-directed must be apparent to the learners themselves via communicative patterns in concert with offering opportunities to exercise influence over instructional outcomes, tasks, and methods of assessment.

Adults bring a wide range of experiences to the learning environment that, consistent with constructivism, affects how new information is interpreted and integrated into expanding knowledge structures. When the diversity of experiences is infused into the learning event itself, the environment becomes richer as the learners become learning resources to others. "Hence, the emphasis in adult education is on experiential techniques—techniques that tap into the experience of the learners, such as group discussion, simulation exercises, problem-solving activities, case method, and laboratory methods instead of transmittal techniques" (Knowles, Holton, & Swanson, 2005, p. 66). In addition, an adult's self-concept is strongly related to his or her experiences. Therefore, an instructor should avoid devaluing these experiences, as this might be interpreted as a devaluation of the learner as a person (Knowles, Holton, & Swanson, 2005).

Personal development is catalyzed by incremental change processes due to lived experiences, while the readiness of someone to grasp new knowledge and skills of increasing complexity is dependent upon the extent of this personal change. "The critical implication of this assumption is the importance of timing learning experiences to coincide with those developmental tasks" (Knowles, Holton, & Swanson, 2005, p. 67). Thus, learning events must be appropriate for the developmental stage of the learners. Readiness, though, can be induced through instructional interventions that bridge gaps to requisite knowledge and skills that are essential for further learning. A good example would be nontraditional adults who may lack the computer skills required for online learning—their technical readiness must be developed so that engagement in the targeted instruction can proceed in an optimal manner. Facilitating readiness helps to build efficacy, reduce stress, and increase the likelihood of persistence.

Knowles, Holton, and Swanson (2005) suggest that adults have a "life-centered . . . orientation to their learning" (p. 67) rather than the subject-centered orientation that is more typical of school children. This assertion assumes that adults are motivated to learn subject matter that is relevant to the context of their lives. Adult educators should integrate learning tasks, objectives, and subject matter into the domain of adult living. As an example, teaching literacy to adults is facilitated by incorporating the language, culture, and requirements associated with successful societal functioning rather than by teaching grammar and vocabulary disconnected from the adult experience.

"While adults are responsive to some external motivators (better jobs, promotions, higher salaries, and the like), the most potent motivators are internal pressures (the desire for increased job satisfaction, self-esteem, quality of life, and the like)" (Knowles, Holton, & Swanson, 2005, p. 68). This perspective suggests that adults are primarily intrinsically motivated to learn/develop even when extrinsic incentives are present. To maximize motivation, the adult educator should relate expected learning outcomes to the learners' personal forms of self-satisfaction rather than solely emphasizing socially constructed reward systems for learning achievement.

Computer-Mediated Communication

Computer-mediated communication (CMC) in learning refers to the many ways in which computers are used to mediate the transfer of information between individuals. CMC can be either asynchronous, e.g., discussion boards, or synchronous, e.g., real-time audio and video. Paulsen (1995) created a framework of four pedagogical CMC techniques:

- One-alone techniques characterize an individual who accesses information (e.g., an online database or journal) for personal study.
- One-to-one techniques refer to learning transactions that are limited to two

people, such as that which occurs when an instructor and student e-mail back and forth for the purpose of sharing information.

- One-to-many techniques are those that have one-way communication from instructor to students, analogous to a lecture, such as when an instructor posts or distributes information for students to read (e.g., attaching a file to a learning Web site or an e-mail sent to multiple recipients).
- Many-to-many techniques refer to communication that occurs between multiple persons (i.e., instructor and students), such as in an online asynchronous discussion board.

Paulsen's (1995) framework provides a repertoire of techniques for the instructor to use for learning modes appropriate to accomplish various educational objectives. Hutchings (2002, pp. 90–91) asserts that each of Paulsen's paradigms supports a unique learning mode. The one-alone paradigm supports independent learning, the one-to-one paradigm supports personalized learning, the one-to-many paradigm supports information transmission learning, and the many-to-many paradigm supports collaborative learning.

Focusing solely on any particular paradigm may neglect important learning objectives. For example, although collaborative activities are important, using only collaborative activities in the instructional design may inhibit fostering learner independence.

Physical presence in a face-to-face environment affords interacting individuals the opportunity to monitor external cues that can moderate communication in a manner that fosters cooperation and politeness. Such cues include environmental indicants of status, body language, and voice quality. Unfortunately, with a reduction of such cues in the online environment, the reduction of social control, coupled with few immediate consequences to inappropriate social interaction, can create opportunities for negative behavior, broadly described as *disinhibition*, which one can define as behavior characterized by a reduction in concerns for self-presentation and critical judgment of others (Joinson, 2006).

Suler (2004) writes of the *online disinhibition effect* that describes how people who communicate online may "say and do things in cyberspace that they wouldn't ordinarily say and do in the face-to-face world" (p. 321). He asserts that this effect can be either benign (e.g., personal disclosures, acts of kindness) or toxic (e.g., the use of abusive or rude language, excessive aggressiveness). Anonymity, a major factor in online disinhibition, is not typically present in course-related CMC (an exception may be end-of-course student evaluations of teaching). According to Suler (2004):

- Invisibility precludes an awareness of disapproving nonverbal somatic cues.
- Asynchronicity prevents immediate reactions to one's postings.
- Solipsistic introjections infuse the characteristics of oneself into the personas of others.

- Dissociating the online world with the real world reduces beliefs of responsibility for behaving appropriately as the cyberworld.
- Minimizing status due to the lack of environmental cues that may define authority can impede healthy, positive social interactions.

One important way in which to minimize online disinhibition and to promote social norms is to nurture a strong sense of community in the online classroom.

Sense of Community

Kreijns, Kirschner, and Jochems (2002) maintain that one cannot assume that desirable social interaction will occur naturally by the instructional design. Online instructors must also attend to sociopsychological objectives that are separate from instructional ones. One such objective is building sense of community in a collaborative learning environment. Wegerif (1998) writes, "forming a sense of community, where people feel they will be treated sympathetically by their fellows, seems to be a necessary first step for collaborative learning" (p. 48).

McMillan and Chavis (1986) describe a sense of community as "a feeling that members have of belonging, a feeling that members matter to one another and to the group, and a shared faith that members' needs will be met through their commitment to be together" (p. 9). Royal and Rossi (1997) argue that common goals and values are also essential elements of community, and Strike (2004) theorizes that normation (i.e., the willingness of students to internalize group-shared expectations) is an important aspect of a learning community. According to Strike (2004):

> Community begins in learning the norms of those who care for and about us, and ends in caring for and about those whose norms we share. . . . [P]eople begin to internalize the norms of communities because someone cares about them enough to share something they value. Normation begins with caring and belonging, not reasoning and not nature. (pp. 221–222)

Social interaction is the primary mode of fostering a sense of community. Students in a classroom setting should have feelings of belonging, trust, safety, participation, and support. More specifically, students should feel that they matter to the other members of their educational group, that they have responsibilities to the group, and that each member's educational needs will be met via a commitment to shared educational goals.

A strong sense of community builds social capital, that is, it increases resources that are available through an individual's social networks to construct new knowledge and understanding. Research (e.g., Rovai & Ponton, 2005) supports the notion "that sense of community and student learning are highly related constructs in ALN [asynchronous learning network] environments" (p. 85). Moreover, major studies on e-learning in higher education provide substantial evidence that active participation positively influences student satisfaction (Alavi & Dufner, 2005) and retention rates (Rovai, 2002).

Thus, a responsibility incumbent upon the online instructor is to create a learning environment that fosters a sense of community via positive social interactions. This goal is supported when the instructor:

- Promotes interaction
- Communicates respect for diverse perspectives and backgrounds
- Monitors interaction and intervenes with nonparticipants in a manner that respectfully addresses psychosocial or structural impediments
- Encourages students to create their own mechanisms of interaction (e.g., online study groups or e-mail)
- Provides timely feedback and maintains teacher presence in the virtual classroom.

Presence

Proximity refers to the physical closeness between participants in an endeavor (Nova, 2003). In a physical environment, proximity facilitates the initiation and frequency of conversations, increases the probability of chance or nonverbally cued encounters that lead to meaningful dialogue, and helps maintain group awareness (Nova, 2003). There are, however, downsides to physical proximity:

> [a] interaction must be synchronous and it privileges people who are nearby . . . [b] the opportunistic and spontaneous communication that is supported is not always welcomed by the participants because of task interruption or loss of privacy . . . [and, c] the face-to-face interaction is costly from a cognitive point of view for both speaker and listener [because] they have to monitor what is being said as well as the feedback which is given. (Nova, 2003, p. 10)

Copresence is related to the concept of proximity. Applicable to either a physical or virtual environment, Nova (2003) defines *presence* as a perception of "being there" (p. 30), while *copresence* refers to a sense of "being together" (p. 29). Nova asserts that copresence "is the cornerstone of collaboration" (p. 11). In a virtual environment, copresence is created solely by social interaction where high-level interaction (i.e., interaction that is timely, frequent, and substantive) fosters a virtual analog to close face-to-face proximity.

Garrison, Cleveland-Innes, and Fung (2004) describe a "Community of Inquiry" (p. 63) model that highlights three important presences necessary for a meaningful online educational experience: social, cognitive, and teacher. Garrison, Cleveland-Innes, and Fung posit that social presence refers to the copresence of students and teacher to create a climate that supports productive CMC to accomplish shared educational objectives (cf. "being together," as per Nova, 2003). They assert that *cognitive presence* refers to an individual student's constructivist learning via CMC and, hence, level of engagement within the course (cf. "being there," as per Nova). Finally, they hypothesize that *teacher presence* refers to the instructor's role in creating an instructional design that promotes social interaction and a concomitant sense of community, thereby catalyzing individual cognitive activity and achievement.

Because an asynchronous learning environment does not support these various presences by scheduled, physical proximity but rather by online interaction, both the student and the instructor require greater degrees of self-directedness. Garrison (2003) asserts that online learners must take more responsibility for regulating the activity, progress, and adequacy of their learning by assuming greater control of monitoring and managing the cognitive and contextual aspects of their learning. In addition, instructors must exert a greater degree of self-directedness in providing timely feedback. Blignaut and Trollip (2003) conclude that "even when instructors are well organized, give helpful, content-related feedback, and challenge learners to stretch intellectually, if they are slow in doing so, learner satisfaction goes down quickly" (p. 166). Garrison also asserts that instructors must incorporate in their instruction opportunities and encouragement for students to assume greater control over their learning so that self-directedness is not just expected but fostered.

Self-directed and Autonomous Learning

The importance of self-directed learning rests in its far-reaching effects on our society of learners. Over 25 years ago, Tough (1982) estimated that approximately 80% of adult learners initiate self-directed learning activities that cover a spectrum from work-related to recreational needs. Today, the Internet provides growing opportunities for numerous forms of online adult learning.

According to Oddi (1987) and Merriam and Caffarella (1999), self-directed learning can be dichotomized into two broad categories: a process perspective and a personality characteristic perspective. These authors assert that the process perspective is the dominant viewpoint that has been adopted by researchers within the field. This perspective generally focuses on the activities in which the learner engages, such as goal-setting, planning a learning strategy, acquiring resources, and monitoring progress (Knowles, 1988; Oddi, 1987). These activities parallel what Zimmerman, Bonner, and Kovach (1996) refer to as "self-regulation," which is the self-generation of activities, both cognitive and behavioral, that a person uses to accomplish his or her educational goals. However, these activities are predicated on the psychological situation of the learner. As Knowles (1988) writes:

> Learning is described psychologically as a process of need-meeting and goal-striving by the learners. This is to say that individuals are motivated to engage in learning to the extent that they feel a need to learn and perceive a personal goal that learning

will help to achieve; and they will invest their energy in making use of available resources (including teachers and readings) to the extent that they perceive them as being relevant to their needs and goals. (p. 56)

These ideas are congruent with Long (1989), who asserts that self-directed learning can be conceptualized along a sociological dimension (addressing learner isolation), a pedagogical dimension (addressing the learner's activities), or a psychological dimension (addressing the learner's mental state). The process description of self-directed learning encompasses both the sociological and pedagogical dimensions. However, Long (1998) asserts that only "the *psychological conceptualization* is both necessary and sufficient to explain SDL [self-directed learning]" (p. 10). He explains:

The psychological conceptualization implies that fundamentally learning is a self-initiated, self-directed, and self-regulated cognitive process whereby the learner can choose to ignore instruction, to merely absorb it by casual attention, to carefully memorize without critical reflection, or to seek to change or create an understanding of information. (p. 9)

One aspect of the psychological dimension consists of the learner identifying needs that serve as motivational inducements to formulate learning goals. Another aspect of this dimension is the learner's personality characteristics.

Imagine two students working diligently on a Friday night. They appear to be involved in a similar self-directed learning activity: searching the Internet for material, reading articles and e-books, taking notes, evaluating their information, and seeking additional information. However, there is an important difference between them. The first student is studying due to several weeks of procrastination and now has an assignment due on Monday. The second student is studying because an interest was generated about a topic casually mentioned during an online discussion. This difference can be explained by the concept of *learner autonomy*.

The concept of autonomy (Knowles, 1988; Merriam & Caffarella, 1999) exists under the personality characteristic rubric of self-directed learning. Chene (1983) defines *learner autonomy* in terms of independence. Such independence is based upon an individual's personal will to learn something of perceived value that results in the learner's discretion of how best to accomplish the desired level of learning. Thus, learner autonomy can be defined as the characteristic of the person who independently exhibits agency in learning activities where independence is the characteristic of the person who controls his or her own actions, control being "a state of mind, as well as of one's environment" (Sheldon & Elliot, 1998, p. 546).

Now, although both of the students mentioned above exhibit some degree of autonomy (after all, it *is* a Friday night), the major difference between them is not in the process of self-directed learning (i.e., identifying a learning goal, planning a learning strategy, gathering learning resources, and evaluating learning progress).

Rather, the major difference is that these processes represent manifestations related to their personality characteristics as learners (i.e., the second student has independently chosen to learn something of perceived value). These manifestations represent *autonomous learning* (i.e., *learner autonomy* can be viewed as the psychological undergirding that leads to the behaviors associated with the process of *autonomous learning*) that include initiative, resourcefulness, and persistence. Confessore (1991) refers to these factors as conative (i.e., intentional) because the manifestation of each is predicated on an individual's desire to engage in a learning activity. He asserts that individuals who exhibit these conative factors in their learning activities "possess traits which are essential to successful self-direction in learning" (p. 129).

Ponton and Carr (2000) assert that educators must support the building of necessary cognitive processes within students that further the development of their learner autonomy. These processes include helping students value learning as a means to desired outcomes, understand that the accomplishment of suitably chosen learning goals can lead to desired outcomes, and assume responsibility for one's own learning. Based upon these prerequisite processes, instructors should help students to foster cognitive abilities in doing the following:

- Prioritize learning over nonlearning activities
- Self-evaluate current states to future desired states of learning
- Create suitable learning goals and plans
- Monitor whether or not planned learning activities are leading to desired outcomes, and adjust plans accordingly
- Solve the problems that interfere with learning
- Create the opportunity, time, importance, urgency, and means for one's own learning activities

They further suggest that these processes can be reinforced within the student regardless of educational level (i.e., primary or postgraduate) or the instructional environment (i.e., face-to-face or virtual).

Diaz (1999) recognizes the important role that self-directed learning plays in the theory of andragogy, as well as the implication that the adult learner needs to be part of the instructional design process. He suggests the autonomous adult learner who desires self-directed study should respond favorably to online learning environments that require independence of thought and action and an increasing degree of participation in the identification, design, and assessment of learning activities. However, although instructors become partners with their students in designing some aspects of the online course, instructors still have the primary responsibility for learning "how to construct a [distance] learning environment that stimulates student motivation and promotes skills that encourage self-directed and independent learning" (Diaz, ¶ 6).

Social Equity

Almost a century ago, Dewey (1916) wrote the following, emphasizing the important role of education to advance social equity:

> A [democratic] society to which stratification into separate classes would be fatal, must see to it that intellectual opportunities are accessible to all on equable and easy terms. . . . A society which is mobile, which is full of channels for the distribution of a change occurring anywhere, must see to it that its members are educated to personal initiative and adaptability . . . [or the] few will appropriate to themselves the . . . externally directed activities of others. (pp. 87–88)

In this context, *democracy* does not refer to a form of government but rather a process to further egalitarianism and social justice by overcoming socially contrived markers used to stratify groups and impede full participation and benefit in all opportunities that society has to offer. Social justice does not necessarily require equal educational outcomes, but it does require equal opportunities to learn. The "few" that Dewey refers to can refer to groups separated by race, national origin, religious practices, age, ethnicity, disabilities, or gender, where disenfranchisement is overcome when every such group is "educated to personal initiative and adaptability," or, in other words, is provided equitable educational opportunities that promote self-directedness.

Self-directedness enables personal achievement in individually chosen pursuits where self-directedness in learning facilitates the acquisition of requisite knowledge and skills. As Albert Bandura (1997) asserts:

> Development of capabilities for self-directedness [in learning] enables individuals not only to continue their intellectual growth beyond their formal education but to advance the nature and quality of their life pursuits. . . . The rapid pace of technological change and the accelerated growth of knowledge require continual upgrading of competencies if people are to survive and prosper under increasingly competitive conditions. . . . Self-development with age partly determines whether the expanded life span is lived self-fulfillingly or apathetically. These changing realities call for lifelong learners. (p. 227)

When instructional designers incorporate methods that further the development of self-directed learners, and when the institution of education provides learning opportunities that are available to all members of society, students are transformed into lifelong learners who are enabled to reach increasing levels of achievement long after matriculation. Social equity is the result of self-directed learning that permits every individual to choose a life trajectory by developing in personally meaningful ways.

The efficacy of self-directedness to enact personal transformations is affected by the availability of learning resources. When certain socially classified groups

of individuals share common narratives that preclude participation in traditional educational programs, entire populations can be deprived of formal education. However, Lagier (2003) asserts, "institutions are realizing the potential
of the Internet and other forms of distance-learning delivery to reach entirely
new populations" (p. 180). The reduction of temporal and geographical impediments in asynchronous learning environments increases access to learning
opportunities by persons who are unable to subscribe to the scheduling and
location demands of traditional instruction. Distance learning provides not
only an opportunity to learn, but also a greater opportunity for democracy in
education.

While the institution of education must work to systematically ameliorate
limitations to participation in distance education due to the lack of computer technologies or deficiencies in computer-related skills, instructors must also reduce the
effects of psychological and social impediments that may prevent social equity (i.e.,
full participation and full benefit) within the course itself, such as discriminatory
practices based on factors such as race, national origin, religious practices, age,
ethnicity, disabilities, and gender. An example of a psychological impediment is
incongruence between the student's dominant perceptual modality and text-based,
online instruction (as would be the case for an auditory learner), thereby diminishing the perception and processing of written information. Another example is
introversion that prevents interaction.

Educators who place social equity at the forefront of their practice recognize
the importance of context and understand that developing a broad and inclusive
worldview is important to promoting social justice in our society. Teaching for
social justice means providing students with a supportive learning environment
that is just and fair.

ELECTRONIC TOOLS

Online instructional design that draws on the theories described above must utilize computer-based electronic tools to effect communication and collaboration.
Typically, the learning management system, such as Blackboard, will consist of
multiple asynchronous and synchronous tools that are available to the instructor
and learners. Table 1.1 provides a listing of common tools used in online teaching
and learning. They are identified as communication tools or collaboration tools.
The glossary provides descriptions of each.

Strijbos, Martens, and Jochems (2004) suggest that designers of CMC-based
instruction should determine the best usage of computer-related technologies to
facilitate interaction and associated learning. This suggests that available tools
should be chosen based upon the accomplishment of learning objectives rather than
adopted wholesale.

TABLE 1.1. List of Common Electronic Tools

Communication Tools	Conferencing Tools
Blog	Audio conferencing
E-mail	Discussion board
Instant messaging (IM)	Multiuser domain (MUD)
Rich Site Summary (RSS)	Object-oriented multiuser domain (MOO)
	Video teleconferencing (VTC)
	Virtual world
	Virtual whiteboard

CONCLUSION

The Internet provides numerous opportunities for adult learning. Adults can informally pursue information based upon personal or professional interests, exchange information with geographically displaced others, or enroll in formal forms of education that may lead to academic credentials. Approximately 147 million adults use the Internet for reasons that include improving job performance, gathering health-care information, and pursuing information related to hobbies and interests (Pew Internet, 2006a, p. 3). The purpose of this book is to inform distance educators and administrators of the salient issues that affect the planning, design, implementation, and evaluation of successful online learning environments.

Topics discussed in this chapter include self-directedness and autonomy that support social equity, and an understanding of adult learners that includes constructivism, andragogy, sense of community, and factors that influence presence. As this chapter suggests, the design of a distance learning environment able to promote adult learning requires:

- The development of suitable learning objectives
- An understanding of the learners, what they bring to the endeavor, and what they expect from the endeavor
- Knowledge of the tools deemed suitable by the instructional designer to bridge the gap from the learner's entry condition to the exit condition.

The next two chapters add to this discussion by describing, in turn, how and why gender and culture influence learning and behavior in an online classroom environment, and outlining strategies that can be used to level the playing field and promote social and academic equity.

CHAPTER 2

Gender

When considering the development of effective online education, instructors not only should consider the technologies involved but also the appropriate instructional design models to serve an increasingly diverse student population. One significant factor that is often overlooked in the design of online instruction is the effect of the instructors' and students' gender on the virtual learning environment. This is ironic, since distance education programs have been extensively marketed to women since the days of correspondence courses (Kramarae, 2003). The anytime, anyplace convenience of distance and online learning is touted as particularly beneficial to women who might not otherwise be able to attend traditional education; yet, despite such target marketing, there is little evidence that most online instructors consider the effects of gender on the learning experience. According to von Prümmer and Rossié (2001), "if gender is not seen as relevant, the system will not be equally accessible to women and men and will offer men more chances to succeed" (p. 137).

An important goal of higher education is to provide a fair and equitable opportunity for each student to achieve academic success. When one considers gender issues in education, one often thinks of sexual harassment. Institutions need to maintain a learning environment that is conducive to learning and guard against a hostile environment of sexual harassment. In particular, online behavior to be avoided includes sexual advances and/or verbal conduct of a sexist nature when it is intimidating, threatening, or offensive, and sufficiently severe to interfere with a student's education. However, there are also more subtle instances where factors related to gender can adversely impact fair and equitable learning opportunities in a distance education program.

This chapter identifies gender-differentiated communication patterns and educational characteristics as a means of offering instructional design, delivery, and support strategies. Both instructor and learner dynamics are considered in light of current research as a means of promoting social equity.

BACKGROUND

A well-known 1993 *New Yorker* cartoon shows a canine sitting in front of a computer declaring to another "on the Internet, nobody knows you're a dog." Indeed, people on the Internet are often identified not by their proper name (which is often a tip-off to gender) but by their login account or e-mail address. An instant message from gb135 could be from 60-year-old Greg Butler, a retired executive in

Washington, D.C.; from fifth-grader Ginny Bradshaw, who lives in Boston; or, for that matter, from former president George H. W. Bush. Such a cryptic moniker lacks the demographic details that are traditionally used to identify individuals.

Such potential anonymity raises the possibility that individuals can construct online identities that are unrelated to their physical ones. More significant is the question of whether such attributes lack meaning in the virtual world. In 1996, an MCI television commercial declared, "There is no race. There is no gender. There is no age. There are no infirmities. There are only minds. Utopia? No, Internet." Although such grandiose proclamations are less common today, new advances in online technology (such as blogs, wikis, podcasting, or virtual worlds) are invariably presented as means of eliminating traditional barriers to communication and promoting a new culture of understanding. Putting aside the question of whether such a so-called utopia is even possible, is a raceless, genderless, ageless, mind-only world preferable for an effective educational environment? Is not one of the major benefits of online learning the opportunity to connect the course content with personal experiences in accordance with constructivism and adult learning theory, rather than reducing education to mere information transfer? Is there a relationship between one's online and offline identities, and how do they manifest in the virtual classroom?

Early online communication literature hypothesized that the limited social cues present in a largely textual environment would minimize gender differences (e.g., Kiesler, Siegel, & McGuire, 1984). On the contrary, Herring (1996a) found significant communication differences by gender and theorized that gender-based communication styles, and the power dynamics and biases associated with these styles, carry over into online environments. Postmes, Spears, and Lea (1998) suggest that rather than encouraging the liberation of individuals from social influence and general social norms, individuals interacting online tend to engage in heightened stereotypical behavior, conform to group norms, commit to the group, and engage in "us versus them" behavior, given the relatively impersonal online environment.

In order to develop online learning environments that facilitate the interaction of diverse groups and accommodate individual and group differences without sacrificing or silencing other members of the learning community, one must first consider gender-differentiated communication patterns and educational dynamics. The issue of cultural differences is addressed in the next chapter. The aim of this chapter is to direct instructors toward the development of learner-oriented pedagogical structures that promote equal opportunities to learn.

GENDERED IMPACTS OF ONLINE TECHNOLOGIES

While males generally view technology in positive terms, females tend to view technology more negatively (Jackson, Ervin, Gardner, & Schmitt, 2001). A number of studies on gender differences in computer skills, use, and attitudes among elementary, secondary, and college students (e.g., Shashaani, 1994; Lee, 2003) reveal that, on average, women are less confident, less experienced, and hold less favorable attitudes toward computers than men.

Kantrowitz (1996) suggests that men tend to be seduced by the computer technology itself and often brag about the power of their computers, while females tend to think of computers as machines that are to be used, like microwave ovens. She claims, "Men typically imagine devices that could help them conquer the universe. . . . Women want machines that meet people's needs, the perfect mother" (p. 140). These two viewpoints underpin the potential ambiguity and uncertainty surrounding the gendered impacts of online technologies.

Herring (1996b) addresses the phenomenon of flaming, which is the use of "derogatory, obscene, or inappropriate language and personal insults" in computer-mediated communication (p. 149). She points out that it is almost exclusively males who engage in this type of communication behavior online. She argues that women place a high value on consideration for the needs of others, while men assign a "greater value to freedom from censorship (many advocate absolute free speech), forthright and open expression, and agonistic debate as a means to advance the pursuit of knowledge" (p. 150). Consequently, she concludes that men and women

> constitute different discourse communities in cyberspace—different cultures, if you will—with differing communicative norms and practices. However, these cultures are not "separate but equal" as recent popular writing on gender differences in communication has claimed. Rather, the norms and practices of masculine net culture . . . conflict with those of the female culture in ways that render cyberspace—or at least many "neighborhoods" in cyberspace—inhospitable to women. (pp. 151–152)

Many of the same gender-linked communication patterns identified in face-to-face interactions appear in online interactions as well. Studies reveal that women use more qualifiers, conditional and parenthetical statements, as well as pronouns to sustain dialogue; in contrast, men use fewer qualifiers and more intensifiers (Fahy, 2002). Comparing computer-mediated interactions of male and female undergraduates, Wolfe (1999) reports that women tend to ask more questions, produce more agreements, and offer fewer responses to opposition than their male counterparts. In examining online class discussions, Rovai (2001) found similar differences by gender. He describes the tone of men's messages as generally more confrontational, autonomous, certain, abstract, and arrogant while women's posts tend to be more empathetic, relational (i.e., they mentioned self, family, or spouse), and cooperative. Herring (1996b) describes this difference as the tendency for women to be considerate of the "face" needs of others, while men often threaten the "face" of others.

GENDER-SPECIFIC TEACHING ROLES

Several studies have explored teaching styles, including communication patterns within the classroom, and found differences between men and women. Men use the lecture method more often than women, whereas women feel more committed to a participatory or collaborative approach (Lacey, Saleh, & Gorman, 1998). Fox (1990) also suggests that men feel more comfortable in a lecturing role than women—a role that is learned at an early age through role models. Accordingly, Lacey, Saleh, and Gorman (1998) describe men as fitting a "provider style." Such a style suggests that the teacher "knows best" what learners need and that they have the information required to satisfy those needs. Not surprisingly, students report that male professors are less interpersonally caring and tend to engage in more negative and offensive behaviors than women (Crawford & MacLeod, 1990).

In contrast, women describe a preference for participatory teaching styles in which students become involved in coaching relationships and gain opportunities to define and participate in their own assessment (Davis, 1999). Women also prefer an enabler style, or "guide on the side" approach, that allows learners to define what they need to learn, and how they wish to learn it, as well as decide on the process for exchange (Gunter, 1995). Women also tend to place a high value on interaction with other students, invest a significant proportion of academic time in preparing to teach, and use a broad range of evaluation techniques. Students report that women professors give them more time and personal attention, and are considered warmer, more nurturing, and more supportive than male professors.

In general, female faculty members are more likely than male faculty members to describe their classrooms as two-way (dialogic), collaborative, process-based, experiential, egalitarian, interactive, empowering, connected, relational, and affective (Tisdell, 2000). Whereas female professors tend to view students as collaborators and contributors to the learning process, male professors are more likely to focus on ways to present the material more effectively and efficiently. This is consistent with communication literature that suggests that most women seek to establish intimacy in a relationship, while most men seek to establish status in a hierarchy (Tannen, 2001).

In light of these and related differences, women may be more open to various constructivist teaching styles that are recommended for online delivery approaches where facilitation, collaboration, egalitarianism, and high interactivity are emphasized (Stanley-Spaeth, 2000). Pedagogical differences identified in the traditional setting may further translate into different uses of and attitudes toward technology-mediated enhancement in online user settings (Ausburn, 2004). Given the hierarchical culture of traditional postsecondary institutions and the constructivist nature of Web-based instructional strategies, male faculty may be more resistant to reconceptualizing their role in terms of creating democratic learning environments.

Gender-based communication differences may, in turn, translate into different uses of online classroom technologies. For instance, males use the Internet primarily for information-gathering or surveillance (Gefen & Straub, 1997) and women use it primarily for e-mail and other forms of personal communication (Jackson, Ervin, Gardner, & Schmitt, 2001). Given that males and females view technology differently and that such views lead to different uses, the assumption is that male and female university faculty will view, and possibly use, technology differently when it comes to teaching online. Given their preference for collaborative and student-centered learning, women may be more likely to develop means of student interaction and flexible assessment, which are valued components of online pedagogy. Given their concern for relational development, they may also be more likely to engage in various online community-building activities than men. Men, who are more predisposed to lecture-based instruction, may be more likely than women to use the online course structure for knowledge presentation than assessment, knowledge construction, or community-building efforts.

Such gender-related differences underscore the need for deployment of professional development activities for online faculty members to guide their decisions about which classroom interventions to implement. Online practitioners must also be given the tools to distinguish interventions that are supported by scientifically rigorous evidence from those that are not.

GENDER-SPECIFIC LEARNING DIFFERENCES

Males and females also tend to have different learning-style preferences. These preferences can be categorized as connected versus independent communication and field dependent versus independent. Moreover, these differences become apparent when examining relational and group dynamics as well as academic achievement. Each of these areas is discussed below.

Connected Versus Independent Communication

Belenky, Clinchy, Goldberger, and Tarule (1996) theorize that there are two developmental paths in adult learning, which result in two different communication patterns. The first is the relational, connected, or interdependent path, which reflects the majority of women (and some men). The second pattern is the self-sufficient, autonomous, or independent path, which is typical of the majority of men (and some women). This model suggests that many female students place emphasis on relationships and prefer to learn in an environment where cooperation is stressed over competition. The connected voice nurtures classroom community-building, while the independent voice does not. In particular, the professional literature suggests that most women seek to establish intimacy in a relationship, whereas most men seek to establish status in a hierarchy, measured in terms of independence (Tannen, 2001).

Gilligan (1993) points out that her voice is characterized by an ethic of caring that men as well as women can espouse. Noddings (2003) elaborates this ethic of caring as "feminine in the deep classical sense—rooted in receptivity, relatedness, and responsiveness" (p. 2). For Noddings, caring is based on reciprocity—one caring and one cared-for—and recognizes "human encounter and affective response as a basic fact of human existence" (p. 4). In this framework, both parties contribute actively to this relationship of caring. Cole and McQuin (1992) describe the ethic of caring as "a predisposition to nurture, a ready capacity for emotional involvement, a need to be sensitive about relationships and how they generate different varieties of responsibility to others, and a willingness to value particularity, connection, and context" (pp. 2–3).

This assertion is consistent with the findings of Rovai (2001), who concluded that the voice of students engaged in online courses is related to gender. The majority of men (and some women) exhibited an independent voice, and the majority of women (and some men) used a connected voice. "The independent voice tends to be impersonal and assertive, that is, it possesses an authoritative tone. The connected voice, on the other hand, is generally supportive and helpful without being assertive" (p. 45).

Communication patterns may also be related to patterns of thinking or cognitive style. Baxter-Magolda (1992) studied college students' ways of knowing and reasoning. She discovered patterns of thinking that are related to gender and that parallel the communication patterns identified by Belenky, Clinchy, Goldberger, and Tarule (1996). Baxter-Magolda (1992) identifies four stages of knowing: absolute, transitional, independent, and contextual. At the lowest or absolute stage, the learner sees knowledge as something that is held by an external authority. Females at this stage tend to function as receivers, taking notes and studying, whereas males engage in interaction with the instructor. At the transitional stage, females are more likely to engage in interactivity, relying on the opinions of others to help construct their own knowledge. Males, on the other hand, are more likely to use the opinions of others as material for debate. At the independent stage, females have their own interpretations but value interactivity, whereas males tend to rely on independent processing. Learners at the most advanced stage of contextual knowing judge knowledge on the basis of evidence in context. For females, connection to others is a central feature of contextual knowing by integrating the views of others. Male contextual knowing is more impersonal, and is based on the premise that students are ultimately responsible for their own judgments and constructed perspectives.

According to Belenky, Clinchy, Goldberger, and Tarule (1996), women are more likely than men to use connected knowing, while men are more likely to use separate knowing. They also assert that individuals who utilize a separate way of knowing distance themselves from the object of knowledge and place an emphasis on objectivity, reason, doubting, analysis, and evaluation. On the other hand, those who utilize a connected way of knowing emphasize understanding, empathy, acceptance, and collaboration, suggesting a stronger sense of community within a learning environment.

Online instructors' strategies for thinking and knowing can differ from those of their students, and they have a role to play in helping students adopt new ways of thinking. They can and should intervene to make a difference between what students will learn on their own and what they can learn with guidance (e.g., Lindemann, 2001). Moreover, instructors must promote the integration of knowledge and experience among all learners.

Field Independence Versus Dependence

Field dependence theory addresses the degree to which a person's perception of information is affected by the surrounding perceptual contextual field (Witkin & Goodenough, 1981). It explains differences in cognitive styles and uses the term *field independence* to describe individuals who are more likely to have been socialized with an emphasis on autonomy over conformity, are more internally directed, and accept ideas through analysis. On the other hand, field dependent or field sensitive individuals prefer working in groups, are externally directed and more pragmatic, and accept ideas as presented.

Research (e.g., Merriam & Caffarella, 1999; Witkin & Goodenough, 1981) provides evidence that females tend to be more field dependent while males tend to be more field independent. These differences suggest that females learn better in a personal, practical, hands-on learning environment where feelings and relationships are allowed to develop. Table 2.1 summarizes major differences in cognitive style by gender, based on field dependence theory.

Relational and Group Dynamics

Gender also appears to influence online interpersonal and relational communication dynamics. Hiltz and Turoff (1993) theorize that people perceive a high degree of impersonality when they are online. This depersonalization might also have a number of effects, including flaming and a willingness to express opinions or ideas that would not be expressed in a personalized setting. Even within the online environment, however, Postmes, Spears, Sakhel, and De Groot (2001) observed different behavior in anonymous groups versus identifiable groups in which members shared personal biographies or photos with group members. They found that identifiable groups are less susceptible to conforming to a primed norm than their anonymous counterparts.

Postmes et al. (1998) noted that one flaw in the oft-cited egalitarian view of online communication is that it fails to consider that social norms are not merely

TABLE 2.1. Gender-Related Cognitive Style Differences

Most Females, Some Males	Most Males, Some Females
Field dependent	Field independent
More likely to use inductive reasoning	More likely to use deductive reasoning
More pragmatic and applied	More abstract and theoretical
Learn best by watching and thinking	Learn best while doing and either thinking or feeling
More organized	More undirected
Connectedness through intimacy and physical proximity	Connectedness through social competition

externally applied, but are also internalized boundaries that influence personal behavior. "Although CMC gives us the opportunity to traverse social boundaries, paradoxically, it can also afford these boundaries greater power, especially when they define self- and group identity" (p. 689).

Women are more likely to seek supportive communication environments and, thus, are likely to have significantly different expectations when it comes to the frequency and nature of communication online. Instructors who are attempting to enhance interaction must also keep in mind that messages from males engaged in online discussions tend to be more certain, controlling, and confrontational than messages from females, which tend to be more compassionate, close, and cooperative.

Herring (2000) found that female students participated more when the instructor actively promoted a civil and focused discourse. Shea, Fredericksen, Pickett, Pelz, and Swan (2001) examined students in the SUNY Learning Network and found that female students had higher levels of learner-instructor and learner-learner interaction than their male counterparts. Both gender and communication style influenced levels of interactivity, and immediacy-producing behaviors were more consistent with female online communication than with male communication. Such findings are consistent with other research that highlights differences in communicative and relational patterns between men and women. Such differences are, thus, likely to have an impact on the development of an online learning community as well as individual reactions to the virtual classroom experience.

Academic Achievement

Although online communication patterns by gender are evident in the professional literature, gender differences have not been as consistent with regard to student achievement or satisfaction. Ory, Bullock, and Burnaska (1997) found no significant gender differences in student attitudes toward asynchronous learning networks after a year of implementation in a university setting. Gunn, McSporran, Macleod, and French (2003) concluded that women often perform better than men in online learning settings. Lim (2001) considered the influence of gender along with a number of other factors (e.g., computer self-efficacy, academic self-concept, age, academic status, and so forth) and concluded that computer self-efficacy was the singular predictor of student satisfaction. Clay-Warner and Marsh (2000) found that gender was not a significant influence on students' acceptance of the use of online communication in instruction. In contrast, Shea et al. (2001) discovered that females in the SUNY Learning Network were more satisfied with online learning than their male peers.

In a study of 109 online learners, Anderson and Haddad (2005) found that women reported deeper perceived learning online than in face-to-face courses, largely due to increased comfort expressing their views in class and the belief that those views were valued. "Our research suggests that, for females, this greater perceived learning occurs because of the role that voice plays in strengthening perceived deep learning in both online and face-to-face courses" (Section V, ¶ 1). They also found that the professor was influential in establishing this confidence and sense of voice among online learners.

STRATEGIES FOR OVERCOMING GENDER CHALLENGES TO LEARNING

Curricular Strategies

Research suggests that males tend to dominate conversations with females due to their desire to achieve a one-up position in the social environment and to achieve status (Tannen, 2001). Additionally, Herring (2000) found that female students often participate more than male students in online discussion boards in which the professor, even when the professor is a male, acts as a moderator who is entrusted with maintaining civility and focus in the group. She notes that:

> The need for such insurance, rather than reflecting a weakness on the part of women, points to the fundamental failure of "self-regulating" democracy on the Internet to produce anything like equitable participation: when left to its own devices, libertarianism favors the most aggressive individuals, who tend to be male. (Herring, 2000, p. 5)

This creates a challenging curricular situation: It is educationally valuable to both men and women to use constructivist-style discussions within the online environment, and yet, those discussions require active participation by the instructor to ensure equity in the online dialog. Accordingly, gender-sensitive online curricular design includes:

- Providing structured opportunities for students to contribute both original content and discussion material
- Using a combination of independent and collaborative assessment tasks to serve both field independent and dependent learners
- Including opportunities for private self-assessment so students can build up their mastery of the course content in a nonthreatening environment
- Clearly announcing the rules of civility for online discussions, perhaps in the form of an online discussion rubric as addressed in Chapter 7.

Teaching Strategies

Effective consideration of gender issues in online teaching cannot be expected to develop if faculty have not given attention to their own pedagogical philosophies and attempted to reconcile them with current opportunities. This does not mean that all faculty need to become constructivists, but the transition to online instruction should provide an impetus for faculty to closely examine their teaching philosophy and practices in light of the gender differences described above to ensure that they are as effective as they would wish and that they exhibit and promote immediacy behaviors and equal opportunities to learn. When the technologies dovetail with the pedagogical philosophy and teaching strategies, it is likely that positive attitudes will result. Such teaching strategies include:

- The use of personal narrative (on the part of both instructor and learner) to connect course content with practical application
- The use of relevant discussion questions to promote collaborative reflection on the course content
- Collaborative discussions with teacher presence to remind the learning community members of appropriate interactive behavior
- Greater emphasis on collaborative rather than competitive discussions
- The use of project-based learning, case studies, and other means of applying the content to real-world situations.

Institutional Strategies

In a study of gender differences in computer experiences and attitudes among secondary-school-age children, Shashaani (1994) found a positive association between students' computer experiences and their attitudes toward computer-related activities. She argues that the association between experience and attitude suggests that "more exposure to computers may help to break the cycle of 'computer dislike' and lack of computer experience" (p. 360). In fact, experience may account for gender differences in computer attitudes and use. While negative reactions to computer experience come mainly from females, gender differences in attitudes toward computers should diminish with increased experience using computers.

Experience with Web-based courseware may not solely predict faculty use and attitudes, but the nature of the experience may be important as well. Spotts, Bowman, and Mertz (1997), in a study that examined gender differences in technology use by university faculty, detected gender differences in responses to knowledge/ experience in multimedia and computer-assisted instruction. Male faculty rated their knowledge about/experience with multimedia and computer-assisted instruction as significantly higher than female faculty. In terms of factors influencing use, females indicated that ease of use, increased student learning, time needed to learn how to use a technology, training for faculty in technology use, and information on material available in the discipline as being significantly more important to influencing their use of instructional technology than did their male colleagues. Spotts, Bowman, and Mertz (1997) suggest that training may interact with gender; that is, training may emerge as a more salient predictor of use and attitudes for female than male faculty. It is not unreasonable to expect that faculty who are trained in course learning management systems will be more likely to use the various tools and will hold more favorable attitudes towards the system than faculty without formal training.

Another factor influencing the effective use of online learning management systems is computer self-efficacy. Men have stronger Internet self-efficacy beliefs than women. When asked how comfortable they were using computers and how they felt about their computer skills, college freshmen males reported greater comfort with computers and greater feelings of competence than females, with some evidence that the effect is diminished with experience and computer instruction (Cooper & Weaver, 2003). In a study examining the association between Internet self-efficacy and resistance to Web-based instruction, Thompson and Lynch (2003) reported that people with weak Internet self-efficacy tend to resist Web-based instruction, and that men report more confidence in their ability to organize and execute the tools needed to complete a Web-based course.

Although much attention has been paid to getting technology into the traditional classroom, there has been considerably less attention paid to helping teachers make the transition into a technology-rich learning environment that would, in turn, impact student learning. According to Twigg (2001), instructors tend to take a traditional course and "put it up" on the Web with little or no change in presentation style. Many teachers, especially more experienced teachers, have been unable to find effective ways to use technology in their classrooms (Smerdon, Cronen, Lanahan, Anderson, Iannotti, Angeles, & Greene, 2000). One possible explanation for this lack of success is that the use of online technologies has been viewed in terms of simple skill acquisition instead of as a change process that affects the behavior of individuals on a very profound level. As a result of these findings, institutions should promote effective online learning by:

- Providing structured training opportunities to help faculty master learning management systems

- Offering mentors to help new faculty make the transition to online instruction
- Developing tutorials for new online learners to master the online course environment and learn appropriate standards of behavior
- Providing instructional design and media development support to faculty rather than expecting them to master all of the online technologies
- Pilot testing new online instruction in a mixed-gender environment
- Promoting cross-gender team design models so that male and female faculty can collaborate on more effective online courses
- Seeking student feedback on courses and disaggregating the results by gender as one of the means of analysis.

CONCLUSION

Missing from fully online programs (particularly those designed around largely textual, asynchronous courses) are many of the personal connections formed between students and among students, professors, and staff in socializing while waiting for class to start, in personal exchanges that take place during visits to the offices of faculty and staff, and in numerous other seemingly insignificant encounters. Faceless interaction without the nonverbal components such as smiles and nods that typically accompany conversation can promote antisocial feelings. Moreover, conversation based on efficient use of words may not be the most effective. Consequently, Palmer's (1998) assertion that deep listening should include mirroring is especially relevant to CMC. Those who are listening need to reflect back on what they believe they have heard, to make certain that communication is complete and correct.

If online instructors are to design and teach using an inclusive student-centered pedagogy, they require additional training about various models of online instruction, as well as detailed information about student differences and how those influence learning. For example, in a study of a blended online learning environment, Ausburn (2004) found that females are significantly more desirous than males of a course that provides an anchor or home base and fosters a sense of belonging and involvement. What other such design factors are differentially preferred by gender? What other personal characteristics influence the online learning experience, and how can instructors create more suitable online courses?

One framework that might be useful for considering a number of these issues at once is Hofstede's (2004) five-dimensional model of national culture. The first dimension is power distance, which reflects the acceptance level by the less powerful in society of an uneven distribution of power. The second dimension is individualism versus collectivism, a scale that considers the importance of the individual versus the larger group. The third dimension is masculinity versus femininity, which reflects the importance placed on traditional gender-related values. (The United

States, for example, is a moderately masculine culture.) The fourth dimension is uncertainty avoidance that relates to the level at which a culture attempts to minimize uncertainty through structure. Finally, the fifth dimension is long-term versus short-term orientation. Although only one of these dimensions explicitly identifies gender, many of the characteristics inherent in the five dimensions (e.g., individualism versus collectivism) are evident in the gender-related literature. Such a multifactor framework might serve as a useful model for instructors and institutions to better understand the personal and cultural dynamics within the student population and, thus, enable the development of better-suited online learning environments.

CHAPTER 3

Culture

Advances in information technology and the massification of higher education have combined to create a culturally diverse national student population. Additionally, as an artifact of globalization, new programs are being designed and delivered to satisfy local needs worldwide, and new certifications are being conferred. Clearly, educational providers and students are moving across borders as the world enters an era of global distance education. Effective cross-culture and cross-border communications are essential elements of effective teaching and learning in this global environment.

However, individual access to and skills in the use of technology are moderated by factors such as socioeconomic status, gender (as described in the previous chapter), ethnicity, and culture. Although Americans of every demographic group have experienced increases in computer ownership and Internet access over the past decade, actual rates as described in this chapter temper the optimism suggested by these results. According to the *Pew Internet and American Life Project* (2006b), the digital divide between members of the dominant White non-Hispanic culture and minority cultures has not closed, as Blacks and Hispanics remain less likely to use the Internet than their White peers. Additionally,

> as education is still largely a cultural process embedded in diverse national, ethnic, religious, linguistic settings, there are risks that cross-border provision does not acknowledge and respect cultural sensitivities. (Organisation for Economic Cooperation and Development, 2004, p. 23)

The previous chapter identifies and discusses issues of gender in distance learning environments. This chapter examines the challenges faced by students who do not belong to the majority culture served by their school. The major sections of this chapter discuss two related topics. The first topic is the situational and dispositional challenges that confront many minority and cross-border students in distance education. The second topic is a discussion of the multicultural communication and educational strategies that promote social equity and social justice.

BACKGROUND

The Association of American Colleges and Universities (2002) asserts that we are verging on universal college attendance, as a college degree becomes the equivalent of what a high school education was 100 years ago. Large state universities are, thus, becoming more diverse and are mirroring the diverse populations of their states. As a result, more colleges reflect our country's growing multicultural population.

The *Minorities in Higher Education: Twenty-Second Annual Status Report* (2006) reveals that total minority enrollment in U.S. colleges and universities increased by 50.7% between 1993 and 2003, with minority students making up 27.8% of postsecondary students.

This multicultural learning environment results in diversity among the cultural styles that are present in a classroom. For example, Falicov (1996) provides the following description of the interactive style of Mexican-American students:

> Indirect, implicit, or covert communication is consistent with Mexicans' emphasis on family harmony, on "getting along" and not making others uncomfortable. Conversely, assertiveness, open differences in opinion, and demands for clarification are seen as rude or insensitive to others' feelings. The use of third-person ("One could be proud of . . .") rather than first-person ("I am proud of . . .") pronouns is a common pattern of indirectness, and is viewed as a way of being selfless as opposed to self-serving. Thus Mexican Americans sometimes are left guessing rather than asking about the other's intentions; they often make use of allusions, proverbs, and parables to convey their viewpoints, which may leave an impression of guardedness, vagueness, obscurity, or excessive embellishment, obsequiousness, and politeness. (p. 176)

Consequently, classroom interactions that involve competition, emphasize individual accomplishments, or promote excessive directness are likely to silence Mexican-American students in particular and Hispanic students in general in ways similar to those in which such interactions tend to silence females, as discussed in the previous chapter.

Postsecondary institutions have been wrestling with how to cope with such cultural differences on campus and in online programs, but few scholars have delved deeply into how the learning environments of such schools are impacted by student diversity (Gallien & Peterson, 2004). Fabos and Young (1999) assert that although "the Internet holds the potential to link classrooms to exchange cultural information and critically address various problems . . . [it may instead] encourage students to see the world through an Imperialist lens" (p. 237). They provide evidence that illustrates how some educators' use of electronic technologies misrepresents other cultures because teachers do not provide substantive background knowledge of the contexts of other cultures, question dominant culture assumptions, or examine the impact of global economic and political systems.

For culturally responsive teaching to be effective, there must be a partnership in the classroom. Students must take ultimate responsibility for their learning, but teachers must also accept responsibility for the effectiveness of the delivery of the curriculum to a diverse audience. Schools must provide culturally responsive, fair, and equitably distributed learning environments so that all students have equal chances to achieve academic success. The following sections identify potential situational and dispositional challenges that can adversely influence minority student achievement (see Figure 3.1).

FIGURE 3.1. Challenges to Learning

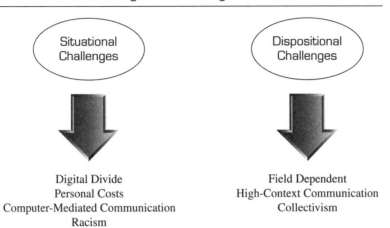

Situational Challenges	Dispositional Challenges
Digital Divide Personal Costs Computer-Mediated Communication Racism	Field Dependent High-Context Communication Collectivism

SITUATIONAL CHALLENGES

According to K. Patricia Cross's (1992) model of barriers or challenges to adult learning, situational challenges are those arising from one's situation at a given time and include both the social and physical environment surrounding one's life. This chapter discusses situational challenges to successful minority participation in distance education in terms of the digital divide, personal costs, computer-mediated communication (CMC), and racism.

Digital Divide

The term *digital divide* can take on several meanings, but at the most basic level, it refers to the division between those who can easily access the Internet and those who cannot. Table 3.1 shows U.S. Internet usage by race/ethnicity, household income, and education. Racial and ethnic differences in education and income contribute substantially to the gap in Internet access rates. Individuals on the wrong side of the digital divide are often denied the option to participate effectively in new high-tech jobs, in technology-enhanced education, and in using technology to access knowledge (e.g., Fairlie, 2004; U.S. Department of Commerce, 2000). From an educational perspective, the groups most disenfranchised by the digital divide are the same groups that have been historically disenfranchised by education in general.

As more individuals use the Internet, it becomes less useful to discuss the digital divide in terms of access only (DiMaggio & Hargittai, 2001). One also needs to examine differences in people's online skills. Such skills are directly related to people's ability to use the medium. Although economic, cultural, and social fac-

TABLE 3.1. Internet User Demographics

Population	Internet Use
Total adults	70%
Race/Ethnicity	
White non-Hispanic	72%
Black non-Hispanic	58%
English-speaking Hispanic	69%
Household Income	
Less than $30,000/year	49%
$30,000 to $49,999/year	75%
$50,000 to $74,999/year	90%
$75,000 and over/year	93%
Education	
Less than high school	36%
High school	59%
Some college	84%
College graduate	91%

Source: Compiled by the *Pew Internet and American Life Project,* 2006b, using data collected by its December 2006 survey.

tors have a greater role to play in narrowing the gap in the first level of the digital divide, educational factors are more important in closing the gap in online skills.

When one examines the digital divide in terms of the ability of university students to use computer technology effectively, Farrell (2005) writes that the majority of minority college freshmen at schools such as UCLA are unequipped to manage the digital workplace. Consequently, regardless of how one examines the digital divide, minorities appear to be at a disadvantage, and this situation can adversely impact their academic achievement, especially as technology-based education grows.

Personal Costs

The next consideration, personal costs, refers to the monetary and human costs associated with pursuing an online academic program. Distance education students encounter many of the same rising financial costs for education as their on-campus peers, as well as costs involving the acquisition of the technology needed to participate efficiently in online learning. Often, minorities and the poor have the greatest need for such aid. However, to cope with potential legal issues associated with minority-targeted financial aid programs, many universities have adopted a more holistic approach to determining financial aid by including considerations such as income, being the first generation to go to college, and the overcoming of obstacles, in addition to race and ethnicity. Consequently, eligibility for financial aid has become more competitive for minority students.

While distance education may open higher education opportunities by permitting better coordination of work and school schedule through the convenience of the anytime, anywhere nature of asynchronous learning environments, human costs involving the expenditure of time and energy are also present. The poor and minorities, who may not have been exposed to the same levels of technology and schooling as their White peers, need technology training, online tutoring, and access to timely online technical support to facilitate access to and successful completion of their online academic programs. The result is the need for many minority students to devote more time than their White counterparts to their academic programs. Moreover, text-based CMC is more time-consuming than verbal communication for all students, and family and work responsibilities often compete for the time needed to achieve educational goals. Consequently, persistence in distance education programs is often 10–20 percentage points lower than in traditional programs (Carr, 2000). Additionally, according to the U.S. Department of Education (2000), minorities tend to have more of the risk factors associated with postsecondary persistence, i.e., delayed enrollment, no high school diploma (including GED recipients), part-time enrollment, having dependents other than a spouse, single-parent status, and working full-time while enrolled.

Computer-Mediated Communication (CMC)

CMC is another situational challenge. Schools rely heavily on CMC as the primary mode of communication for distance education courses. It is generally regarded as effective because CMC supports the interactivity and collaborative online work that is valued in a constructivist learning environment. However, text-based CMC, which is the backbone of Internet-based e-learning, has both strengths and weaknesses.

Morse (2003) includes flexibility, communication openness/access, opportunities for reflective thought prior to participating in a discussion, and post-participation review/access to written discussions as strong points. However, this communication medium also presents challenges. Morse (2003) identifies these challenges as frustrations regarding the use of technology, coordination issues for group work, delays in receiving responses in asynchronous communications, and potential computer and writing skill deficits. One additional challenge, particularly relevant to a multicultural CMC text-based learning environment, is the reduction of nonverbal cues, such as facial expressions and gestures, during the text-based communication process. Consequently, the result of communication at a distance, particularly among members of a multicultural online learning community who have not previously met, is often a less accurate representation of the participants and their messages.

Cross-cultural interactions can therefore result in miscommunication. Because of the global reach of distance education, different cultures within the same country, as well as cross-border cultural differences, must be considered. Cues that some students need to determine how to interact in a given communication situation may be missing in a CMC environment. As a result, these students may feel uncomfortable, frustrated, or reserved because, without context cues, they cannot determine how to react in a specific communication situation. Therefore, they may become silent or reserved in order to avoid offending other participants in an exchange.

Racism

Marable (1992) defines *racism* as "a system of ignorance, exploitation, and power used to oppress African Americans, Latinos, Asians, Pacific Americans, American Indians and other people on the basis of ethnicity, culture, mannerisms, and color" (p. 5). Chesler, Lewis, and Crowfoot (2005) describe Black student perceptions of racial tension and conflict on-campus in terms of racial stereotyping, marginalization in social relations, pressure to assimilate, White resentment of affirmative action and supposed undeserved gains, and the unwillingness of many White students to engage in meaningful discussions or relationships with Blacks. These perceptions can also occur in the virtual environment of distance learning, with its reliance on use of CMC tools.

Racial discrimination can manifest itself in ways such as adoption of an "us versus them" outlook, positive self-presentation of the dominant group, and negative presentation of the minority group. These attitudes lead to the ability of the dominant group to control the flow of communication and to influence the behavior and thought processes of others.

Teachers are not exempt from biased attitudes and racial stereotyping. Some teachers are vulnerable to using stereotypical perceptions of student characteristics for which they hold different expectations. In educational settings, racial stereotypes are often used to justify:

- Having low educational and occupational expectations for minority students
- Placing minority students in separate tracks or classrooms
- Dumbing down the curriculum and pedagogy for minority students
- Expecting minority students to one day occupy lower status and levels of occupations. (Solorzano & Yosso, 2001)

Such low expectations are often blamed on the minority students themselves and their culture, rather than on society and its institutions.

Racism, including racial stereotyping, can thus result in diminished status for minority students. Elizabeth Cohen (1994) suggests that students with relatively low status with their peers will interact with classmates less frequently and will learn less than high-status students. She explains:

> High-status individuals are expected to be more competent than low-status individuals across a wide range of tasks that are viewed as important. . . . Since in our culture people of color are generally expected to be less competent on intellectual tasks than Whites, these racist expectations came into play in [cooperative group activities]. (pp. 33–34)

DISPOSITIONAL CHALLENGES

In addition to the situational challenges described above, many minority students are also faced with culturally related dispositional challenges. According to Cross (1992), dispositional challenges are those related to the characteristics, attitudes, and self-perceptions of the adult learner. The three potential dispositional challenges described in this chapter are the field dependent (or field sensitive) cognitive style, high-context communication preference, and inclination toward collectivism of many minority cultures in the United States.

Field Dependent Cognitive Style

Field dependence theory (Witkin & Goodenough, 1981) and its notion of field independent and field dependent cognitive styles have been used to describe two different learning orientations. Using an analogy, field dependent adults focus on the forest, while field independent learners focus on the trees within the forest. However, the terms *field dependent* and *field independent* reflect a tendency, in varying degrees of strength, toward one end of a continuum (field dependent) or the other (field independent). Research suggests that field independent learners are more typically White males, while field dependent learners are often female, African-American, Hispanic, or Native American students who need to connect their new learning with previous experience or other familiar information (Anderson, 1988).

Ibarra (2001) claims that minority students who demonstrate field dependency often have highly developed social skills and are sensitive to the social elements of the learning environment. Field dependent learners also benefit from examples and contextual and cooperative learning environments that relate learning materials to students' personal experiences rather than casting them in an abstract, decontextualized manner (Ibarra, 2001). Such characteristics contrast those of field independent learners who demonstrate success in individualistic, competitive, and more decontextualized learning environments (Ibarra, 2001). Field independent learners approach learning more as an independent activity than as a social or communal activity. Consequently, they may be inattentive to relational and affective aspects of the learning environment, and their strength often lies in abstraction (Bennett, 2006).

High-Context Communication Preference

Knowing the identity of the individual with whom one is interacting can often be crucial to knowing how to communicate. Edward T. Hall (Hall & Hall, 1990) notes that the way in which individuals communicate within the same setting can vary along cultural lines. These setting-based variations on cultural communication behavior form the foundation of Hall's theory of high- and low-context cultures.

According to Ibarra (2001), low-context cultures make little use of nonverbal signals, value direct communication with explicit verbal messages, and depersonalize disagreements. High-context cultures rely extensively on nonverbal signals; see communication as an art form in which indirect, implicit, and informal verbal messages are valued; and personalize disagreements (see Table 3.2). Low-context cultures use language with great precision and economy. In contrast, high-context cultures use language more loosely, since words have relatively less value. Ibarra (2001) claims that minority cultures tend to be characterized by high-context communication, while the predominant U.S. culture is one of low-context. Because the language of communication is English, low-context communication is presumed, thus perhaps disadvantaging those whose cultural background relies on high-context communication (Morse, 2003).

Copeland and Griggs (1985) developed a high-/low-context scale that identifies the position of various cultures (see Figure 3.2). This scale shows that Japanese and Chinese cultures are high-context societies and, by implication, Japanese Americans and Chinese Americans who have not become fully acculturated in the predominant U.S. culture are also high-context cultures. Although not listed on this scale, African-American culture is a high-context culture. The further apart two cultures are on this scale, the more difficult it is for effective intercultural communication to take place.

One expects different learning behaviors in a computer-mediated environment as a result of differing cultural backgrounds. According to Morse (2003),

> low-context individuals, acculturated toward environmentally related learning variables anticipate that their role in learning is to attain some minimum level of competence which to some extent sees these individuals competing on an individual basis against a standard that may grow or change rapidly over time, and perhaps to a lesser

TABLE 3.2. Comparisons Between Low-Context and High-Context Cultures

	Low-Context	High-Context
Interaction	Low use of nonverbal signals; direct communication; messages are explicit; disagreement is depersonalized.	High use of nonverbal signals; indirect communication; messages are used to engage with others; disagreement is personalized.
Association	Personal commitment to people is relatively low; task orientation; success means getting recognized.	Personal commitment to people is high; getting things done depends on personal relationships and group process; success means being unobtrusive.
Temporality	Work is done on a schedule; speed and efficiency are valued; promptness is valued; time is a commodity.	Needs of people may interfere with schedules; accuracy and completion is more important than speed; time is a process.
Learning	Analytical thinking is important; learning is oriented to the individual; scientific, theoretical, and philosophical thinking is emphasized; academic style is teacher-oriented.	Comprehensive thinking is important; learning is group-oriented; practical thinking is valued; academic style is student-oriented.

Source: Adapted from Ibarra, 2001, pp. 69–76.

degree, with their peers as well. On the other hand, those from high-context cultures might expect formal communication to prevail, expect a single definitive or information specific form of assessment and expect to be directed where to obtain supplemental information, which would then be integrated into the body of knowledge for them. (p. 43)

The challenges presented by CMC, with its reduction of nonverbal cues, suggest that minorities may be adversely affected in an online learning environment vis-à-vis their White, non-Hispanic peers. This situation suggests the need for online course designers and teachers to adopt a multicultural education strategy that promotes an equitable learning environment.

Collectivism

Hofstede's (2004) model of national culture, introduced in Chapter 2, also applies to a multicultural classroom environment. One of the most important behavioral distinctions observed among various cultures is the difference between collectivism

FIGURE 3.2. High/Low-Context Scale

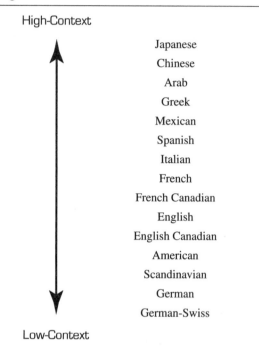

High-Context

Japanese
Chinese
Arab
Greek
Mexican
Spanish
Italian
French
French Canadian
English
English Canadian
American
Scandinavian
German
German-Swiss

Low-Context

Source: Adapted from Copeland and Griggs, 1985, p. 107.

and individualism (Triandis, Chen, & Chan, 1998). Individualism-collectivism represents two extremes along a continuum (Hofstede, 2004). The U.S. national culture is individualistic, while many minority subcultures are more collectivistic. In particular, many cross-cultural psychologists (e.g., Phinney, 1996) maintain that collectivist values continue to influence African-American, Asian-American, Hispanic-American, and Native American cultures, although variations do occur in each culture based largely on the amount of acculturation of individuals into the dominant White culture.

Members of individualistic cultures tend to be candid and task-related issues take priority over relationship-related issues. During group discussions between members of the White majority culture, views are expressed frankly, and individuals, regardless of status, resist attempts by others to influence them. However, in a multicultural environment, collectivist individuals attempt to maintain harmony and relationship concerns tend to prevail over task-oriented concerns. Lower-status individuals are more likely to yield to influence attempts by those in higher status, in order to avoid confrontation. This situation can often result from racial discrimination.

MULTICULTURAL EDUCATION

When eight experts on higher education policy were asked to comment on account-ability in higher education by *The Chronicle of Higher Education* (2004), none of them spoke about the need for indicators of equitable educational outcomes for racial and ethnic minorities. Unlike the K–12 school environment and the No Child Left Behind Act that mandates closure of the achievement gap by race and ethnicity, there is no similar emphasis on achieving academic equity in higher education.

In order to promote academic equity and excellence, curriculum and instruc-tion must respond to the varied needs of a diverse student body. The aim of multi-cultural education is to level the academic playing field by responding to the diversity in educational institutions, to include addressing the situational and dis-positional challenges to minorities discussed above.

Banks and Banks (2004) describe multicultural education as

> a field of study . . . whose major aim is to create equal educational opportunities for students from diverse racial, ethnic, social-class, and cultural groups. One of its im-portant goals is to help all students to acquire the knowledge, attitudes, and skills needed to function effectively in a pluralistic democratic society and to interact, ne-gotiate, and communicate with peoples from diverse groups in order to create a civic and moral community that works for the common good. (p. xi)

This description is consistent with the fundamental purpose of higher education, which is to prepare responsible adults to assume productive roles in our society.

Institutional Strategies

Responding to the global nature of distance education, Labi (2005) describes qual-ity-assurance guidelines for cross-border higher education promulgated by the Organization for Economic Cooperation and Development and the United Na-tions Educational, Scientific, and Cultural Organization. These guidelines include ensuring that academic programs take into account the cultural and linguistic sen-sitivities of the receiving country. Such distributed multicultural learning requires deliberate and well-planned strategies to be effective.

According to William G. Bowen, the 2004 Thomas Jefferson Foundation Dis-tinguished Lecturer at the University of Virginia, the challenge for universities re-garding minority students is to move beyond finding effective ways to enroll more minority students to finding effective ways to educate a diverse population of mi-nority and majority students (Foley, 2006). Chesler, Lewis, and Crowfoot (2005) offer a rational model for institutions to achieve this goal by emphasizing:

- Strategic planning
- Multicultural audits

- Alteration of leadership roles to include diversity and multiculturalism as areas of responsibility
- Use of multicultural leadership teams to provide direction to and promote changes within the institution
- Movement of colleges and universities from monocultural to multicultural institutions, especially by providing multicultural instruction in the classroom.

To achieve the goal of multicultural education, institutions must also find ways of supporting students' desire to succeed by providing necessary social supports and academic scaffolding. Kemp (2002) reports that life events and external commitments are not highly correlated with lack of student persistence, but the coping abilities of students are important to student retention. Consequently, inclusion of university services to assist students in developing their coping skills takes on added significance.

To be effective in a multicultural environment, teachers must first learn to become culturally responsive. The institution has a role to play by assisting faculty in this area through professional development activities that focus on the affective domain of learning in order to change the value teachers place on teaching culturally diverse students. The emphasis of these activities should be on self-reflection. By examining their attitudes and beliefs about themselves and others, teachers can begin to confront biases that may have influenced their existing value system. According to Villegas and Lucas (2002), the aim of such professional development activities is to produce culturally responsive teachers who:

- Possess an understanding that people's ways of thinking and behaving are deeply influenced by factors such as race, ethnicity, social class, and language (Banks, 1996)
- Have affirming views of students from diverse backgrounds by seeing them in an affirming light and acknowledging the existence and validity of diverse ways of thinking, talking, behaving, and learning
- See themselves as responsible for and capable of bringing about change to make learning more equitable
- Understand how learners construct knowledge and are capable of promoting knowledge construction
- Know about the lives of their students
- Design instruction that builds on what their students already know, supporting students who need help, and stretching students who need a challenge.

Design Strategies

Because computer-mediated asynchronous communication is textual and not visual, it is a relatively low-context communication medium, as noted above. Consequently, in a multicultural classroom in which there is a representation of both low- and high-context cultures, the impact of a low-context learning environment can be reduced by enriching existing course content with high-context features such as graphics, audio and video clips, podcasting, and synchronous two-way audio and video. Vendors, such as Wimba, offer a variety of supporting audio, video, instant messaging, collaboration, and content display tools that enable instructors to add important elements of interaction that cannot be provided in an exclusively text-based course. Enriching the CMC environment provides improved opportunities for high-context communication to occur.

Another design tool is class broadcast Web logs (blogs) where students write about their learning, their perspectives on the subject, and the learning process itself. Blogs are more useful than traditional journals because the instructor and fellow students can read one another's entries and, thus, gain more understanding about beliefs, perspectives, culture, problems, and successes, all of which contribute to students' sense of community.

However, because these media fall outside many normal institutional offerings, the instructor must take into account availability, levels of support, cross-platform compatibility, minimal student computer configurations, plus the technical ability and savvy of the students. This is particularly important for minority students, many of whom are unequipped to manage the digital learning environment because of relatively low computer knowledge, skills, and experiences, which can adversely impact their academic achievement. Therefore, instructors and designers who believe nonmainstream technologies may further enhance the effectiveness of online programs and courses should naturally be concerned with the implementation viability of each tool.

Curriculum and Instruction Strategies

Multiculturalism suggests the development of knowledge systems that reflect a plurality of worldviews. Michael Vavrus (2002) argues that successful multicultural educators have learned how to engage the uneasy coexistence of a transformed and a more traditional curriculum within a single school: "Transformative multicultural education pragmatically recognizes and engages this tension as an inherent aspect of meeting multicultural education goals" (p. 7). Thus, the challenge in many institutions is learning how to engage this tension in pragmatic and productive ways, such as designing learning communities for particular groups of students, using learning communities as sites for curriculum transformation, and developing instructional practices that support diverse learners.

In achieving this purpose, it may be necessary for students to make the most significant kind of knowledge transformation: a perspective transformation or paradigm shift in order to erase vestiges of racism and cultural bias. Jack Mezirow (1991) describes such a transformation as:

> the process of becoming critically aware of how and why our assumptions have come to constrain the way we perceive, understand, and feel about our world; changing

these structures of habitual expectation to make possible a more inclusive, discrimi-
nating, and integrating perspective; and finally, making choices or otherwise acting
upon these new understandings. (p. 167)

According to transformative learning theory (Mezirow, 1991), changing perspectives is related to several conditions and processes that must be met:

- An activating event that exposes the limitations of a student's current perspective, such as providing students with conflicting viewpoints or a dis-
orienting dilemma
- Opportunities for the student to identify and discuss the underlying assumptions in the student's current perspective
- Critical self-reflection as the student considers where these underlying assumptions came from and how they influence or limit understanding
- Critical discourse with other students and the instructor as the learning
community examines alternative ideas and perspectives
- Opportunities to apply and evaluate new perspectives.

Resistance to perspective transformation is common (Illeris, 2003). Consequently,
to facilitate transformative learning, instructors must create an environment that
encourages and rewards intellectual openness (Taylor, 1998).

Banks and Banks (2004) suggest a strategy consisting of curriculum content
changes for promoting multicultural education. They identify four levels or
approaches:

1. At the contributions level, the teacher uses examples from different ethnic
groups that focus on heroes and holidays.
2. At the additive level, the number of examples is increased so that the information fills an entire unit or class.
3. At the transformation level, the nature and purpose of the curriculum
changes, and students view subject-matter concepts from different racial
and cultural perspectives.
4. At the social action level, students are guided toward decision making in
their world based on what they have learned.

Cose (1997) recommends that online teachers find ways to motivate minority students, convince them that their teacher believes in them, teach them study
skills, challenge them with practical material, provide adequate scaffolding, and
demand that they perform. Cohen (1994) suggests that instructors pay particular
attention to unequal participation of students in group work and discussion and
employ strategies to address student status inequities. She recommends that instructors delegate authority to students, through norms and roles, to generate student interactions. The instructor intervenes indirectly to equalize students' status

in the classroom by raising the status of those students with lower status. The idea is that when status is equalized, all students in the group interact equitably and all will learn.

Assigning competence to low-status students means that the teacher publicly recognizes the work they have accomplished. Cohen (1994) suggests that the teacher makes the case to students that everyone needs one another for successful completion of the classroom work and no one has all the abilities necessary for a collaborative assignment but each student possesses some. Moreover, instructors need to attend to nurturing student attitudes, such as interest in projects and pride in success.

Additionally, Banks and Banks (2004); Gay (2002); Rovai, Gallien, and Stiff-Williams (2007); and Williams, Goldstein, and Goldstein (2002) suggest the following activities for culturally responsive teaching:

- Acknowledging students' differences as well as their commonalities
- Respecting the diverse talents of students and their ways of learning such as:
    Allowing students to choose project topics
    Incorporating diverse views into courses
    Allowing students to participate in assorted types of assignments (e.g., independent work and collaborative work)
    Giving students a choice in their assignments
- Validating students' cultural identity in classroom practices and instructional materials
- Educating students about diversity
- Promoting equity, mutual respect, and sense of community among students
- Encouraging student interaction within a constructivist learning environment by providing clear guidelines for student participation and by grading online course participation
- Relating course materials to multiple social and cultural environments
- Providing handouts to assist students
- Encouraging student-student interactions
- Improving faculty-student contacts
- Arranging student study groups or research projects
- Assessing students' ability and achievement validly
- Motivating students to become responsible for their own learning
- Encouraging students to think critically
- Challenging students to strive for excellence as defined by their potential
- Improving minority student integration within the institution.

CONCLUSION

Research shows that White students enter colleges and universities, especially top-tier institutions, without much experience relating to persons of color, especially in a setting of "relative equality" (Chesler, Lewis, & Crowfoot, 2005). Many broaden their perspectives about race relations during their time as students. These changes are generally tied to the frequency of contact with minority students and their willingness to grow at a personal level. Consequently, it is important that online program directors and instructors facilitate a positive interaction among members of a learning community at the beginning of a program. When a member of a majority group initially meets with a minority group member and the experience is a positive one, Allport's (1954) contact hypothesis suggests that an attitude change occurs on two levels. First, there is an attitude change that is target-specific. That is, initial assumptions about the other that arise from the (negative) stereotypes associated with his or her group are replaced by more positive attitudes regarding the individual. Second, these new positive perceptions will become extended to that individual's group as a whole, thus reducing negative attitudes toward the group.

Allport (1954) identifies four key conditions for such a meeting: equal-group status within the situation, common goals, intergroup cooperation, and institutional support. Additional conditions were later added, the most important of which are voluntary interaction and intimate (i.e., socioemotional) contact. Moreover, research shows that, when effectively implemented, these conditions do lead to a positive attitude change that is target-specific (e.g., Hewstone & Brown, 1986), although evidence is weaker regarding an attitude change toward the individual's group. In particular, Hewstone and Brown (1986) argue that a general contact is likely to be perceived on the interpersonal level and therefore not have any impact on the intergroup level unless individual participants are seen as representatives of their group.

Ibarra (2001) attributes many of the challenges to ethnic minority student success in higher education to academic culture, where the tone is largely set by an upper/middle-class White, non-Hispanic culture.

> The difference is that today we must rethink and reframe the operative paradigm to address the real problem, which is academic organizational cultures that prefer to confront, not collaborate. And in no way are the pipeline programs born in the 1960s capable of dealing with the growing problem of high-context, field sensitive students who are abandoning (or never entering) graduate schools, which are dominated by low-context, field independent professors. (p. 243)

We must be careful not to fall into the "fatalist instrumentalist approach" of assuming that it is inevitable that "social structures will remain unaltered and digital information technologies will be another factor to strengthen the existing structure of social stratification" (Mendoza, 2001, p. 30). We must move beyond complacency to the ethical realm, a realm of rights, equality, the social good, and democratizing information. Here, teaching and learning assume moral concepts that carry with them substantive assumptions of the way society should be and the role of multiculturalism in that society. Every culture, including the dominant culture, has its limitations and benefits from a dialogue with others. Different cultures should both be respected and brought into a creative interplay.

A key element in effective intercultural communication is being aware of the pervasive influence of culture on communications and understanding. Different worldviews, color perceptions, values, and communication patterns. Without an awareness of these differences, intercultural communication can result in misunderstandings, stereotypes, prejudice, and reduced motivation to learn. Consequently, it becomes essential for staff and faculty to know their students well enough to understand what unique obstacles and incentives may encourage or discourage motivation. Allport (1954) claims that familiarity lessens prejudice. Prejudices and stereotypes about others are not removed based on an exchange of knowledge, since individuals are likely to accept only those pieces of information that fit into their preconceived schema of the world. It is through getting to know each other that people may be able to break down their stereotypes, enabling the exchange and exploration of diverse perspectives that enrich lives and promote a strong sense of community.

CHAPTER 4

Strategic Planning

Strategic planning is an umbrella term that encompasses various approaches to the management of organizational decision making. It consists of a process in which an organization envisions its future and develops the necessary strategies, programs, and activities to create that future. In so doing, it seeks to better align itself with its environment. The basic premise is that actions guided by a deliberately planned strategy produce more satisfactory outcomes for the organization than actions chosen by other means (Grace, 1996).

For educational institutions, distance education can mean movement toward new directions, particularly in the growing area of lifelong learning and outreach to a wider and more diverse student population. Strategic planning assists the institution in realizing these outcomes efficiently, and can help provide a solution to the adult educational needs of educationally isolated communities; physically handicapped persons who cannot attend on-campus classes; individuals who move frequently, such as members of the armed forces; and persons whose work and family schedules make it difficult or impossible to attend scheduled classes or commute to campus.

Additionally, corporate training and education needs must be satisfied either in-house or by colleges and universities tailoring programs to satisfy corporate requirements. Online learning has an important potential role to play by supplying the corporate workforce with an up-to-date and cost-effective program that yields motivated and skilled knowledge workers. Corporations can realize substantial savings by replacing in-house, instructor-led training with electronic content delivery and perhaps outsourcing all or part of the training to colleges and universities that are able and willing to work cooperatively with corporate trainers in producing and delivering online training.

Implementing a distance education program can be expensive, and requires detailed and focused planning, management, program design, and a change in the institution's traditional culture. Integrated and systematic planning is required to determine the extent of the need, to realign institutional activities, and to allocate resources efficiently to meet that need. Moreover, developing or expanding services for off-campus students who are enrolled in distance education programs can be complex and expensive. The purpose of this chapter is to discuss these issues and suggest a flexible framework for addressing distance education within the institution's planning system.

BACKGROUND

Rowley, Lujan, and Dolence (1997) describe strategic planning in higher education as a

> formal process designed to help a university identify and maintain an optimal alignment with the most important elements [of] the environment . . . within which the university resides. [This environment consists of] the political, social, economic, technological, and educational ecosystem, both internal and external to the university. (pp. 14–15)

Strategic planning is a management tool that helps an organization do a better job by focusing its energy, promoting organizational unity of effort, and assessing and adjusting the organization's direction in response to a changing environment (Bryson, 2004). Accordingly, strategic planning is a disciplined effort to produce fundamental decisions and actions that shape and guide what an organization is, what it does, why it does it, and what it should look like in the future. Keller (1997) writes that strategic planning is also about organizational learning and creativity. College and university administrators need to challenge their basic assumptions and consider altering everyday processes.

Effective planning includes broad-based support and participation by all institutional stakeholders and allows colleges and universities to "pursue greater mission differentiation to streamline their services and better respond to the changing needs of their constituencies" (Benjamin & Carroll, 1997, pp. 22–23). The real measure of success is about how to move beyond strategy to implementation and transformation. In so doing, university administrators have become increasingly knowledgeable about the limitations of cookie-cutter planning methodologies (e.g., Mintzberg, 1994). Consequently,

> strategic planning cannot be applied in universities and colleges in the same way it is applied in the private sector. Organizational goals in higher education are often vague and, even when well defined, contested. (Lewis, Massey, & Smith, 2001, p. 135)

Moreover, governance and organizational culture in not-for-profit colleges and universities are decidedly different from those of corporations.

IDENTIFICATION OF PROGRAM NEED

To grow, universities must appeal to more diverse students in an increasingly competitive marketplace. These potentially new students include learners with varying needs, which represent opportunities that can be attained through delivering programs and courses at a distance using technology. It is therefore important to integrate distance education in the institution's overall strategic planning process in order to examine opportunities for growth, and to ensure the proper utilization of technology as a support to teaching and learning at a distance. Without a properly articulated need, an institution should not move ahead with implementation of a new distance education program or make substantial changes to an existing program.

Establishing the need for institutional programs is an important early step in the strategic planning process. Although the notion of "build it and they will come" worked well for actor Kevin Costner in the movie *Field of Dreams*, the simple truth is that this approach is not a reliable substitute for conducting a needs assessment. When the need for a distance education program has been carefully determined and is real, planning and implementation will be effective and meaningful and students will come.

There is no single model for conducting a needs assessment that is universally used. Kosecoff and Fink (1982) describe the following four-step model for conducting a needs assessment that was originally developed by David Satcher (see Figure 4.1).

Step 1: Identify potential objectives. In Step 1, the school compiles a comprehensive list of objectives for a distance education program if one is not presently offered, or a list of objectives to alter or expand existing programs if a distance education program already exists. The professional literature, experts in the field, student evaluations of teaching, faculty and staff surveys, and school self-studies are good sources for identifying objectives. Potential objectives include:

- Increasing distance education student enrollments
- Expanding the number of programs offered at a distance

FIGURE 4.1. Needs Assessment Model

1 Identify potential objectives.

2 Decide which objectives are most important.

3 Assess the nature and type of services currently available.

4 Select and refine final objectives.

- Improving professional development training to faculty and students on the uses of technology
- Providing incentives for faculty participation in distance learning development activities
- Improving ease of navigation of the distance education Web site
- Providing an individualized, dynamic online portal for students to all relevant academic course materials, resources, and student support services
- Improving student evaluation of online teaching
- Increasing the sense of community among distance education learners
- Integrating distance education students in the institution and campus life
- Providing meaningful on-campus residency experiences
- Providing an equitable learning environment that considers issues of gender, ethnicity, and disabilities
- Improving support services for online students.

Step 2: Decide which objectives are most important. In this step, the school selects a sample of potential and/or actual distance education students, faculty, and staff and has them rate the objectives according to relative importance. A market analysis is also useful during this step to determine the market potential for the distance education program and to identify those topics and programs that are in high demand. The school then analyzes and synthesizes the results.

Step 3: Assess the nature and type of currently available services, both internal and external to the institution. The purpose of this step is to obtain information about how well current programs are satisfying the proposed objectives and student/faculty needs. An important issue is how well clients are satisfied with current programs and services. A need can be very important, but if it can be easily satisfied without changing existing services, then the proposed objective should be dropped or relegated to low priority.

Step 4: Select and refine final objectives. In this step, the school synthesizes collected information in order to prioritize objectives and establish supporting strategies, activities, and programs within the strategic planning process.

THE STRATEGIC PLANNING PROCESS

Typically, distance education is fully integrated in the school's overall planning process. Keeping in mind the principle of flexibility, strategic planning activities can be viewed as involving three sequential phases (see Figure 4.2) that comprise a cyclical planning model. Each phase addresses an increased level of strategic focus on the information and issues defined and analyzed in the preceding phase. The process ends with the implementation and monitoring of the strategic plan as a new strategic planning cycle begins.

FIGURE 4.2. Strategic Planning Model

	1	2	3
Phases	Startup	Scanning and Diagnosis	Strategy Formulation and Implementation
Outcomes	Workplan Timeline		

SWOT Analysis
Core Values

Strategies
Refined Mission
Refined Vision
Strategic Goals
Strategic Objectives
Benchmarks
Resource Requirements
Budget Requirements
Strategic Plan
Unit Plans
Implementation
Monitoring

Phase 1: Startup

The startup phase consists of the formation of the strategic planning committee (SPC). The SPC performs the following tasks:

- Identifies the institution's key services, products, and markets, to include distance education, as appropriate
- Reviews strategic plans and reports from the previous strategic planning cycle
- Identifies the broad information needs for the second phase
- Identifies organizational constraints to conducting the strategic planning process.

The output of this phase is a detailed work plan with a timeline.

Phase 2: Scanning and Diagnosis

In this phase, the SPC performs a situational analysis by accomplishing two major tasks. First, it conducts an analysis of strengths, weaknesses, opportunities and threats (SWOT) by diagnosing the internal strengths and weaknesses and external opportunities and threats facing the overall organization and each of its key services, products, and markets (Bryson, 2004). Second, it identifies the core values that form the heart of the school's approach to intellectual, moral, social, and cultural development.

SWOT analysis is conducted using a process of scanning internal and external stakeholders. The objective of this analysis is to recommend strategies that ensure the best alignment between the external environment and internal situation (Hax & Majluf, 1996). Table 4.1 provides examples of SWOT factors that would influence the results of a needs assessment and strategic planning for distance education programs. Naturally, the institution's analysis must be made based on an evaluation of its own unique ecosystem.

Bryson (2004) describes SWOT analysis as a tool for auditing an organization and its environment. It helps planners focus on the strategic issues, that is, the issues that are the fundamental challenges the organization must address to achieve its mission and move toward its desired future. This focus helps the organization relate to what it should be doing to meet the needs of its clients or potential clients. The SWOT analysis is carried out by identifying and assigning each significant factor, positive and negative, to one of the four SWOT categories, allowing an objective look at the environment. This analysis is a useful tool in developing and confirming a strategic vision and supporting goals and strategies.

The SPC also identifies or revises the institution's core values, which largely define organizational culture. For example, shared governance, faculty control of the

TABLE 4.1. Examples of SWOT Factors

Example Factor	SWOT Category
Accreditation status	Strength or weakness
Technology infrastructure	Strength or weakness
School recognition/reputation	Strength or weakness
Student and faculty support	Strength or weakness
Faculty professional development	Strength or weakness
Demand for distance programs	Opportunity
Expansion and improvement	Opportunity
Globalization	Opportunity
Increased student diversity	Opportunity
Inadequate funding sources	Threat
Competition	Threat
Poor communications and planning	Threat

curriculum, and nonproprietary basic research and scholarship detached from revenue considerations are likely to be important values for not-for-profit institutions. In contrast, strong hierarchical organizational structure with centralized power and realization of a profit from operations are valued by for-profit institutions.

One possible method of identifying organizational values is first to examine the values that faculty, staff, and students bring to the school before examining the institution's values. By identifying and publicizing core values, the school makes clear what is expected, and provides the basis for individual accountability. Moreover, the core values become a recruitment tool and allow hiring to address the congruence of the applicant's values to those of the school.

Phase 3: Strategy Formulation and Implementation

In the final phase, the SPC develops a strategic vision and the strategies, programs, and activities that will achieve this vision. The SPC performs the following tasks in this final phase:

- Recommends refinement of the school mission statement, if needed. The mission statement outlines what the school is now. A well-articulated mission statement identifies (a) the needs the organization fulfills, (b) the products and markets required to fulfill the organization's purpose, and (c) unique competencies that distinguish the organization from competitors (Hax & Majluf, 1996).
- Refines the school's vision statement, if needed. A vision statement outlines what a school wants to be. It focuses on tomorrow and provides a clear decision-making standard. A school's vision does not determine how the school will work, but rather how it will look and act if the strategic plan is implemented successfully.
- Sets strategic direction by identifying strategic university goals that lead the school from where it is at present, as defined by its mission, to where it wants to go, as defined by its vision.
- Develops strategic objectives and benchmarks (i.e., targets) that reflect statements of attainable and quantifiable achievements that move the school toward its strategic goals.
- Develops appropriate strategies, activities, and programs to enable key services, products, and markets to best respond to the issues and challenges flowing from the previous phase.
- Develops resource and budgetary requirements. Budgetary decisions are made based on the requirements of processes related to educating students.
- Directs the preparation of unit strategic plans that address implementation of strategic objectives at the departmental level. These plans identify the specific steps that will be taken to achieve the initiatives and strategic objectives and focus on operations, procedures, and processes.

- Implements and monitors the institution's strategic plan and supporting unit plans through institutional research and program evaluations that focus on key performance indicators.
- Directs the refinement of unit plans, as needed, as the result of monitoring activities.

Fornaciari, Forte, and Mathews (1999) propose distance education strategies based on "institution size, tuition cost, and reputation" (p. 709). They suggest that large regional universities with low national reputations adopt cost leadership strategies based on the goal of achieving a lower cost position than the competition to attract out-of-state students by charging them in-state tuition rates. Alternatively, small institutions with strong national reputations can pursue differentiation strategies by offering highly selective distance degree programs. Institutions that do not have the resources to be full-fledged competitors in the broader marketplace often adopt focus strategies. Consequently, they avoid competition and target a specific market or niche instead of competing in the mass marketplace. For example, Fornaciari, Forte, and Mathews (1999) note that the University of Phoenix is a typical focus-differentiator. Its target audience is not all college-age students, nor does it seek to be a comprehensive university. Instead, it offers specific degree and certificate programs to working professionals.

Benchmarking is an important part of this phase, as what is benchmarked heavily influences implementation.

> Benchmarking implies measurement . . . of the industry best practices. [Then] the practices can be quantified to show an analytical measurement of the gap between practices. This metric is often the single-minded measurement that most managers want. (Camp, 1989, p. 67)

Several types of benchmarks can be used, to include internal benchmarking that compares similar processes across programs within the institution, competitive benchmarking that compares similar processes to those of competitors, and generic benchmarking that identifies best educational practices (Alstete, 1995).

Appendix A provides an example of what a distance education strategic goal with supporting strategic objectives, benchmarks, and sources of evidence might look like. Naturally, this example would be part of an overall integrated university strategic plan.

DISTANCE EDUCATION CHALLENGES AND STRATEGIES

Institutions that wish to survive and thrive must draw from their strengths and become proactive in identifying and responding to challenges as well as to emerging opportunities. Berge and Muilenburg (2006) report that the three most significant types of barriers to distance education are related to faculty compensation and time, organizational change, and lack of technical expertise and support. The ensuing discussion elaborates the following six strategic planning challenges: startup costs, a new student base, competition, marketing, student support services, and faculty support. These challenges are related to the human, physical, and financial resources of the institution that influence institutional effectiveness.

Startup Costs

Van Dusen (2000) maintains that starting up a distance education program can be expensive and is unlikely to affect institutional cost savings over the short or middle term. The basic infrastructure needed to deliver online courses that adds to this expense includes appropriate basic technologies of servers, wiring, networking connections, computers and software, computer support personnel, and software licensing (Wright, 2002).

Moreover, high startup costs make small-market programs or programs in areas undergoing rapid transition expensive to offer. The expense of frequent upgrades, faculty development, and technical support can ultimately become more expensive than initial hardware and software acquisition costs. Additionally, the costs of high technology are difficult to manage, and the lure of new technology tends to undermine the need for sound educational planning.

Van Dusen (2000) writes that the current assumption that schools will profit through economies of scale with distance learning courses is erroneous due to shrinking budgets and expensive startup costs for the technology. He identifies the following issues that need to be addressed in order for distance education to become economically feasible:

- Evaluating program delivery systems and ensuring integration with other facets of the institution
- Ensuring that the institutional mission supports distance education learning
- Recognizing that the cost of distance education is not just in startup purchases, but includes long-term product upgrades and support systems
- Recognizing that faculty course development is a cost that should be fully supported.

However, costs associated with starting up and sustaining a distance education program can vary greatly. If little support and training is given to faculty and traditional course materials are simply made available online, costs will be relatively low, but so will be the quality of learning. If online courses, supporting materials, faculty, and student support services are designed from the ground up to take advantage of the potential presented by online learning, costs will be substantially higher, as will the quality of learning outcomes.

A New Student Base

An increasing proportion of college students are members of the Net Generation, who grew up using information technology with sensory-rich interactive environments, entertainment-style communication, and immediate feedback, and who prefer experiential activities, virtual or real. Many of these new students rely more on the Internet for information than on libraries. Moreover, they are accustomed to using the Internet for multiuser online activities, such as participation in virtual worlds like Second Life, as well as social networking. These changes suggest that students from the Net Generation and beyond may be more motivated in immersive and authentic learning environments and engaging in flexible and convenient learning activities. For example, instead of reading course material, many Net Generation students may prefer the convenience of listening to a podcast on an iPod while exercising.

As higher education has expanded, the student body has become much larger and more diverse in terms of age, ethnicity, cultural background, and academic preparation. Unlike their on-campus peers, students enrolled in distance education programs attend class at home using computer technology to access course materials and communicate with their instructor and other students. Unless required to attend on-campus orientations or residencies, they may never visit the university campus, and they typically access student support services at a distance. A report by the American Council on Education, Center for Policy Analysis and Educause (Oblinger, Barone, & Hawkins, 2001) cites seven distinct audiences for distance learning:

- Corporate learners
- Professional enhancement learners
- Degree-completion adult learners
- College experience learners (the traditional student)
- Precollege (K–12) learners
- Remediation and test-preparation learners
- Recreational learners.

Research, e.g., Ashby (2002), suggests that distance education students are more likely to be disciplined, married, female (if an undergraduate), enrolled part-time, and isolated from postsecondary school campuses and research libraries. These differences suggest that distance education students have educational and personal needs that differ from those of traditional students. Mupinga, Nora, and Yaw (2006) report that the top needs of online students are:

- Technical help
- Flexible and understanding instructors
- Advance course information

- Sample assignments
- Grading standards, e.g., a rubric
- Instructor feedback
- Interpersonal interaction
- The same learning management system used in a consistent manner by all courses and instructors
- Additional reference materials
- Equal recognition with on-campus students.

Moreover, the global and cross-border reach of distance education suggests that the distance education student population is international. Culture profoundly influences the values, attitudes, and behavior of individuals. Effective planning for cross-cultural teaching and learning does not occur without understanding other cultures, their characteristics, and their learning needs.

Competition

Notwithstanding the massification of higher education, competition among postsecondary institutions for students has intensified as the result of distance education and the emergence of a market structure as a means of regulation. The primary market areas of colleges and universities are no longer limited to the geographical areas in proximity to their campuses. Students are increasingly viewed as consumers, and institutions are marketing directly to them. Among the competitors to traditional universities are corporate universities and for-profit institutions, such as the University of Phoenix, Strayer University, and DeVry University.

According to Meister (1998), hundreds of corporate universities have sprung up in the United States as in-house training facilities because of the growing frustration of business with the quality and content of postsecondary education. Moreover, Meister contends that these corporate universities are evolving into strategic umbrellas for educating not only employees, but also secondary customers and suppliers. Consequently, the corporate university is filling the educational void left by the inability or unwillingness of traditional schools to adapt rapidly enough to the evolving educational needs of a changing labor force.

Additionally, the rising costs of tuition at traditional colleges and universities have stimulated the expansion of for-profit institutions, despite the fact that public subsidies of public higher education historically shield public institutions from serious competition. Within the present competitive higher education environment, public institutions are limited in their ability to reduce tuition, the traditional business response to increase market share in a saturated market. According to Zemsky, Wegner, and Massy (2005), state governments drive up the prices that public institutions charge students whenever the business cycle reduces state revenues and forces state governments to choose between a reduction in educational services, an increase in taxes, or an increase in tuition.

Gerald R. Odening, vice president of Salomon Smith Barney, a Wall Street investment firm, predicts that for-profit institutions will capture 15% to 20% of the higher education market share by 2020 (Strosnider, 1998). Winston (1999) outlines reasons for this projected growth:

> The vision—or specter—is simple. New information technologies and the organizational efficiencies of privatization can lower the cost of producing higher education enough that for-profit schools can compete with existing not-for-profit colleges and universities by offering students a better deal and still making a profit. Or they'll produce an education that students deem more appropriate, improving quality from the consumer's point of view. So, costs and prices will be lower, or the education will be different and better, or both. (p. 13)

Lyons (2003) describes one approach that for-profits use to capture market share as a "skimming" strategy in which they target the most lucrative market segment, e.g., highly motivated working professionals who are older than traditional students and who pursue degrees in highly popular disciplines. Lyons (2004) claims that for-profit institution courses are typically highly standardized and display few gaps or overlaps in content from one course to the next, thus reducing the instructor's preparation time and achieving other productivity gains that help reduce costs.

The implications for traditional colleges and universities that are unable to evolve quickly enough and adapt in response to the changing higher education environment is that they will fall behind the competition and eventually become irrelevant as other institutions emerge to fill the educational and training gaps. As colleges and universities revisit their missions and visions as part of the strategic planning process, it becomes essential that they consider ways of dealing with the expectations of both society and students and fully integrate academic and information technology planning to respond to the changing needs of learners. "Planners may have to come to grips with the possibility of a radical redefinition of their institutions and their missions" (Lewis, Massey, & Smith, 2001, p. 28).

Marketing

Pardey (1991) defines *educational marketing* as "the process which enables client needs to be identified, anticipated, and satisfied, in order that the institution's objectives can be achieved" (p. 12). "The main task of the institution is to determine the needs and wants of target markets and to satisfy them through the design, communication, pricing and delivery of appropriate and competitively viable programs and services" (Kotler & Fox, 1995, p. 8).

The characteristics of adults who are likely to be interested in enrolling in distance education programs—those who comprise the target market—and their academic needs are discussed above. However, the question remains: Who are the best prospects for enrolling in distance education programs? Certainly professionals who are remote from the institution, are comfortable using computer-mediated communication, and have few, if any, opportunities for face-to-face classroom instruction because of work and/or family responsibilities are prime candidates for distance education programs. However, marketing solely to this population is a mistake. Many students, for example, like to mix on-campus and distance study in the same program.

Marketing professionals must align their actions with the strategic vision adopted by the university regarding the role of distance education in its future and adjust its marketing strategies accordingly. Moreover, the school's marketing plan for distance education must take into account the school's distinctive place in the distance education market relative to competing programs (Foskett, 2002). Most importantly, marketing claims must be supported by the programs offered and should not convey misleading expectations, such as emphasizing the convenience of distance education but ignoring the time and work needed to complete a program. Preoccupation with consumer satisfaction is harmful to higher education.

Marketing and student recruitment strategies that emphasize mass marketing can be contrary to the need for a focus on relationship marketing for building and maintaining a long-term relationship with students. There are three levels of relationship marketing (Berry, 2004). At level one, price incentives are used to promote enrollments. Social bonding is used at level two to develop trust in the relationship and loyalty to the institution. At level three, the focus is on building relationships through customized programs that meet the needs of the student and the student's employer. According to Berry, level one and two programs can be replicated by the competition and are not used for developing competitive advantage. However, level three programs are not easily replicable, and are the basis of competitive advantage to the institution.

Student Support Services

High-quality, comprehensive student support services are essential to student recruitment and retention. Students expect convenient access to the same types of support services as on-campus students (see Table 4.2). Access to these services, to the maximum extent possible, should be provided online.

Distance education is a topic that is not being fully addressed by student affairs (Woodward, Love, & Komives, 2000). "Because student affairs work has traditionally been campus based, little consideration has been given to how student affairs might confront the issue of distance education" (Blimling & Whitt, 1998, p. 7). Much of student affairs' online presence in support of distance students involves essential support services, such as admission, registration, financial aid, and help with technology. Student life, student activities, and related services have yet to provide distance students with experiences equitable to those offered to traditional students on-campus. This situation should be addressed in the institution's needs assessment.

TABLE 4.2. Typical Student Support
Services

Support Area	Service
Enrollment	Admissions
	Advising
	Registrar
	Billing Office
	Financial Aid
	New Student Orientation
Instruction	Bookstore
	Library
	Tutoring
	Service Learning
Support	Technology
	Career Center
	Counseling

Schroeder (1999) maintains that the creation of seamless learning environments must be a priority for student affairs. Student affairs professionals should therefore service distance students as they do on-campus students. They need to consider the total environment in which learning takes place. The campus environment is one that exists virtually for distance education students, and it will take more effort to create a virtual community than solely offering independent services that are not integrated into a complete educational experience. Elements of student support services may be supplied by consortium partners or outsourced to other organizations. However, responsibility for performance remains with the institution awarding the diploma.

Faculty Support

The school's faculty members are important stakeholders who should be consulted during the strategic planning process in order to take their views into account and engage them in the process. Research (e.g., Gunawardena, 1990) identifies potential faculty resistance to distance education as a barrier to the continued growth of distance education programs. Common perceptions one may encounter is faculty skepticism about the quality of distance learning, the lack of perceived institutional support (faculty compensation and rewards, incentives, training, and so forth) for course conversion to distance education formats (e.g., Olcott & Wright, 1995), and lack of recognition of the increased time required for high-quality teaching at a distance.

According to Dooley and Murphy (2001), the ability of an institution to adapt to change is influenced by competence (knowledge, skills, and abilities of its faculty and staff) and value (the amount of importance the faculty places on the role of distance education to accomplish teaching and learning). Faculty must also view distance education as congruent with the beliefs and values they hold about university education (Black, 1992). Consequently, training and assistance for faculty members who are not experienced with the distance education model are needed in order to elicit their support.

CONCLUSION

To make the point that the higher education environment is changing and that institutions need to adapt if they expect to remain competitive, Beaudoin (2002) writes:

> Whether or not it embraces the trend, the academy is shifting from a campus-centric to a distributed education model, and while the administrative and instructional infrastructures that presently characterize most of our institutions won't necessarily disappear, they will be utilized in different ways. Those who dismiss this as a passing phase, apparently do not recognize how pervasive these changes already are even within their own institutions, however mainstream they may still appear to be. (p. 133)

The goal of strategic planning is to assist an organization in adapting to a changing environment, to focus its energy, and to ensure that members of the organization are working toward the same goals (Bryson, 2004). However, strategic planning is not without its limitations and critics, especially when implemented as an inflexible system by individuals with superficial understandings of the concepts and various purposes of planning. Institutions of higher education represent highly complex social systems and "organizational strategies cannot be created by the logic used to assemble automobiles" (Mintzberg, 1994, p. 13). Taken too far, the logic of strategic planning can result in the collection and analysis of huge amounts of data and the production of numerous recurring reports, placing an unreasonable burden on the organization. In such a situation, the tail indeed wags the dog. Moreover, the dependence on benchmarking and the use of key performance indicators used in strategic planning tend to focus the planning process only on variables that are easily defined and measured.

Despite these weaknesses, one cannot ignore what Lewis Carroll wrote in *Alice's Adventures in Wonderland*: If you don't know where you are going, any road will take you there. Despite the polemics in the professional literature about strategic planning pitfalls, planning remains an essential element of organizational effectiveness, and a planning process characterized by order and logic is required to help the institution determine where it wants to go and how best it can get there. The key is to tailor the planning process to fit the needs and culture of the school so that the planning process encourages and facilitates changes in predictable increments. Although many authors support the notion of flexible planning, e.g., Mintzberg (1994), the danger is taking this concept too far so that flexible planning becomes daily decision making.

Higher education administrators must learn to think strategically as part of their regular activities. Strategic thinking involves "arraying options through a process of opening up institutional thinking to a range of alternatives and decisions that identify the best fit between the institution, its resources, and the environment" (Rowley, Lujan, & Dolence, 1997, p. 15). Administrators also need to acquire a collection of strategic planning skills if they expect to be successful in their efforts. These skills include conducting needs assessments and market analyses, fitting technology to needs, operationalizing ideas, mobilizing resources, implementing online infrastructure, formulating policy, training the faculty, collaborating with partners, evaluating and accrediting programs, and mentoring the next generation of leaders (Beaudoin, 2002).

CHAPTER 5

Program and Course Design

The first question that many ask when considering distance education is whether it is as effective as face-to-face education. Based on extensive research, the answer is a resounding yes, although it is important to be clear about what is being asked. Does this mean that all online instruction is as effective as all face-to-face instruction? No. Does this mean that all online programs or courses are equally as effective? Certainly not. Does this mean that online instruction is the ideal mode for all students? Of course not. What we know from the literature is that fully online as well as blended instruction produce outcomes similar to those seen with face-to-face instruction, provided that the method and technologies used are appropriate to the instructional tasks, that there is ample student-student interaction, and that there is timely teacher-student feedback. In other words, the research indicates that media or delivery method is not the determining factor in educational effectiveness.

A meta-analysis of 232 comparative studies conducted by Bernard, Abrami, Lou, Borokhovski, Wade, Wozney, Wallet, Fiset, and Huang (2004) concludes that although there is no average difference in achievement between distance and classroom courses, the results demonstrate wide variability. In other words,

> a substantial number of [distance education] applications provide better achievement results, are viewed more positively, and have higher retention rates than their classroom counterparts. On the other hand, a substantial number of [distance education] applications are far worse than classroom instruction. (p. 406)

These findings suggest that appropriate instructional design and good pedagogical practices, rather than the computer-mediating technology itself, are at the center of effective online education.

This chapter highlights design and pedagogical considerations for effective distance education program and course design. In particular, various design models are presented, online learning technologies are discussed, and issues of accessibility are considered.

BACKGROUND

The contemporary models of computer and Internet-based virtual classes have been labeled "fifth generation" distance education by Moore and Kearsley (2005), supplanting the previous generations of correspondence, broadcasting, systems approach, and teleconferencing. Throughout this historical progression, opportunities for interpersonal interaction between instructors and learners (and among learners themselves) have increased as the learning environments have matured. Early correspondence courses enabled learners and instructors to interact, albeit with a significant time lag between message production and reception. Videoconferencing made it possible for learners and instructors to interact in real time, and it also facilitated learner-learner interaction, although the required equipment often made this means of distance education too costly for mainstream use. With the emergence of the Internet, featuring asynchronous and synchronous communication opportunities combined with the potential for simulations and virtual worlds, it became possible to promote high degrees of interaction within media-rich learning environments.

Despite this rich history, one of the limitations facing instructors and institutions when developing online programs and courses is recognizing the variety of types of distance education available. There are, in fact, many different approaches to distance education, ranging from fully online asynchronous courses to synchronous online courses conducted in 3-D virtual worlds, from exclusively textual material to portable audio and video instructional content.

PROGRAM AND COURSE DESIGN MODELS

Most of us have spent enough time in traditional degree programs to know what to expect when we arrive on campus. We are used to the teacher handing out syllabi, writing notes on the chalkboard, and launching into an introductory lecture. Distance education is different, not only from our experiences with traditional courses but also from one course to another. A student could conceivably take three online courses during an academic term and have three substantially different experiences. Programs and courses can be designed with various class sizes, content delivery, classroom environments, and campus time in mind.

Class Sizes

Online courses range in size from a single student to hundreds of students. The four most common sizes of online classes can be categorized as independent studies, tutorials, seminars, and audiences. Table 5.1 highlights the advantages and disadvantages of these categorizations.

In independent studies, students learn with no contact with other students and limited contact with the instructor. Typically, course materials are distributed at the beginning of a course, including lecture notes, books, and assignments, and then students work through the materials at their own pace. These materials may be all online or a combination of offline and online. Furthermore, the actual instruction may be completely computer-led, with online simulations and computer-graded exams, or it may be instructor-led with assignments turned in via e-mail or

TABLE 5.1. Class Size Models

Class Size	Description	Advantages	Disadvantages
Independent study	Single student	Can learn at one's own pace	Can feel isolated
Tutorial	1 to 3 students	Personal attention from the instructor; team learning opportunities	Not as time-flexible as independent study
Seminar	3 to 20 students	Potential for significant class discussion while still engaging the instructor	As the size increases, online discussions can get overwhelming
Audience	More than 20 students	Large support system of fellow students; can result in high-quality class discussion	Students can feel distant from the instructor; online discussions can get overwhelming

the Web. The primary advantage of this approach is that students can proceed at their own pace (or within some established timeframe, such as a semester schedule) and study a highly specialized and/or personalized topic whenever it is convenient. The primary disadvantage is that students lose the feedback of fellow classmates and, very likely, regular interaction with the instructor.

Tutorial-style courses have small class sizes, often one to three students, and involve a greater level of interaction with the instructor. The tutorial model offers more frequent learner-instructor and learner-learner interaction, while still maintaining the time and subject flexibility associated with independent studies. Tutorials are often customized to the needs of individual students or groups of students using a learning contract. Learning contracts may be written by the students, under the guidance of the instructor, and outline the learning objectives, content materials, and assessment tasks that will be undertaken throughout the course. Students maintain regular contact with the instructor, often through weekly or monthly dialogues in which they discuss learning activities.

Seminar-style courses are probably the most common online courses, at least on the university level, and generally involve up to approximately 20 students. The size is usually large enough to support robust class discussion but still small enough to permit personal interaction with the instructor. In many respects, online seminars are not dramatically different from offline ones—seminar instructors often structure the courses identically to face-to-face ones except, of course, that communication takes place online. Class discussions, often taking place using asynchronous threaded discussion boards and sometimes live chat rooms, are commonly used in seminars. This approach offers students the chance to interact with each other as well as the instructor throughout the duration of the course. This feature improves the learning experience as well as the sense of community.

Audience courses have large class sizes—typically more than 20 students—and may even enroll hundreds of students. In many respects, audience courses are the online equivalent of campus courses delivered in large lecture halls. Such courses can reduce the opportunities for personal interaction, though sometimes the course is divided into small groups with facilitators (analogous to recitations with teaching assistants) and then functions more like an online seminar. The challenge for many people who take audience-style courses is they may feel less like students and more like spectators. The advantage of audience courses is that they often provide the best opportunity to learn from leading scholars who might not otherwise be accessible. They are also beneficial to those students whose cognitive style is a good match to the lecture model (i.e., field independent learners).

Content Delivery

Online courses use a variety of online and offline technologies to deliver course content. Although one might imagine that courses touted as Web-based are completely online, the reality is that instructors choose to deliver materials in ways best suited to learning. As a result, it is not uncommon to include a mixture of technologies in online courses, including printed and electronic text, presentation graphics, audio and video clips, videoconferencing, simulations, and virtual worlds. Many textbook companies publish course cartridge content to accompany specific textbooks that are compatible with Learning Management Systems such as Blackboard. Cartridge content often includes slides, documents, quiz questions, and lists of relevant hyperlinks to related Web sites. This content is created by publishers and is available for instructors to download. When students access this content within a course, they are prompted for an access key, which they must purchase.

Most online courses incorporate considerable reading. Textbooks, workbooks, journals, novels, magazines, articles, and individual handouts are used at least as often, if not more, in online courses than in campus-based ones. While face-to-face classes often contain lectures in addition to the books, some online courses increase the amount of reading to compensate for the lack of an online lecture, or perhaps incorporate lectures as podcasts. Typically, students receive a book list at the beginning of the class, and then the syllabus or study guide leads them through the required readings. Sometimes all of the reading materials will be bound into a course pack and purchased by students at the beginning of the course.

Electronic publishing is growing in popularity and is beginning to offer a significant alternative to print publishing. Although it is unlikely that students will abandon printed textbooks in the near future, the use of electronic publications, such as e-books and articles, is growing. Adobe Acrobat Portable Document Format (PDF), the standard for electronic document delivery, is often used by individual faculty members who are looking to provide electronic copies of articles or notes. PDF files are electronic copies that look and print (including text, graphics, and photos) identically to the original hardcopy version. University libraries and academic databases use such files to provide an electronic reserve collection and virtual library for online learners.

Many instructors also present material online through presentation graphics packages such as Microsoft PowerPoint. Sometimes these presentations are annotated with streaming audio, but often they are soundless presentations. While such presentations lack the in-depth content found in other media, they often provide an overview of the key points found in the readings for that week, and can thus serve as an advance organizer. Many instructors incorporate these slide presentations into online courses in lieu of traditional lectures. Some instructors also provide text-based lecture notes that provide a level of detail that cannot be easily included in a PowerPoint presentation.

For those instructors interested in incorporating lectures, audio and video clips fit the bill. While some programs still have audio and video tapes held over from the pre-Web distance learning days, more have moved to the use of streaming and portable media (e.g., podcasting) for such content. They bring the sensations of sight and sound to the online classroom. This not only helps those who profess visual or auditory learning styles but also enriches the overall learning environment for all students. These technologies are addressed further in the online learning technologies section of this chapter.

Packages such as Elluminate, HorizonWimba, and Microsoft NetMeeting make it possible to conduct full-motion videoconferencing courses online. Videoconferencing opens up the possibility of an online learning experience that is similar to a face-to-face one, with the students watching the instructor live, asking questions, and mingling with fellow classmates. Although most online conferencing is one-way (typically with the students watching the instructor), if everyone has high-speed Internet connections, it is possible for everyone to appear live. While the multisite approach is more common in a corporate training program or multi-campus university system (where the high-speed network is already in place), one-way instructor video combined with two-way (or multipoint) graphics, whiteboard, and audio is growing in popularity.

Computer-animated simulations and virtual worlds are not as common in online courses because of the higher development costs and steeper learning curves needed to master the software, but such technologies can significantly enhance the learning experience when they are used. Computer-animated simulations can be used to add depth to many subjects, from math and physics to art and history, and are most frequently used as supplements to text-based material. An increasing number of textbooks include online companion sites with these types of rich media resources that online instructors can use. In addition, 3-D virtual worlds, such as Second Life, offer the opportunity to learn in computer-generated environments that are customized for the online learning experience. For example, a university might create a virtual campus, complete with lecture hall, library, laboratory, and coffeehouse. Students would then log in to the virtual world and listen to the instructor speak in the lecture hall, read the latest electronic articles in the library, work with a simulation in the lab, and then socialize with fellow students in the online coffeehouse. Table 5.2 provides a recap of the various models described above.

Classroom Environments

Communication with the instructor and with fellow students is normally an important part of the online learning experience (see Chapter 7 for a detailed treatment of this topic). There are four basic online environments categorized by the type of opportunities available for discussion: none, audio or video conferencing, synchronous online chat, and asynchronous online discussion. Table 5.3 provides a summary of the different classroom environment models. The class size and instructional delivery methods that the instructor selects often influence the choice of interaction model.

The first approach to classroom discussion is to plan no discussions, so, in essence, there is not a shared classroom environment but rather a group of individuals

TABLE 5.2. Content Delivery Size Models

Instructional Delivery	Description	Advantages	Disadvantages
Text	Printed books or e-books	Familiar; packs a lot of content into the course	Audio and visual learners at a disadvantage
Presentation graphics	PowerPoint-style presentations	Good for overview of material	Less depth of more textual presentations
Audio and video	Portable audio or video or via online streaming	Richer content than with text alone; material can be portable if designed for iPods or MP3/MP4 players	Poor production can hinder learning; may simply stream existing lectures rather than design courses for online delivery
Videoconferencing	Live video delivery; possibly using other conferencing features such as shared whiteboards	Can be very similar to a traditional classroom experience	Requires high bandwidth and synchronous participation
Simulations	Computer-animated materials	Valuable for visual subjects	Higher design requirements; students need robust computer systems to work well
Virtual worlds	Computer-based simulated worlds for immersive instructional experiences	Can create varied learning environments	Difficult to create; high learning curve for students to use the system

TABLE 5.3. Classroom Environment Models

Classroom Environment	Description	Advantages	Disadvantages
No discussion	No interaction	Benefits independent learners	Missing the insights of fellow students
Audio/video-conferencing platform	Live audio or video discussion	Lively group discussions	Can be costly
Synchronous online chat or conferencing	Computer chat or conference room	Low cost; real-time interaction	Slower than verbal chats
Asynchronous online discussion forums	E-mail or message boards	Anytime communication; increased opportunities for reflection prior to communicating; archive of discussions	Less spontaneous than live chats; fewer nonverbal cues

pursuing learning separately. Ideally, this is done by design, as in the case of most independent study courses. Such a model assumes highly independent learners who are most likely to profit without class discussion, and so it is best suited for competency-based programs where students are expected to interact with the material and then take tests, write papers, and demonstrate their mastery of the course content without social interaction. However, this approach minimizes opportunities for social construction of knowledge, which is the heart of the social constructivist philosophy of learning and a major strength of online programs.

Some online courses make use of Internet phone services (e.g., SKYPE), conferencing software (e.g., WebEx, HorizonWimba), or traditional telephone conference calls to add audio or videoconferencing for class discussion. This approach generally requires students to be online (or by their telephone) at a scheduled time in order to participate in the class discussion. The benefit is a rich class discussion that closely emulates a face-to-face experience. Similarly, some courses incorporate live chat rooms to foster live classroom discussion. Chat rooms are the computer equivalent of a conference call—everyone in the class gets online at the same time and then logs on to a chat room for discussion. Instead of speaking to one another, chat rooms are text-based. Students type the entire interaction, which can then be archived for future reference.

Asynchronous discussions are the most common environments for online discussion. These interactions are time-delayed, like the message postings on a bulletin board, and do not require that everyone be online at the same time. Students post their message onto a discussion board at a time that is convenient to them and then others read it when they are online and post their response. Since students do not have to be online at the same time, they can participate in class discussions whenever it is convenient for their schedules. Furthermore, for the students who need time to consider a question before answering, asynchronous discussion forums provide just such an opportunity. This approach also provides an archive of all discussions throughout the course, so participants can reference, or resume, any conversation throughout the course.

Campus Time

While a significant growth in distance education over the past decade has been with online courses, there is a growing interest in combining online and face-to-face instruction into a blended learning model. According to Colis and Moonen (2001), blended learning is a hybrid of traditional face-to-face and distance learning so that instruction occurs both in the classroom and at a distance and the distance component becomes a natural extension of traditional classroom learning. Blended learning is a flexible approach to program and course design that supports the blending of different times and places for learning, offering some of the conveniences of distance courses without the complete loss of face-to-face contact. The result is a potentially more robust educational experience than either traditional or fully distance learning can offer. Moreover, the reduced seat time of blended learning is attractive as a cost savings approach for institutions coping with shrinking budgets and reduced classroom space (Brown, 2001). Clearly, institutions are moving in this direction, as 81% of all institutions of higher education and 97% of all public institutions currently offer at least one blended course (Allen & Seaman, 2003).

From a program design perspective, a blended program can lie anywhere along the continuum anchored at opposite ends by fully traditional and fully distance learning environments. The traditional component can be either on the main university campus or faculty can travel to a remote site in order to meet with students. There are essentially two models that are used for blended learning, with many variations possible for each model: the blended program model and the blended course model.

In the blended program model, blending is designed at the program level and each course can be offered either fully at a distance or blended. The distinguishing feature of this model is that all students enrolled in the program are required to physically meet at a central location, typically the main university campus, for one or more residencies during the program. Annual residencies during the summer are a common program requirement for both undergraduate and graduate programs. Typically, the initial residency serves a purpose similar to that of the "freshman experience" used in many undergraduate programs. That is, the purpose of the initial residency is to introduce students to the university, to each other, and to faculty and staff; integrate students in university life; and provide information and impart skills that will promote and support academic success. Such a residency is consistent with various student development theory models (e.g., Tinto, 1987) that focus on academic involvement, student-faculty interaction, campus involvement, and student-peer interaction. These elements have been shown to have an impact on student persistence when included as part of an initial university experience.

Subsequent residencies build on the initial residency and can be used to provide opportunities for guest presentations and discussions by distinguished scholars on topics significant to the program. Additionally, they can be used to conduct cooperative learning experiences that emphasize teamwork and promotion of leadership skills and involve small group face-to-face discussions and projects, nurture intra-cohort and inter-cohort community-building, and conduct proctored, high-stakes testing.

The blended course model, in contrast to the blended program model, consists of blended learning designed for each course. A blended course is suitable when all students live in proximity to each other. Martyn (2003) describes a successful blended course as consisting of an initial face-to-face meeting, weekly online assessments and synchronous chat, asynchronous discussions, e-mail, and a final face-to-face meeting with a proctored final examination. A variation to this model consists of an initial weekend face-to-face meeting and monthly meetings throughout the term, culminating in a final meeting with a proctored final examination. Between meetings, students and learners meet in a virtual online classroom with weekly assignments and discussion topics.

Selecting a Model

It is important to recognize that the variety of online courses means that not all online learning experiences will be identical. There is no single "best" model that should be employed for all online programs or courses. One program may be better suited for an asynchronous learning environment combined with annual campus residency sessions while another may work better in a synchronous conferencing environment with no campus time whatsoever. Depending on the needs of the student population, and the pedagogical and technological sophistication of the institution, one might develop various combinations of class sizes, content delivery, classroom environments, and campus time.

INSTRUCTIONAL DESIGN APPROACHES

Once the overall online program and course models are selected, the task then shifts to the actual design and development of the instruction. Although individual courses can be effectively taught online by a few motivated faculty, successful online programs also require the proper planning, commitment, and support of key administrators. In traditional education, instructors do all aspects of course design and development by themselves. After all, they are the content experts and are best equipped to design a quality learning experience for their students. In fact, many institutions insist that teachers do not need instructional design assistance, since educational software is so easy and powerful. Although this is a mistaken notion, it is nevertheless common. The typical faculty member is trained in his or her particular field, not in instructional design. It is simply unrealistic, and a poor use of resources, to expect a faculty member to be content expert, Web developer, multimedia designer, and systems administrator all rolled into one.

Just as businesses have learned the value of work teams, so too should online instructors team up with instructional designers and other support staff to develop a quality course. In a team approach, the faculty member is partnered with one or more instructional designers and multimedia developers. These individuals should be well trained in their field and bring a customer-focused attitude toward their work. Instructional designers bring insight into how to design the contents to maximize student learning. They will have the most insight on the media selection, layout of Web pages, and overall instructional approach, and can help the faculty member translate his or her content into a quality course to be delivered at a distance. Multimedia developers not only can convert much of the content into an online format (e.g., creating audio podcasts or video clips of a classroom lecture or guest speaker), but they can also bring a sense of style to the course design. This is no small undertaking, as it requires a commitment not only from the instructor to collaborate on the course design (which is likely a new, and somewhat unsettling, experience) but also from the institution, which needs to commit the resources necessary for instructional design support.

In general, when developing online instruction, the process is more efficient and effective when a systems design model is followed and a team works on the project. It requires a greater institutional commitment of resources up front, including money for design, equipment, and media resources, as well as increased staffing, but the end result is an instructional product that can be used in a variety of contexts, such as instructor-led online courses, self-paced learning, or modules in a blended environment. In many respects, it is akin to the creation of textbooks and other course materials that we regularly use in face-to-face courses. It takes a significant amount of time and energy to produce the resource, but once it is complete, it can be used in many situations.

ONLINE LEARNING TECHNOLOGIES

When developing distance education programs, designers should consider the characteristics of various technologies and select those that best suit the teaching and learning process under consideration. Different technologies may be better suited to different applications within the educational endeavor. For all of the benefits of the Internet, for example, there are many valuable characteristics of printed text. Numerous asynchronous online courses depend almost exclusively on text—a decision often rooted in faculty technological skill (or lack thereof) and bandwidth limitations, rather than a deliberate pedagogical choice.

E-mail, Web pages, word processors (e.g., Microsoft Word), and presentation software (e.g., Microsoft PowerPoint) are common tools that are used extensively in online learning. More recently, however, there have been technologies that have changed the online learning experience from a high-tech correspondence approach to a more interactive and collaborative learning experience. Some of the leading tools are learning management systems, blogs, wikis, podcasting, and virtual worlds. Although several have been mentioned already, each warrants particular attention when planning online programs and courses.

Learning Management Systems

A course learning management system (LMS) is a computer software program designed to support the delivery of online instruction. Blackboard is perhaps the most popular LMS used in U.S. higher education, although a number of competing products are also available. An LMS enables instructors and learners to post content, participate in discussions, maintain a grade book, keep a roster, track participation, and generally engage in and manage learning activities in an online environment.

An LMS can also refer to a content management system. Unlike a true course management system, a content management system is not limited to instructional content, nor is it necessarily organized around course units. Rather, a content management system is a program that enables the storage and organization of various content (text, audio, video, and so forth), often using a database as a backend organizational system. Content management systems tend to have an online publishing orientation and are thus likely to be used for online newspapers and databases as they are for online learning. Nevertheless, such tools enable institutions to create virtual classroom spaces for online and blended learning.

One result of the open source software movement is the development of open source course and content management system software programs that anyone can use for their own purposes. For example, some schools that cannot afford commercial products or choose not to commit to a proprietary platform have turned to Moodle (http://moodle.org) or Sakai (http://sakaiproject.org) as an alternative. These platforms are open source software that are free to use (presuming, of course, that one has access to a Web server on which to install it) and thus makes it possible for virtually anyone to develop and offer online courses without requiring the purchase of commercial LMS software. Similarly, numerous organizations have used open source systems on which to develop their Web sites, so they are easier to manage than using several flat-files developed with Web publishing programs, such as Microsoft FrontPage or Microsoft Expression.

Blogs

A *blog*, short for "Web log," is a place where anyone can post a running commentary on just about any topic (usually accompanied by links to Web pages). A common feature of blogs is the option to copy content from one site to another using the Really Simple Syndication (RSS) standard. This makes it possible for someone to create a newspaper-style Web site that pulls headlines from several individual blogs. Blogging plus RSS makes it possible for anyone to syndicate content that can be freely picked up by anyone for publication on their Web site.

Although political blogs have received much media attention because of their role in various elections, there is nothing inherently political about blogs. They can easily be used for educational purposes. Blogs can be used by instructors to share thoughts on current events, articles, and activities with students. Students can also manage their own blogs and use them for reflective journals, WebQuest narratives, electronic notebooks, or a host of other instructional efforts. Finally, since there are numerous educational blogs, there are many excellent resources to be found in existing blogs.

Wikis

Whereas a blog is primarily one person's online diary with visitor replies, a wiki is a Web site where anyone can add or edit Web pages without needing special administrative access rights. This would be the equivalent of a large chalkboard on campus where anyone could add, edit, or remove content at will. A wiki is a great online tool for collaborative writing. Once the author establishes the wiki Web site, it can be set to allow anyone to participate or only registered users. Either way, everyone who writes content for the wiki shares in its growth. Along the way, the wiki software tracks all the changes and who made them. If some content is lost, it can be added back by reverting to an earlier version. Through the combined efforts of a small group of people, or a great many, the wiki's content can grow.

Although there are numerous wiki sites online, Wikipedia (http://www.wikipedia .org) is perhaps the most substantive. Wikipedia is a remarkably fast-growing online encyclopedia with increasingly robust articles and perhaps the most elaborate wiki around, although there are numerous other wiki sites with subjects ranging from technical support to classical music. Like a print encyclopedia, it is a collection of knowledge. Unlike a print encyclopedia, it seemingly has no end to the extent of its entries because its depth and breadth go as far and wide as the personal interests of the people who add to wiki's content.

As a teaching and learning tool, the wiki is a powerful tool for online communication and collaboration. It allows a group of people to produce or work toward a final product. It is easy to learn and use, not requiring special software coding knowledge or software other than a standard Web browser. Wikis offer a relatively easy and fun way to hook a class into utilizing one of the exciting changes that technology is bringing to the education world. Moreover, wikis can be used by learners and instructors to create a searchable and reusable resource that extends beyond the duration of any individual course.

Podcasting

Podcasting is the automated delivery of prerecorded digital audio files via the Internet, to individual computers. Many have likened podcasting to creating an online radio program. The convergence of freely available software, mobile audio and video technology such as Apple's iPod and iPhone, and available hosting sites on the Internet has contributed to the explosive growth of podcasting in particular and mobile learning in general.

While many existing LMSs enable one to upload digital content (including audio), there is a significant advantage to hosting one's audio on a podcast-friendly site. That advantage is RSS. Just as blogs use RSS to publish headlines from one site to another, if an instructor makes his or her podcasts available via RSS, then students can subscribe to the audio podcasts and be alerted when new audio content is available. From an educational perspective, this means that instructors and institutions can post content that any student who has subscribed to the corresponding RSS feed will know about almost instantly. Rather than having to log in to, say, Blackboard to see whether an instructor has posted something, students can have their own RSS subscription and be alerted anytime that something is new.

Apple's iTunes is perhaps the biggest player in the podcasting industry. One can run iTunes on Macs or PCs and listen to (or watch) podcasts while on one's computer, or offload them to one's iPod or MP3 player. While anyone can host their podcast somewhere and contribute a free link to iTunes for listing in their system, Apple has also partnered with universities to create iTunesU. iTunesU is based on the iTunes store and enables educational institutions to publish audio and video files available to the public or just to their enrolled students. Unlike the general iTunes store, iTunesU lets colleges and universities build their own branded sites where material is grouped by course. Faculty can post audio and video content, students can download podcasts, and online learning becomes highly mobile.

In addition to being podcast listeners, students can also produce their own podcasts. When students are assigned the task of creating a podcast, they are given the opportunity to engage in authentic, constructivist learning. The process of creating a podcast provides important learning experiences for students, and builds on previous experiences, thus helping students develop their own understanding, create tangible products (that could potentially become reusable learning content), engage in problem solving, and work collaboratively with other classmates. Developing podcasts also appeals to a variety of learning styles, as well as providing an opportunity for developing proficiency with the technology.

Virtual Worlds

Until recently, online virtual worlds were largely text-based environments such as Multiple User Domains or Dungeons (MUDs) and Object Oriented MUDs (MOOs). When used for online learning, MUDs and MOOs offer students the opportunity to learn in computer-generated virtual worlds customized for the online learning experience. Recent years have seen the emergence of a graphical, 3-D virtual world called Second Life. Second Life was created by Linden Labs in 2003 and has grown significantly, with numerous commercial and governmental organizations establishing a presence in the Second Life virtual world. Essentially, it is a graphical world where participants customize their appearance via an avatar (i.e., a graphical image of a user), purchase land, construct buildings, socially interact, and basically live in a virtual world. From an educational perspective, Second Life provides a unique and flexible simulated environment that can be used for experiential learning, multiperson scenarios, simulations, and a host of social networking options.

Selecting Instructional Technology

Distance education systems should lag behind the technological cutting-edge; technology must be readily accessible to students. When considering instructional technology, one should realize that not everyone believes that technologies are neutral; there are some competing schools of thought. One can argue that technology itself is neutral and that the real issue is how people use the technology. A different perspective comes from Marshall McLuhan and others, who insist that media have particular biases associated with them. One of McLuhan's famous quotes, besides "the medium is the message," is from his book *Understanding Media* (1964) in which he writes:

> Our conventional response to all media, namely that it is how they are used that counts, is the numb stance of the technological idiot. For the "content" of a medium is like the juicy piece of meat carried by the burglar to distract the watchdog of the mind. (p. 18)

The use of video is a good example. If an instructor presents content such as a lecture using video, rather than just via a textual presentation, new dynamics are introduced into the learning environment. Even if the actual words are the same, students can see the instructor's face and hear his or her voice, which adds personality and a greater sense of instructor immediacy that would be lacking if the lecture were presented exclusively in written form.

COPYRIGHT AND FAIR USE STANDARDS

Distance education presents complex copyright issues related to both the ownership of the newly created course design and materials, e.g., course syllabi, as well as the fair use of existing materials that are used in the course, e.g., journal articles. The Technology, Education and Copyright Harmonization Act (2002), also known as the TEACH Act, amends sections of the Copyright Act and outlines the terms under which educators may clip pieces of text, images, sound, and other works and include them in a distance education course. Works primarily produced or marketed for the digital distance education market, works not lawfully acquired or made, and works such as textbooks and course packs typically purchased by students are not covered. According to the TEACH Act, it is not a copyright infringement for teachers at accredited, nonprofit educational institutions to transmit performances and displays of copyrighted works as part of a course if certain conditions that are analogous to traditional teaching are met. If these fair use conditions are not or cannot be met, permission from the copyright holder(s) must be obtained.

The Copyright Act describes the reproduction of a particular work to be fair use if it is used for teaching, scholarship, and research, provided that four factors are considered in determining whether or not a particular use is fair:

- The purpose and character of the use, including whether such use is of commercial nature or is for nonprofit educational purposes
- The nature of the copyrighted work
- Amount and substantiality of the portion used in relation to the copyrighted work as a whole
- The effect of the use upon the potential market for or value of the copyrighted work

One method of providing protected materials to students for use in an online course is through the supporting library's electronic reserve service. Typically, fair use of copyrighted material held on electronic reserve is limited to one article from a journal issue and one chapter, or less than 10% of the content, of a book. Copyright permission is required when an article is needed for more than one academic term, when multiple articles from the same journal are needed, when one chapter of a book is needed for more than one academic term, or when multiple chapters of a book are needed. Another popular method that allows students access to copyrighted material is to provide a durable link to the copyrighted document in the online course materials area, assuming the material is available online. This can be accomplished by obtaining the Internet address of the copyrighted document (i.e., the URL) and making it available to students as a hyperlink.

The relevant statutes require that each institution provide notice to students that materials used in connection with the course may be subject to copyright protection. The law anticipates that students will access academic sessions within a prescribed time period and will not necessarily be able to store the materials, review them later, or redistribute the works to others. As many of the provisions of the TEACH Act focus on the behavior of institutions, each institution must develop its own policy, impose restrictions on access, and disseminate copyright information. It is beyond the scope of this book to provide such detailed information.

Consequently, faculty who teach distance education courses must obtain such information directly from their institutions in order to avoid copyright infringement.

ACCESSIBILITY IN DISTANCE EDUCATION

For individuals with disabilities, the Web can either increase access to information or decrease it. Some have found a new sense of freedom online. Rather than being dependent on others to read aloud or convert materials into Braille, students can use voice-box-equipped computers and listen to newspapers, magazines, journals, and numerous other publications, as well as educational content such as lectures and podcasts. However, poorly designed online course sites can make it difficult, if not impossible, for those with disabilities to experience the full richness of the Internet.

"Providing accessibility means removing barriers that prevent people with disabilities from participating in substantial life activities, including the use of services, products, and information" (Bergman & Johnson, 1995). If a classroom lacks a wheelchair ramp, then a physically disabled student would be shut out of a potentially valuable learning opportunity. If an online educational video lacks open or closed captioning, then a deaf student would likewise miss out. From publishing academic catalogs and course materials online to electronic research and Internet-delivered distance learning, the Web has become a significant tool in both formal and informal education.

Ironically, if steps are not taken to ensure that academic Web pages are available to those with disabilities, schools could not only inhibit such advances but actually move backward. A student who could read the Braille version of the printed college catalog might be completely incapable reading the online-only version of the same catalog if it is not formatted for screen readers. If genuine concern for students is not enough reason for educational institutions to make Web pages universally accessible, there are legal pressures as well. Laws such as the Americans with Disabilities Act (ADA) require that businesses and public accommodations "take steps to ensure that disabled individuals are not excluded from or denied services due to the absence of auxiliary aids" (Freed, 1996). When institutions fail to recognize that inaccessible Web pages exclude those with disabilities, they are at risk of being found out of compliance with the ADA (Young, 1998). While it is questionable whether schools and universities could realistically be prosecuted for failure to make Web pages accessible, it is clear that the legal trend has been in the direction of providing universal access and the ethical obligation goes without saying.

Distance education program developers should design courses and support systems with ADA compliance in mind. Creating online educational environments that are universally accessible not only eliminates barriers to students with disabilities but may actually result in courses that are easier to use and better understood by all students (Nielsen, 2000). Furthermore, by addressing accessibility concerns when originally designing the courses and creating online materials, significant time and money is saved over the alternative of retrofitting the courses with accessibility features.

CONCLUSION

Even students in the millennial generation, or the "digital natives" (Prensky, 2001), have a sizable history with traditional classroom-based education. Accordingly, one would expect that their idea of learning in new environments would be influenced accordingly. While some students would likely relish a move toward immersion in virtual worlds or fully on-demand education, others might be more comfortable with traditional models. We do not know whether they expect that such models will be enhanced versions of their current classrooms (as is typically the case with today's online blended courses) or something entirely different that looks more like searching Google on a Blackberry or iPhone. Perhaps the next generation looks toward blended and online learning activities with a less traditional view of the classroom and a different set of expectations. However, during this time of transition and change, it is critical that institutions develop high-quality distance programs and courses that effectively use the varied resources available. Limiting a distance degree program to a pedagogically or technologically narrow approach without due consideration of the educational needs of diverse students or the academic support structures required by the faculty will ultimately hurt both. While the current environment is such that simply offering an online degree may be enough to attract students and fund the program, thoughtful consideration of appropriate program and course design models will ensure the development of a quality program that will last.

CHAPTER 6

Assessment of Student Learning

Assessment is used to determine if, in fact, learning is occurring, to what degree, and whether or not teaching or learning processes should be modified. Taylor and Nolen (2008) describe the multiple facets of assessment as follows:

> *Assessment events* . . . describe the myriad situations in which a teacher gathers information about student learning, *assessment tools* . . . refer to the tests, assignments, and so on that the teacher uses to gather information, *assessment processes* . . . refer to the strategies used to evaluate the success of students and of instruction, and *assessment decisions* . . . [refer to] the decisions made using the results of these evaluations]. (p. 7)

Graded assessment tools provide an overall metric of student accomplishment and can stimulate student motivation due to the high-stakes implications of grades. Formative assessment events that may or may not be graded provide feedback to both the instructor and students by highlighting ineffective as well as effective teaching and learning strategies with the primary aim of improving teaching and learning.

The purpose of this chapter is to provide a description of general assessment principles that are relevant to distance education learning environments. Just like instructional strategies, there is no presumption of a "one size fits all" model. Students are complex, thinking is constructivist, learning objectives are multidimensional, and the effectiveness of any instruction is dependent upon multimode transactions between unique instructors and students; thus, no single assessment approach can judge this entire process validly, reliably, and fairly. Nonetheless, assessment represents an essential component in judging student achievement, and must be intelligently incorporated in all instructional designs.

Compared to the face-to-face environment, the online environment does present some special challenges. Some of these include anonymity that not only eliminates nonverbal cues as indicants of student understanding but also poses threats to identity security (i.e., students actually doing their own work). Although the latter exists in all learning environments, computer technologies have certainly improved a student's ability to construct plagiarized submissions. Of course, such technologies have also improved an instructor's ability to detect plagiarism. This chapter will conclude with a discussion of academic dishonesty and related issues that are particularly relevant to the online learning environment.

BACKGROUND

Assessment represents the process of gathering information to determine whether student learning has occurred. Rovai (2000) indicates that the measurement (or *norm-referenced*) model of assessment generally consists of traditional, selected response assessment tools (e.g., multiple-choice items) that test recall and use norm-referencing to emphasize comparative judgments and assessment reliability; however, the standards (or *criterion-referenced*) model "emphasizes mastery, validity, and the variety of ways in which students can demonstrate their mastery of the standards" (p. 143). Stiggins (1987) asserts "performance assessments call upon the examinee to demonstrate specific skills and competencies, that is, to apply the skills and knowledge they have mastered" (p. 34); thus, performance assessments typically fall under the criterion-referenced model. Often, constructed response tools that require the student to create his or her response to prompts (e.g., open-ended questions) are associated with performance assessments—the constructivist perspective supports the utility of these types of tools, as it results in a more authentic representation of the student's individual construction of knowledge (Rovai, 2000).

Lee (1998) advocates performance-based assessments over selected-response tests, but claims that most assessments are designed and administered from a Eurocentric perspective. Battiste and Henderson (2000) describe such an approach as "cognitive imperialism," which occurs when Eurocentric thinkers automatically assume the superiority of their worldview and ways of learning, and attempt to impose them on others. Consequently, ethnic minority students tend to do poorly on tests constructed from such a perspective. However, "performance-based assessments have been deemed 'authentic' in the sense that they require students to tackle complex problems that have some real-world currency over an extended period of time" (p. 268). Although they can also be developed from a Eurocentric perspective, they offer the flexibility of allowing students a measure of freedom in their performances. Lee suggests that once these assessments are designed with the students' background in mind, teachers can expect an increased likelihood that they will see greater student achievement.

Stiggins (1987) asserts that "all performance assessments are composed of four basic components: a *reason* for assessment, a particular *performance* to be evaluated, *exercises* to elicit that performance, and systematic *rating* procedures" (p. 34). In actuality, these components can characterize assessments from either the norm-referenced or criteria-referenced models where the major difference is the level of learning to be assessed. All of these components are multifaceted, with implications that need to be considered to realize a successful (i.e., valid, reliable, and fair) assessment strategy. As Anderson, Ball, Murphy, and associates (1975) indicate,

> Assessment, as opposed to simple one-dimensional measurement, is frequently described as multitrait–multimethod; that is, it focuses on a number of variables judged

to be important and utilizes a number of techniques to assay them (tests, question-naires, interviews, ratings, unobtrusive measures, etc. [capitalization and italicization removed]). Its techniques may also be multisource . . . and/or multijudge. . . . (p. 27)

Stiggins (1987) defines the reason for the assessment in terms of the associated decisions to be made based upon the findings. Biggs (2001) contrasts the decisions for using norm-referenced versus criterion-referenced assessment models as follows: The former is used to differentiate students from each other, thereby informing selection decisions; the latter is used to measure student learning of desired outcomes and inform decisions that judge achievement. Biggs supports the criterion-referenced model by arguing that education should be about learning rather than selection, and he is against current measurement models that are based upon parametric statistical assumptions such as the normal distribution. However, Pieper, Fulcher, Morrow, and Thelk (2002) counter Biggs and provide arguments in favor of measurement models as part of an assessment process and suggest "measurement is much broader and more complex than Biggs describes" (p. 4). Both norm-referenced and criterion-referenced assessments have important roles to play but must be consistent with the reason for the assessment. With the current emphasis in education on accountability, even "the larger assessment context" must be considered (Pieper et al., p. 4).

Both norm-referenced and criterion-referenced assessments can be used for two different instructional purposes within a course. Rovai (2000) indicates that assessment findings can be used for summative (e.g., to inform achievement such as by assigning a grade) or formative (i.e., to inform learning progress) purposes. Assessment feedback from the formative perspective (i.e., formative feedback) is used to modify teaching or learning strategies or motivate additional effort so that desirable learning outcomes are better achieved. By incorporating formative assessments to improve deficient practices and maximize student achievement, summative assessments with high-stakes implications may be viewed as a fairer procedure.

The second component of any assessment is attention to the important content and skills to be learned with respect to learning objectives (Stiggins, 1987). Content is closely related to information to be learned, while skills may involve not only learning processes (e.g., critical thinking, the ability to use an online data-base) but also other developmental processes. An example of the latter is as follows: In collaborative learning, not only should achievement in learning the subject matter be assessed but also "student participation in group processes" (Barkley, Cross, & Major, 2005, p. 88). As Barkley et al. assert,

[because] more faculty recognize the importance of collaborative skills for the work-place and good citizenship, these skills are becoming part of the teaching goals in many disciplines. Ways to grade achievement in content is well understood and accepted in higher education, but teachers are still developing effective ways to grade group process. (p. 88)

Constructive group interaction can foster a sense of community and help field dependent learners whose most efficient learning modality is associated with group activities. In addition, these skills are of particular importance to students in those fields, such as business, whose ultimate professional success will depend upon successful team endeavors.

Of course, the importance of learning group processes does not discount the importance of learning and assessing self-directedness as another important developmental process. Macdonald (2004) writes, "e-learning courses with constructivist approaches will by definition demand the development of a self-directed approach to study" (p. 216). She supports the notion that developing self-directed learners in a traditional setting is a long, gradual process, but that increasing e-learning opportunities at earlier stages in one's formal education offers the opportunity to foster self-directedness at a younger age. Macdonald further asserts that self-directed online study requires a personal ability to identify, locate, evaluate, and use requisite information (i.e., "information literacy") but that collaborative learning can support the development of these self-directed skills through modeling processes and vicarious learning (p. 217).

The remainder of this chapter will focus on the third and fourth components of assessments: types of assessments and factors that affect assessment procedures (e.g., the purpose of assessment, the purpose of feedback, academic integrity, and issues unique to online learning). When compared to face-to-face instruction, online instruction lacks certain informal assessment events. Bassoppo-Moyo (2006) suggests:

> Face-to-face interactions enable teachers to use informal observation techniques to gauge student response, obtain feedback, and [evaluate] progress toward prescribed goals. This lack of nonverbal cueing, a technique rampant in traditional delivery systems, poses a great challenge to online assessment. (p. 8)

In addition, other than proctored examinations that require student identification, there are no guarantees that any work submitted online, which includes individual contributions to discussions, are actually attributable to the registered student. Therefore, online instructors must pay particular attention to the results from multisource assessment events and tools in order to compensate for the lack of nonverbal indicants of student understanding and verifiable methods of online student identity so that student learning is accurately evaluated.

TYPES OF ASSESSMENTS

Similar to face-to-face courses, online courses can incorporate many of the same types of formal (i.e., graded) assessment tools. Students can create individual deliverables as well as collaborate on group projects. Submitted work is evaluated, feedback provided, and final grades ultimately determined. However, there are nuanced differences in the instructional purpose between different (a) types of deliverables, (b) persons performing the assessment, (c) types of feedback, and (d) interpretations of grades. This section will attempt to address many of these instructional implications.

In addition, there are informal assessment events that provide the instructor with opportunities to assess student learning. In an online environment, these events are typically associated with the content of text-based contributions to discussions; however, similar to a face-to-face classroom, an individual student's contribution can be the result of an instructor prompting greater degrees of critical thinking. Informal assessment findings can inform both the instructor and student as to the need for modifying or enhancing teaching and learning practices.

Independent Work

There are many types of graded deliverables that students independently prepare to help evaluate their individual learning: exercises, papers, compilations of work (i.e., portfolios), and examinations. Anderson et al.'s (1975) "multimethod" perspective supports the position that assessment must take varied forms to truly evaluate the complexity of student achievement.

Requiring graded deliverables not only provides information for assessment, but also catalyzes motivation. As Macdonald (2004) writes, "the only time when most students will undertake activities is when they are linked to assessment [i.e., a grade]" (p. 220). This, of course, is related to the "high-stakes" nature of summative grades that (a) characterize academic and personal achievement, (b) influence perceptions of self-worth, (c) impact continued matriculation in programs of study, and (d) inform future academic and vocational selection processes.

With respect to ungraded deliverables, fostering motivation can be a greater concern for the online instructor when compared to his or her face-to-face counterpart. "In a classroom situation there is some expectation that students, once in the classroom, will participate, at least to some extent, in the activities set for them. Distance learners are not the same" (Macdonald, p. 219). This, of course, suggests that online students must elevate their self-directedness in order to maximize the benefit of all learning opportunities, particularly those that are not graded. To do this, instructors must catalyze self-motivation. Ponton and Carr (2000) highlight the importance of helping students understand the relationship between course performances in all activities and valued personal outcomes, thereby fostering motivation and supporting the development of learner self-directedness.

In general, every assessment item (i.e., graded or not graded) will fall into one of two categories: selected-response or constructed-response. That is, the assessment will either provide responses from which the student will *select* his or her response to the prompt, or the assessment will not provide any solutions and the student must *construct* a response. Multiple-choice, true/false, and matching items generally characterize selected-response assessments; open-ended questions, statements, or scenarios that prompt short answers, essays, or papers characterize constructed-response assessments. Even within the scope of assessments that are not formally graded, students can be asked questions as part of a discussion board with or without a range of possible responses. Note that even selected-response assessments can require critical thinking in choosing correct responses rather than simple recall; however, the evaluator would be unable to differentiate a fortuitous guess from a considered choice. Therefore, a constructed-response assessment is the preferred method to accurately assess a student's ability to think critically.

The formative perspective supports the usage of ungraded before graded assessments. Instructors should initiate dialogue with students, stimulate their construction of knowledge, and query for evidence of understanding and thinking (i.e., perform an assessment). There are at least three advantages that online learning has over face-to-face learning in support of this formative activity: more regular interaction, more reflective interaction, and widespread dissemination of feedback.

In a traditional face-to-face course, classes meet a few times each week—sometimes only once—at a prescribed time; in an online course, every day is a potential meeting, with new discussions generated throughout the day on discussion boards. Thus, the online instructor is afforded a continuous stream of assessment events to scrutinize student learning and provide formative feedback. In addition, dialogues posted on discussion boards provide all students with an opportunity not only to interact but also to observe and learn from the comments of their peers and instructor. For the face-to-face instructor, widespread dissemination of feedback triggered by questions or discussion is available only during class meetings or by mass mailings; thus, online instructors are better able to regularly and efficiently provide consistent feedback to all students.

Informal assessment not only provides students with feedback to improve their learning but also provides information to the instructor regarding student weaknesses. This information may warrant altering the instructional strategy, prompting thinking from a different perspective, or providing electronic attachments of additional readings. Formative assessments can help improve not just learning but also teaching; consequently, formative assessments are often viewed as assessments *for* learning instead of assessments *of* learning.

Whether the assessment is graded or ungraded, feedback must match its intended purpose. Brookhart and Nitko (2007) offer a typology of feedback and recommendations for usage from both the formative and summative perspectives. They assert that feedback can vary based upon (a) comparison type, (b) result or process attribution, and (c) function. More specifically, Brookhart and Nitko's (pp. 124–125) typology is as follows:

1. Comparison Type
   - Norm-referenced feedback: A comparison between performance and that of other students (e.g., "Your paper is average for the class")

- Criterion-referenced feedback: A comparison between performance and a desired standard (e.g., "You do not understand correlation")
- Self-referenced feedback: A comparison between performance and a previous performance (e.g., "Your discussion this week shows a better understanding of John Dewey's perspective as compared to your postings last week")

2. Result or Process Attribution
   - Outcome feedback: An indication of the resultant evaluation (e.g., "You earned a C on your paper")
   - Cognitive feedback: A description of how aspects of the assignment are connected to the student's demonstrated achievement (e.g., "You did not use the online database adequately to find relevant literature")

3. Function
   - Descriptive feedback: Provides information about the submitted work itself (e.g., "You used existing research well in supporting your argument on the importance of motivation")
   - Evaluative feedback: A judgment (e.g., "Excellent work")

Brookhart and Nitko suggest that criterion-referenced, self-referenced, cognitive, and descriptive feedback types are best used for formative purposes. In addition, they assert that such feedback should be clear, specific, and supportive to increase not only its functional utility but also to reduce psychological impediments to learning, such as a weak sense of self-efficacy (i.e., a perceived lack of capability).

For some students, outcome feedback and evaluative feedback can also support the formative function. For example, a student who earns a "C" (i.e., outcome feedback) and is told that he or she demonstrates "poor adherence to the American Psychological Association writing style" (i.e., evaluative feedback) may heighten personal efforts to learn by accessing supportive materials (e.g., the *Publication Manual of the American Psychological Association*), thereby improving future deliverables (one would hope). However, such feedback lacks specificity that may be required by the student to know where to focus augmented efforts. Thus, in the spirit of facilitating learning, formative assessments should be provided whenever possible. However, instructors should also help students understand that it is part of their personal responsibility as learners to use feedback, even outcome and evaluative feedback, as an opportunity to improve study habits, increase effort, and increase the likelihood of attaining desired learning outcomes. Building beliefs of personal responsibility supports self-directedness.

In addition to instructor assessments, student self-assessments should also be performed. Consistent with adult learning theory, adults desire participation in the design and evaluation of learning activities. In addition, self-regulatory learning, which includes self-reflective outcome assessments, supports self-directedness. Zimmerman, Bonner, and Kovach (1996) provide a cyclic model of self-regulated learning that involves the following processes: (a) self-evaluation and monitoring,

(b) goal-setting and strategic planning, (c) strategy implementation and monitoring, and (d) strategic outcome monitoring (p. 11).

Self-evaluation and monitoring occur when a student compares current levels of learning to desired levels. Instructors facilitate this process when an accurate assessment is performed to indicate the discrepancy between a student's current and desired levels of achievement. Typically, this process occurs whenever assessments are performed and feedback is provided. However, the ultimate goal of this process is for self-directed students to independently identify desired learning outcomes and be able to identify not only discrepancies between current and desired future states but also to target effective learning strategies based upon past learning successes.

Goal-setting and strategic planning refer to establishing learning goals and planning learning activities that will lead to desirable learning outcomes. Autonomous goal-setting and planning skills are developed through the evaluation of the effectiveness of past learning strategies—strategies that were initially modeled by the instructor in courses but later tasked to the student in course-related activities. Outside of formal instruction, such strategies become a repertoire of learning processes from which self-directed learners choose to accomplish desired levels of learning.

After a plan is developed, *strategic implementation and monitoring* refer to the implementation of the plan and subsequent evaluation as to the accuracy of the implementation. As a simple example, a student who establishes a plan of reading discussion board postings for one hour every night needs to monitor his or her efforts to determine if, in fact, the planned reading is occurring for the intended duration. Establishing a specific plan and a method of assessment, e.g., a reading log, provides formative feedback as well as motivation, due to the clear determination of a potential discrepancy between current and desired performances.

Strategic outcome monitoring refers to the process in which the learner makes an assessment as to whether adopted performance goals and plans are leading to desired outcomes. Following the above example, the student might ask, "Does reading one hour every night lead to satisfactory levels of understanding?" This self-assessment provides formative feedback to modify study practices.

In self-directed learning activities, self-assessments are critical in providing feedback as to whether adopted goals and plans are adequate for desired levels of learning. Students need to be encouraged to reflect upon outcomes, goals, and the adequacy of learning strategies. Self-directedness is dependent upon the learner's ability to initiate these processes independently subsequent to successful modeling activities provided by the instructor.

Group Work

Students are often assigned tasks that require them to interact in groups, e.g., discussions and group projects. In a collaborative learning model, the instructor defines a task and creates groups that require each member to contribute equally to the workload so that learning goals are accomplished and individual learning occurs. The collaborative learning model, however, is in contrast to the cooperative learning model (Bruffee, 1995). Although often viewed as interchangeable, Bruffee asserts that each has a different pedagogical purpose. The variation in purpose also has assessment implications.

Bruffee (1995) writes that "cooperative learning began with the observation that competition among students sometimes impedes learning" (p. 16). Following this perspective, instructors incorporating the cooperative learning model of group work would assert a greater degree of control over group activities, such as by assigning distinct roles to members, monitoring group work closely, intervening regularly, "and [would] sometimes . . . reward groups with a common grade for the degree to which the group as a whole has arrived at the correct answer or solution" (Bruffee, pp. 16–17). This model tends to be more appropriate for teachers of children in situations where the children may need to learn how to work together cooperatively while often tackling problems that have well-defined solutions.

At the college level, however, the social constructivist perspective that recognizes the relevance of a constructed perspective of knowledge suggests a different group work paradigm. As Bruffee (1995) opines,

> "Liberally educated" people accept as a premise that most questions, answers, methods, and criteria are subject to challenge, discussion, and change. A major part of a college and university teacher's responsibility is to marshall [*sic*] students' competence in "associated life" so that they can cope interdependently with the intellectual challenges generated by and within this encompassing community of uncertainty, ambiguity, and doubt. (p. 16)

The collaborative learning paradigm began with the observation that the traditional hierarchical structure within a classroom can impede learning because teacher interference can reduce or eliminate student-to-student interaction and dialogue (Bruffee, 1995). Thus, an instructor who incorporates the collaborative learning paradigm reduces or eliminates his or her involvement in group activities, thereby promoting unfettered discussion and group member negotiation of interdependent roles. Such a model "helps students become autonomous, articulate, and socially and intellectually mature . . . and it helps them to learn the substance at issue not as conclusive 'facts' but as the constructed results of a disciplined social process of inquiry" (Bruffee, p. 17).

Of course, even at the college level, the cooperative model may be as appropriate as the collaborative model. The determination of which model to use is based upon the degree to which individual perspectives that are no more correct than others can meaningfully contribute to the discussion and task at hand. The greater this degree, the more appropriate is the collaborative model.

The importance of this discussion of collaborative versus cooperative learning with respect to assessment is that each model has a different (a) epistemological perspective that influences the desired learning outcome at the individual level,

(b) expectation of group dynamics, and (c) degree of instructor oversight and intervention. The epistemological perspective associated with the cooperative learning model is a presumption that there is a single "best" answer—the collaborative model makes no such presumption. Thus, if each group member in the cooperative model has attained the learning goal of the task, there would be homogeneity of perspectives; in theory, any one person could be randomly tested and represent the group perspective. However, in the collaborative model, each group member may still (and likely will) vary in perspective—no individual member can offer a group perspective, because none truly exists. This does not mean that an instructor cannot use the collaborative model for producing a group project; rather, it suggests that such a project will be the product of a multitude of perspectives (i.e., socially constructed).

The cooperative model maintains an expectation of cooperation, while the collaborative model encourages each member to challenge the thinking of others in thoughtful, respectful discourse. These variations in purpose suggest that cooperation should be part of the assessment in one model, but quality of discussion should be assessed in the other. From a formative perspective, maintaining a cooperative climate is best facilitated by an ever-present instructor who intervenes regularly; however, supporting constructive discussion is best facilitated by a more invisible instructor who intervenes only occasionally to challenge thinking when stagnation develops. Of course, if instructor invisibility is created by implementing an unobservable collaborative model (i.e., group interaction outside of the LMS), opportunities for formative assessments are eliminated. Therefore, implementing the collaborative model within the discussion board framework is recommended so that formative assessments are possible.

Specific assessments of group work are consistent with all of the concepts discussed in the previous section for individual work. That is, an instructor can create assessment events that incorporate selected or constructed response tools administered either to the entire group or to individual group members; an instructor can provide formative or summative feedback to the entire group or individual group members; and students can engage in self-assessment, thereby improving learning skills and self-directedness. However, group work does provide additional assessment considerations that are distinct from individual work.

When a group is tasked to prepare a single deliverable for an instructor's assessment (e.g., a report), an equitable contribution by all group members is impossible to assess if that is all the information available to the instructor. Disparate contributions suggest disparate student engagement, a lack of individual learning, and undeserved credit/blame for someone else's effort/laziness. Thus, instructors must use multiple methods to assess individual efforts: Discussion board participation and peer evaluation provide two good methods.

Geographically distributed students can also engage in e-mail or telephone communication to which the instructor is not privy. This additional private information, coupled with the public information, gives group members the opportunity to accurately evaluate the contributions of other members. To facilitate this process, the instructor should help novice peer evaluators by defining assessment criteria. The instructor must also decide to what degree the peer evaluation will influence the final assessment for each individual.

ACADEMIC DISHONESTY

Duggan (2006) identifies several reasons for academic dishonesty among students: poor time management, desire for higher grades, misunderstanding of plagiarism, and different international standards of behavior. Institutions that offer online learning must certainly recognize the possibility of cultural antecedents and pro- actively educate students as to what is acceptable by the host institution. Duggan asserts,

> Tackling these issues effectively requires a holistic approach, in which detection is undoubtedly an element, and through which institutions consider the nature and role of assessment needed to reduce the opportunities for plagiarism, develop fair and transparent policies and procedures to ensure identified incidences are dealt with consistently across the institution, and develop mechanisms for information and feedback to students to prevent plagiarism arising from misunderstanding and con- fusion. (p. 152)

The computer technologies and distributed environment of online learning pro- vides nontraditional opportunities for identity fraud and plagiarism. Assessment procedures that can detect and deter these forms of academic dishonesty are dis- cussed below.

Identity Fraud

It is certainly true that even in a face-to-face course, the instructor has no way of knowing for certain that work completed at home was actually performed by the registered student. To compensate for this, proctored, in-class assessment events can be used to corroborate student learning. However, in an online course, such triangulation is virtually impossible (pun intended), because even discussion board postings, let alone online tests, cannot be attributed to a particular student with complete certainty.

One way to deal with this situation is the usage of proctoring services, par- ticularly for high-stakes summative tests (Rovai, 2000). Due to their very nature, high-stakes tests would likely increase the motivation to cheat. Many postsecondary institutions offer proctoring services primarily designed for their own students who were absent from tests, but also for outside students for a small fee. The student is required to show some form of identity for the proctor's certification. Another solution might be to administer periodic proctored exams (e.g., after completing a finite number of credits or courses) at the host campus. Obviously, these proctoring options require physical copresence.

Electronic copresence can also be used when an instructor is familiar with his or her students' voices or appearances. In conjunction with written submissions, oral examinations can be conducted via the telephone or Internet-based videoconferencing software. This multiple method approach can help the instructor determine whether or not the student's thoughts and communication patterns are consistent across different media.

Another approach that may help avoid identity fraud is to create individualized constructed-response assessments. As an example, assigning a paper that requires the student to relate a specific theory to his or her experience as a missionary in Africa reduces the possibility of identity fraud, as it is unlikely that someone other than the student would be in a good position to construct such a deliverable. Although someone else certainly could help with aspects of the paper (e.g., writing, theory), nevertheless, the instructor would have a greater degree of confidence that such an individual assignment would necessitate a high level of agency by the student, due to the personalized nature of the assignment.

A final approach is to reduce the emphasis on high-stakes summative assessments. Low-stakes assessments that either contribute a reduced percentage to the final grade or are ungraded and formative may reduce the motivation to conceal ignorance, incompetence, or lack of diligence. Coupled with formative feedback, low-stakes assessments can support an emphasis on learning rather than high grades.

Plagiarism

Plagiarism describes a situation in which a student misrepresents another person's creative work or ideas as his or her own. Unlike identity fraud, as discussed in the previous section, plagiarism does not involve a complicit second party and, therefore, represents a property right violation in addition to a lack of integrity. Repercussions can occur many years after graduation, particularly when student work is archived (e.g., a dissertation) and is, therefore, available for scrutiny at any time in the future. Professional style guides offer guidelines on how to properly cite the work of others in one's own writing (cf. American Psychological Association, 2001).

The large amount of text-based information available on the Internet that can easily be copied and pasted into student work via word-processing software tempts students to plagiarize "even before one takes into account the explosion in commercial 'essay bank' sites offering ready-made solutions for those with money to spend" (McKeever, 2006, p. 156). However, as McKeever points out, while the Internet has facilitated plagiarism, "it has also made it much easier to detect" (p. 156). Plagiarism detection software uses search engine techniques to compare the text in submitted papers against Web pages, previous student papers, or journal articles. While any detection software is limited by the size of the comparison database, nevertheless interest in such software is increasing, with limited research suggesting that students are in favor of its usage (Dahl, 2007).

Depending upon the detection software, verbatim or even slightly modified copying can be detected (McKeever, 2006). Some examples of commercial detection software can be found at the following URLs:

- http://www.canexus.com
- http://www.catchitfirst.com
- http://www.copycatchgold.com
- http://www.integriguard.com
- http://www.ithenticate.com
- http://www.mydropbox.com
- http://www.turnitin.com

Search or metasearch engines in the public domain can also be used to detect plagiarized Web documents. Note that plagiarism is not limited to full-length papers, as even short answers to unproctored test questions or discussion board postings can also be plagiarized. The reader is left to explore the available options and determine what is suitable for his or her particular needs.

Plagiarism has significant costs that include not only the sanctions against the perpetrator, but also the resources required to detect and prosecute. In addition, dealing with plagiarism incidents as well as any other form of academic misconduct requires educational institutions to move away from the mission of teaching and learning. Therefore, as with other crimes, the detection of plagiarism is second to deterrence. Students must be made aware not only of what constitutes plagiarism, but also why plagiarism is wrong. As Macdonald and Carroll (2006) assert, "students [need] to be engaged with the nature of academic culture . . . [and be provided] the guidance to signpost the values of scholarship and nature of originality" (p. 240).

CONCLUSION

It is not enough to design instruction and assume that learning will occur. Assessments must be performed to determine whether learning objectives are being met. Assessment findings can be used either to provide formative feedback to improve student or instructor strategies or to provide a summative metric of accomplishment (e.g., a grade). Ideally, formative feedback to students will precede summative assessments, thereby maximizing the probability of student success. Selected-response assessment tools are generally used to test recall, while constructed-response tools are used to assess critical thinking consistent with a constructivist perspective of knowledge; however, both can form the basis for either formative or summative feedback. Additionally, assessment tools can be used to evaluate either individual or group work with feedback provided at the appropriate level of agency.

The lack of physical copresence in the online environment provides new opportunities for identity fraud that can be dealt with by incorporating proctored assessments or oral examinations administered telephonically, or by Internet-based videoconferencing. In addition, computer technologies facilitate plagiarism as well as its detection. The motivation to commit either identity fraud or plagiarism may be reduced through the use of low-stakes instead of high-stakes assessments.

Regardless of the amount of specific, supportive formative feedback provided by the instructor or the adequacy of the instructional design, students must be active participants in the learning process. Therefore, students must not only be active learners but also active self-assessors by scrutinizing their learning strategies to determine if adopted strategies are being implemented authentically and are leading to desired learning outcomes. While instructors can help in this process by providing formative feedback, self-directed learners engage in these self-regulatory processes autonomously. Therefore, instructors should help their students to model the formative assessment process to promote self-directedness. In addition, instructors should encourage every student to view summative assessments through the formative lens, thus emphasizing the importance of developing as a learner. True learner-centered instruction attends to the developmental needs of the emerging self-directed learner and is supported by assessment events that identify developmental opportunities.

CHAPTER 7

Online Discussions

Alexander Astin's (1997) influential book *What Matters in College? Four Critical Years Revisited* examines more than 25,000 students and more than 190 environmental variables that influence student success as measured by cognitive and affective variables. He reports that the most important predictor of student success in higher education is active student involvement in the learning process, supported by interpersonal interactions. Similarly, the most important predictor of a successful distance education course, as measured by educational outcomes, is required and consistent interaction.

One can define *interaction* as two-way communication between objects, such as individuals and groups, as well as an exchange between an individual and technology. Michael Moore (1989) draws from this view and identifies three types of interaction in a distance education environment:

- Learner-content, which is "the process of intellectually interacting with content that results in changes in the learner's understanding, the learner's perspective, or the cognitive structures of the learner's mind" (p. 2)
- Learner-instructor, in which students and the teacher communicate with each other, and which is "regarded as essential by many educators and highly desirable by many learners" (p. 2)
- Learner-learner, which is "between one learner and other learners, alone or in group settings, with or without the real-time presence of an instructor" (p. 4)

Learner-learner interaction is especially important in group work where students at different times are required to engage in peer teaching and have content explained from different student perspectives instead of relying solely on the teacher. Moreover, peers may often be in a better position than the instructor to understand common misconceptions of the content. However, without the establishment of teacher presence through learner-instructor interaction, there is a danger that students will assume that the instructor possesses an uncaring attitude and has no concern for their learning.

Various authors have made additions to the types of interactions listed above, to include:

- Learner-interface interactions, which occur between the learner and the technology used by distance education (Hillman, Willis, & Gunawardena, 1994)
- Vicarious interactions, or self-talking, which take place when learners participate internally by silently responding to questions and discussion topics. (Sutton, 2001)

The importance of interaction is also highlighted by the constructivist philosophy of learning discussed in Chapter 1, which posits that knowledge and understanding is created or constructed by the learner through his or her interactions in the environment. Consequently, all the types of interaction listed above are important for learning. Moreover, learning in computer-mediated virtual classrooms implies a focus on social rather than independent learning. This focus distinguishes online learning from both the behaviorist and the instructivist traditions that reflect earlier approaches to the relationship between information and communication technology and learning (Stahl, 2006). The purpose of this chapter is to focus on learner-instructor and learner-learner interactions by addressing how to plan, facilitate, and moderate discussions in an online learning environment. The focus is on small-group asynchronous discussions, although many of the strategies described in this chapter also apply in varying degrees to synchronous online discussions using tools such as synchronous chat.

BACKGROUND

Asynchronous communication is the dominant delivery mode for online instruction. Ideally, however, an online course should use a mix of both synchronous and asynchronous communication tools. Research evidence suggests that synchronous communication generates higher levels of social and community-building responses, but is less useful in building cognitive presence or task accomplishment (Hrastinski, 2006). Asynchronous communication, on the other hand, encourages more time on task and promotes reflective interactions among members of a learning community because of the delay between receiving and replying to a communication.

Wegerif (1998) describes participation in asynchronous discussions as being like taking part in a developing conversation. Many of the replies are much more considered than might be the case had the same people met face-to-face and talked together over several hours. This process can be characterized by what Lipman (2003) terms *reflective thinking*, or "thinking that is aware of its own assumptions and implications as well as being conscious of the reasons and evidence that support this or that conclusion" (p. 26). It is this thinking about thinking, or metacognition, that promotes the ability of learners to construct deep personal knowledge.

Reflective thinking is essential for nurturing cognitive presence. Matthew Lipman's (2003) model of a community of inquiry provides an excellent theoretical basis for the social and reflective learning environment that should exist in the virtual classroom. In such a classroom, students listen to one another with respect, build on one another's ideas, challenge one another to supply reasons for otherwise unsupported opinions, assist each other in drawing inferences from what has been said, and seek to identify one another's assumptions (Lipman, 2003). Such an environment has the goal of promoting critical thinking skills as the instructor works cooperatively with the students, providing guidance when needed, but mostly acting as a catalyst in the students' pursuit of the truth. In a community of inquiry, the moderator does not lead the discussion. According to Lipman (2003), the argument does the leading. He maintains that the moderator should allow the natural process of the argument to unfold with very little or merely procedural influence.

However, there are several issues that can hinder the natural progression of an inquiry. The instructor must be mindful of the issues associated with different gender-related voices and culture-related communication patterns and cognitive preferences among members of the learning community described in Chapters 2 and 3. Because communication has both verbal and nonverbal components, some cultural groups show their feelings more readily than other groups, and some individuals rely more on nonverbal messages to communicate, which are reduced and subject to misinterpretation in an online environment. Such differences can have unintended negative consequences in cross-cultural interactions and can isolate students who are not fully acculturated in the majority culture. Consequently, members of the learning community must learn to care for and value dialogue in order for it to achieve its full potential. According to Noddings (2003), caring is the element that helps each participant accept different points of view, a particularly important aspect of effective cross-cultural communication.

PLANNING STUDENT ENGAGEMENT

Productive interpersonal interaction does not automatically occur in an online course. Researchers (e.g., Hewett, 2003) report that without adequate planning and implementation, online discourse tends to be fractured, isolated, haphazard in topic development, and lacking in evidence of higher-order thinking. Moreover, maintaining interaction is more challenging in online learning environments than in face-to-face learning contexts because of the time and space separation allowed by the technology. Planning for interaction is, therefore, an essential precursor to effective online learning. Strijbos, Martens, and Jochems (2004) suggest that to design online instruction for optimal interaction, instructional designers should first determine the following:

- Learning objectives
- The appropriate interaction required to accomplish learning objectives
- Tasks that promote the required interaction
- The degree of structure required to promote interaction
- Optimal group size
- The best usage of computer-based technologies to facilitate interaction and associated learning.

The design of spaces for interaction is crucial to the success of computer-mediated learning. Accordingly, the online instructor should not present course content and simply await students' questions regarding the content. If the instructor does this, the interaction process is likely to be inconsistent, content-driven, and dominated by learner-instructor interactions.

Interaction strategies that are available to an instructor will largely depend on the institution's technology infrastructure, the learning management system adopted by the school, e.g., Blackboard or WebCT, and the communication tools available within these systems, such as asynchronous discussion boards and e-mail, and synchronous chat and instant messaging. It is the planning of specific course activities using available tools that results in effective interactions. Students look to the instructor, the syllabus, and the course design to shape their participation in online discussions.

Computer conferencing systems can be asynchronous or synchronous and open (i.e., public) or closed (i.e., private). Typically, such systems, also called bulletin boards or threaded discussion forums, are closed. Guests are usually not allowed access. Only the instructor and students enrolled in the course can read postings and participate in the discussions. However, students need to know the extent of guest access, if any, and the extent to which their written remarks are protected by confidentiality and nonattribution outside the learning environment. A reasonable policy for distance education programs is to announce to students up front that all postings are nonattributable outside of the course. Such a policy will help build trust within the community of inquiry and promote open interactions and a sense of community.

Online instructors must plan for interactions in ways that will encourage learners to think harder about their learning. Learners should be reflective about their own performance, the learning experience received, and their learning-style preferences. Interaction should be design-driven and carefully planned before the start of the course, in order to:

- Promote a proper balance between learner-instructor and learner-learner interactions
- Ensure that the instructor implements an effective and well-thought-out interaction strategy that encourages discussion
- Provide separate areas for socioemotional and task-oriented discussions.

Socioemotional Interactions

Online courses frequently include a separate discussion forum to get acquainted and to engage in socioemotional discussions. In other words, it is used to humanize the online learning experience at the beginning of the course, and allows the members of the learning community to visualize one another as individuals. According to Garrison, Anderson, and Archer (2000), the expression of emotions, feelings, and moods is a characteristic of social presence, and providing an opportunity for such expressions should promote both social presence and community-building. Typically, this forum goes by the name of "Water Cooler," "Welcome Area," or "Break Area," and the instructor uses it to welcome students to the course, introduces himself or herself, and asks each student to do the same. The postings allow everyone to share information about their family, interests, hobbies, pets, job, sports, and so forth, as appropriate. Such mutual self-disclosure is an important component for the formation of a strong sense of community. Additionally, this initial contact between learning community members, if positive, can also improve intercultural relations and help reduce negative ethnic stereotyping.

Affect is expressed by humor as well as by self-disclosure. Cues suggest that the appropriate frame is one of humor. In face-to-face interactions, cues include tone of voice, facial expressions, body posture, and laughter (Palmer, 1994). Teacher immediacy literature identifies the use of humor as a contributory factor to immediacy and, subsequently, to learning (Baker, 2004). It can also facilitate the creation of common understanding and help generate solidarity and group identity (Palmer, 1994).

However, instructors should exercise care on how they use humor in text-based CMC, because a comment that is intended to be amusing and positive can be difficult to decode in the absence of nonverbal cues and may be perceived as negative by others. Consequently, instructors should focus on positive humor and avoid negative humor. Martin, Puhlik-Doris, Larsen, Gray, and Weir (2003) posit that positive humor consists of affiliative humor (e.g., using humor to say funny things and using jokes to amuse others to facilitate relationships) and self-enhancing humor (e.g., reflective of a generally humorous outlook on life). Negative humor, on the other hand, consists of aggressive humor (e.g., using humor to hurt or tease other people, such as with sarcasm and ridicule) and self-defeating humor (e.g., using humor to amuse others through saying self-disparaging things).

Socioemotional forums can also be used as places where members of the learning community can hang out and "shoot the cyberbreeze" about any topic they choose throughout the academic term by creating threads and posting messages. Consequently, the use of such forums has the added benefit of keeping the task-oriented forums free of non-task-related postings.

Task-Oriented Interactions

Task-oriented discussions are needed to support peer learning and to establish cognitive presence. McKeachie and Svinicki (2006) observe that there is substantial evidence that peer learning and teaching is extremely effective for a wide range of goals, content, and diverse students. However, students often find it difficult to acknowledge peers as teachers. Students instinctively believe that the person who teaches has the status and authority to teach, and peers do not. Consequently, it takes time and encouragement from the instructor for a student to learn to openly acknowledge that he or she has learned something from a peer.

There are two broad types of task-oriented course activities that involve peer learning: the systematic and prescriptive variety known as cooperative learning and the less-structured dialogue-based variety known as collaborative learning, as introduced in the previous chapter. Both types rely on learner interaction, but differ primarily in the "degree of involvement of the teacher . . . [and] the extent to which students need to be trained to work together in groups" (Matthews, Cooper, Davidson, & Hawkes, 1995, p. 36). There are numerous cooperative strategies. MacKnight (2000) lists several representative ways to group students for task-oriented peer learning:

- Small discussion groups led by the instructor or a designated student moderator (usually 10–15 learners per group)
- Buzz groups (two or three learners interact for brief periods of time; even normally silent students are likely to contribute in such small groups)
- Case discussions
- Jigsaw groups (members of groups break into buzz groups and then go back and share the information they learned with their groups)
- Mock trials.

Perhaps the most common collaborative learning activity is the online discussion group initiated by instructor-generated discussion topics for task-oriented discussions. Gallimore and Tharp (2005) refer to this strategy as "assistance questioning." They posit that assistance questions are inquiries made in order "to produce a mental operation that the [student] cannot or would not produce alone" (p. 182).

The assistance questioning topic should be problem-oriented and should not be answered by a simple "yes" or "no" response. Instead, the topic should permit multiple perspectives to be argued. Additionally, the topic should entail higher levels of cognitive learning, e.g., application, analysis, synthesis, or evaluation. Addressing higher levels of content-related affective learning is also appropriate, e.g., to value the benefits of educational research in an online statistics course. Typically, the instructor posts a new problem-oriented topic in task-oriented discussion forums at regular intervals throughout the academic term. He or she monitors learner interaction in the groups and provides assistance, clarification, and encouragement as required. Either the instructor or a designated student can moderate each forum.

Productive discussions require good topics that help students develop critically informed understandings about topics and problems. The first message in each task-oriented forum should be a focused discussion topic posted by the instructor. Angelo and Cross (1993) provide a useful list of topics for instructors to include or adapt in their courses that have the added benefit of providing formative feedback to the instructor regarding learning. These topics include:

- One-sentence summaries: Students select and articulate only the defining features of an idea.
- Most important point: Students describe the most important point of a reading assignment and why it is important to them.
- Muddiest point: Students identify the least-understood point in a reading assignment.
- Test questions and model answers: Students write plausible test questions and model answers for specified topics.
- Self-confidence surveys: Students assess their self-confidence regarding specific skills.
- Benefits analysis: Students describe how the skills learned relate to their goals and interests in life.

Questions and problems stimulate the natural curiosity in all learners and encourage critical thinking in student postings. Critical thinkers do not take things for granted. They are willing to reflect upon matters and engage in reasoning before they make a judgment. In doing so, they base their understanding on objective standards and recognize their biases and prejudices. Collison, Elbaum, Haavind, and Tinker (2000) identify the following five types of questions that can promote critical thinking:

- Questions that probe the "so what?" response—relevance, interest level, urgency, and context
- Questions that clarify meaning or conceptual vocabulary—ambiguity or vagueness and common concepts
- Questions that explore assumptions, sources, and rationale—qualities assumed and study evidence
- Questions that seek to identify causes and effects or outcomes—primary or secondary and causes, internal or external factors
- Questions that consider appropriate action—weigh different courses of action. (p. 143)

Such questions do not simply ask learners to regurgitate facts. Instead, they require learners to reflect upon a situation and provide a reasoned response. Consequently, learners need adequate time to reflect on the question and compose their response. Additionally, the instructor must take care not to overwhelm the group with a series of questions.

In research where active instructor participation in online discussions was either limited or absent, Kanuka and Anderson (1998) report learners rarely engage in critical discussion and appear to avoid areas of contradiction. Gerber, Scott, Clements, and Sarama (2005) report a significant relationship between instructor stance in online discussions and the extent of both referencing and reasoning in learner postings. They report that regardless of topic, a challenging stance adopted by the instructor can facilitate student use of references and increase critical thinking.

When students work together in groups, it is important to differentiate between group products and individual learning outcomes. A group outcome is a group product that is related to the functioning of the students as a group, e.g., satisfaction with the process or satisfaction with the outcome. The quality of the group's outcome can be measured in terms of the original task, e.g., the correctness of a decision, the creativity of a set of ideas, or the degree of consensus in the group. There are situations in which cooperative projects are needed in order to build and assess teamwork skills. However, if the focus is on individual achievement, effective cooperative learning strategies, such as positive interdependence, and individual accountability should be employed to ensure the successful learning of all students (Lou, Abrami, & d'Apollonia, 2001).

Feedback

> Most learners crave teachers' responses to their coursework and their examinations. Learners see the quality and quantity of feedback on their work as an important part of their relationship with their professors and educational provider. (Salmon, 2004, p. 113)

The giving and receiving of feedback is an essential aspect of online learning. In the absence of immediate feedback, there is a degree of uncertainty in online communication regarding how one's posting is perceived by others. This uncertainty can result in anxiety if left unattended for extended periods of time. Feedback is not merely a matter between the instructor and the learner; it is also an important aspect of learner-learner interaction, and can become a positive learning experience. However, the learner must first develop and internalize learning goals and, thus, be intrinsically motivated to learn if feedback is to be most effective in the learning process.

Effective feedback provides the learner with two types of information: verification and elaboration (Kulhavy & Stock, 1989). *Verification* represents the judgment of whether a response is correct or incorrect, complete or incomplete. *Elaboration* provides relevant cues to guide the learner toward a correct or complete response.

Salmon (2004) posits that achievement in online teaching and learning involves five different stages, each with its own unique type of feedback. See Figure 7.1. In stage one, at the start of the course, feedback is often technical and focuses on online access issues and providing motivation and encouragement to learners to actively participate in course activities. In stage two, feedback is directed toward promoting socialization and explaining how online interactions contribute to learning. Feedback at this stage should nurture a sense of community. In stage three, feedback encourages examination of particular aspects of problems and issues. Salmon argues that at this stage, moderators should provide concise feedback that clarifies direction in the mass of discussion board postings so that learners do not

FIGURE 7.1. Five-Stage Model of Teaching and Learning Online

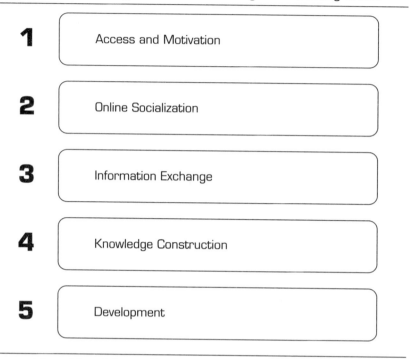

Source: Adapted from Salmon, 2004.

feel overwhelmed by information overload. In stage four, feedback takes the form of woven summaries. Finally, in stage five, the highest level of achievement in online learning and teaching, Salmon writes, "e-moderators and participants are essentially using a constructivist approach to learning. . . . Challenge and argument at this stage will foster deeper thinking and reflection" (p. 48).

Burnout

In planning a discussion strategy, the instructor should not place himself or herself at the center of all discussions. Higher education faculty already perceive teaching online as involving more work and time than teaching a traditional course (Hislop & Ellis, 2004), and placing oneself in the center of all discussions substantially increases the workload and can become a major workplace stressor for the faculty member that can result in teacher burnout, with its emotional exhaustion and feeling of low personal accomplishment. Moreover, numerous postings to read, along with significant textbook readings and written assignments, can result in student burnout, which is related to reduced student engagement and attrition.

Maslach (2003) describes burnout as job-related and a prolonged response to chronic emotional and interpersonal stressors on the job. Maslach and Jackson (1986) identify three burnout dimensions: (a) emotional exhaustion, (b) depersonalization, and (c) a reduced sense of personal accomplishment and satisfaction. Careful management of teaching loads and number of students per online course and skillful facilitation of online discussions to maintain efficient levels of public interaction can help avoid burnout. More postings are not necessarily better than fewer postings, and at some level, the sheer number of postings can become exhausting.

Placing emphasis on student-student interactions and rotating students as moderators of small-group online discussions can decrease instructor workload and increase student interest, motivation, and learning. Humor can also moderate the effect of stressors on members of the learning community (e.g., Lefcourt, 2003) and help preempt teacher and student burnout.

Neumann, Finaly-Neumann, and Reichel (1990) conclude that college students may experience burnout due to learning conditions that demand excessively high levels of effort and do not provide supportive mechanisms that facilitate effective coping. They suggest that the "development of learning environments that improve learning flexibility and students' involvement" (pp. 29–30) can reduce this burnout phenomenon. They recommend strengthening the flexibility of academic programs by emphasizing electives, self-directed learning, independent study, and courses concerned with critical questions. Within a course, flexibility can be achieved by allowing students to select discussion topics and flexibility in determining which discussion topic they respond to.

Participation Rubrics

Regardless of the type of activity used for group work, students must know what is expected of them so they can engage in appropriate behavior and be successful. Consequently, the instructor should provide the ground rules for online discussions at the start of the course by including active learner participation in the overall course assessment strategy and by clearly describing course expectations regarding active learner participation in course discussions. These expectations must be communicated to learners in a clear, concise, and cohesive manner, particularly if discussions represent a graded course component, so that they can be accurately and objectively measured consistently and fairly. A participation rubric is an excellent choice for communicating these expectations. A challenge for the instructor is to motivate students to engage in productive discussions and not merely to motivate students to post a minimum number of messages in order to achieve a good course grade.

Rubrics can be holistic, producing a single score, or analytic, producing scores for several distinctive dimensions. Such rubrics employ the concept of analytical trait scoring by judging a learner's performance several times along different dimensions. Typically, the scores for each dimension are combined into an overall score that is given a suitable weight in determining course grade. Appendix B contains an example of a participation rubric. The example rubric is analytic with three dimensions: social presence, cognitive presence, and writing skills.

The weight given to course participation is based on the instructor's professional judgment after considering the curriculum, desired student learning outcomes, instructional strategies, and other learning activities. Rovai (2003a) reports the results of a causal-comparative investigation of three discussion grading strategies in 18 online graduate courses in which discussions are not graded, discussions represent 10–20% of the course grade, or discussions represent 25–35% of the course grade. He reports that grading strategies influence online discussions and that discussions are directly related to students' sense of community and satisfaction. A significant increase in the number of student messages per week was noted between courses in which discussions are not graded and those in which discussions account for 10–20% of the course grade. No additional benefits were noted when this weight was increased to 25–35% of the course grade.

CONDUCTING ONLINE DISCUSSIONS

Online learners may feel isolated and abandoned if there is too little discussion. On the other hand, too much interaction can create overload and frustration as students attempt to sift through many postings in order to locate the teaching points and follow an often circuitous discourse. As a result, it is necessary for online instructors to identify a proper balance of interaction strategies. Dunlap (2005) suggests:

> One way to reduce discussion facilitation workload is to use a synchronous communication tool such as chat to meet with small groups of learners each week. Weekly, synchronous meetings can be used to discuss readings, assess project status, ask and answer questions, and so forth. For example, if there are 30 learners in a course, there could be six groups of five learners. Instead of tracking learners asynchronously all week long, an instructor can meet with each group synchronously for one hour per week. (p. 24)

The major purpose of facilitating and moderating online discussion is to establish teacher presence in the virtual classroom and, by doing so, to promote both social presence and cognitive presence. However, in establishing teacher presence, the instructor must nurture development of a community of inquiry in which he or she moves away from center stage by promoting collaboration and cooperation. Accordingly, Collison, Elbaum, Haavind, and Tinker (2000) suggest three principles for moderating online discussions:

- Moderating takes place in both professional and social contexts.
- The style of guide-on-the-side is more appropriate than sage-on-the-stage.

- Moderating online discussions is an art that has general guiding principles and strategies that can be learned by new online faculty members.

It is through active and appropriate intervention by a teacher that communication tools such as computer conferencing and cooperative learning become useful instructional and learning resources (Garrison, Anderson, & Archer, 2001).

The professional literature makes a distinction between moderating and facilitating discussions, although there is a measure of overlap between the terms and some writers use these terms interchangeably. Often, it is the same person who fulfills both roles. When a distinction is made, the moderator is the instructor or student who is in charge of leading the discussion. The facilitator, most often, the instructor in an online environment, creates a student-friendly online environment that promotes and provides structure to the discussion and participates in discussions as a subject-matter expert when needed. Facilitator responsibilities in online discussions include:

- Dividing a large class into small groups
- Creating separate forums for each discussion topic or project
- Establishing group goals
- Developing and posting each discussion topic or project requirement
- Assigning students on a rotating basis to moderate each conference for a grade
- Providing learners with suitable scaffolding so they know what is expected of them, typically in the form of procedures and a grading rubric
- Establishing a date when discussions terminate for each topic
- Monitoring all interactions
- Maintaining a social presence in all active conferences by periodically providing words of encouragement and content-related critiques
- Pointing out themes that learners fail to identify in the course of their discussion
- Coordinating activities with the moderator
- Using the discussions to assess class mastery of instructional objectives and to identify weak areas that require reinforcement
- Balancing serving as the content expert and resource with allowing learners to construct deeper understanding through primarily learner-learner discourse
- Training moderators as required.

The manner in which the moderator responds to students is critical to the course of the discussion thread. Formality creates distance, while informality fosters interaction and approachability. Although the moderator has the responsibility to guide the discussion procedurally, he or she should not lead the discussion down a predetermined path. The moderator engages in group-building and maintenance, which are oriented toward the functioning of the group as a group (Benne & Sheats, 1978). These functions are designed to alter or to maintain the group's way of working and to strengthen, regulate, and perpetuate the group as a group.

Some of the group maintenance roles that the moderator can assume include encourager, harmonizer, compromiser, gatekeeper, standard setter, observer, or follower. At times, the moderator also challenges, widens horizons, and becomes the devil's advocate. Collison, Elbaum, Haavind, and Tinker (2000) suggest that moderator roles also include generative guide, conceptual facilitator, reflective guide, personal muse, mediator, and role-player. The situation generally dictates the role that the moderator chooses to adopt at a specific time. Naturally, the role will change as the situation changes. Skill in performing these roles is useful in maintaining critical group discussion and in promoting a sense of community. Collison, Elbaum, Haavind, and Tinker (2000) view effective online teaching as a kind of improvisational casting, sending the best persona into the drama of teaching and learning as the drama unfolds.

Robert Tinker, director of the Concord Consortium (Collison, Elbaum, Haavind, & Tinker, 2000), outlines a progression of stages that can increasingly involve participants in online activities. Learners are first asked to respond to simple, straightforward questions that are easy to answer. Next, learners begin to interact with the moderator and one another, as they engage lightly with the content. At this stage, the course requires discussion forums that are dedicated to course content and task-oriented discussions. Finally, learners are ready to take on demanding questions, delve more deeply into the issues, and interact with one another more strenuously. At this stage, the discussion topics posted by the instructor in the content forums elicit progressively more critical thinking on the part of the learners. Accordingly, the moderator typically has the following responsibilities:

- Introducing the topic
- Closely monitoring the discussions by accessing the active conferences at least twice a day
- Setting a tone for an enthusiastic, smooth discussion
- Adopting an empathetic and nurturing approach for those learners who are struggling with course content or technology
- Eliciting postings, as needed
- Responding to procedural and organization issues as they arise
- Recognizing high-quality contributions
- Maintaining a social presence without becoming dominant or appearing authoritative
- Ensuring that all learners are encouraged to participate in the ongoing discussion
- Attending to issues of social equity based on different culture- and gender-related communication patterns

- Allowing learners time for reflection
- Identifying areas of agreement and disagreement
- Helping in the sorting of ideas and helping participants focus on key points
- Working toward reaching a consensus
- Giving timely and supportive feedback
- Bringing closure to the discussion topic by summarizing discussions and providing one last opportunity for learners to make final comments.

Finally, the responsibilities of learners who participate in computer conferencing include:

- Accessing the discussion board frequently
- Reading all postings
- Stimulating critical discussions, as needed
- Participating in discussions in accordance with established procedures and the discussion rubric
- Using discussions as an opportunity to clarify understandings of the content area and to ask relevant, task-related questions.

CONCLUSION

Cooperative and collaborative learning allows students at various performance levels to work together in small groups toward a common objective. The goal of such work is to share alternative viewpoints and challenge, as well as help develop alternative points of view (Sharan & Sharan, 1992). Social learners are responsible for one another's learning as well as their own. According to Slavin (1989), for effective cooperative learning, there must be group goals and individual accountability. Each group member depends on the others to accomplish a shared goal or task. Thus, the success of one student helps other students become successful. When the group's task is to ensure that every group member has learned something, it is in the interest of every group member to spend time explaining concepts to members of the group.

In order to promote quality cooperative learning, planners, facilitators, and moderators of online discussions need to consider the following strategies.

- Place emphasis on learner-learner interactions.
- Promote social presence by increasing familiarity among learners, and help develop favorable social relationships.
- Assist members of the community of inquiry in caring for one another in a pedagogical sense and value the interaction process (Sharp, 2004).
- Establish teaching presence to help learners make the transition from social to cognitive presence (Garrison, Anderson, & Archer, 2001).

- Share teaching presence responsibilities by appointing learners as discussion topic moderators (Garrison, Anderson, & Archer, 2001).
- Create a variety of social learning activities that allow multiple opportunities for demonstrating knowledge and skill proficiencies designed to address the diverse range of learning preferences and communication patterns that students bring to instructional environments (Bangert, 2004).
- Require learners to reflect periodically on their own performance, the learning experience received, and their learning-style preferences.
- Recognize and respond to communication patterns that can silence some students. For example, recognize put-downs and alienating or competitive dialogue, and respond privately to offending students and encourage them to be more inclusive (Rovai, 2007).
- Intervene indirectly to equalize students' status in the virtual classroom by raising the status of those students with lower status by recognizing the importance of their roles and creating problems or discussion topics that require multicultural perspectives (Cohen, 1994).
- Publicly recognize the work students have accomplished, paying particular attention to low-status students, through actions such as giving praise, citing student contributions, and assigning significant roles in group projects (Cohen, 1994).
- Encourage the use of a connected voice and teamwork. For example, a grading rubric can be used to describe instructor expectations for students to use a connected voice where cooperation and interdependence are stressed over competition and independence (Rovai, 2007).
- Discourage competition among students, as competition creates both winners and losers, and that can create hurt feelings and alienate and silence sensitive students (Rovai, 2007).
- Encourage and reward group activities and cooperative efforts.
- Encourage all students to participate in discussions; use the telephone or e-mail to confer privately with students who remain silent, in order to determine the cause (Rovai, 2007).
- Consider cultural differences by designing learning strategies that encourage the open sharing of views and establish a classroom climate in which one set of values is not automatically given precedence.
- Avoid sexist or culturally biased language. For example, avoid language that reflects sexual or cultural stereotyping or adoption of a single cultural perspective.

CHAPTER 8

Program Evaluation

Quality assurance of distance education programs is a matter of national interest and accountability. Institutions of higher education need to evaluate the effectiveness of their distance education programs and use the findings to improve programs and services and to document evidence for program accreditation. The importance of maintaining quality programs takes on added significance as institutions of higher education seek "a competitive edge in a student-based, consumer-driven market" (Oblinger, 1997, p. 31). Moreover, some researchers (e.g., Rowley, Lujan, & Dolence, 1997) maintain the existence of a growing gap between what the public wants and what traditional universities provide. Therefore, strategic planning in general and program evaluations in particular must address both student needs and quality assurance by showing that distance learning outcomes meet student needs, are appropriate to the rigor and breadth of the degree or certificate awarded, and that distance education programs support the school's strategic vision. Accordingly, distance education program evaluations should address such diverse issues as:

- Inputs, such as quality of incoming students, student support services, and technology infrastructure
- Processes, such as quality of the provided education, teaching effectiveness, and cost-effectiveness
- Outputs and outcomes, such as student persistence; number of graduates; alumni achievement; and student, alumni, employer, and faculty satisfaction.

The purpose of this chapter is to provide and describe a framework for planning and evaluating distance education programs. It discusses the principles of program evaluation, provides the framework for developing an evaluability assessment in order to determine if a program can be evaluated for results, and describes the major types of program evaluation within the context of distance learning.

BACKGROUND

Chapter 4 describes strategic planning as a long-term, future-oriented process of goal-setting, strategy-building, and assessment that maps and monitors an approach to anticipating the future that is both desirable and achievable. An important goal of this process is to improve the chances of reaching desirable outcomes that achieve the organization's vision of itself for the future. As such, it is a systematic and disciplined effort to produce basic decisions that guide and shape what the organization is, what it does, and why it does it. It is also a participatory process that considers the needs of clients and stakeholders in defining its mission and vision as well as determining the goals, objectives, and standards needed to achieve that vision. Inherent in this process is the development and/or refinement of strategies, activities, and programs to satisfy its strategic goals and objectives and, ultimately, to achieve its vision.

The Joint Committee on Standards for Educational Evaluation (1994) defines a *program* as a "standing arrangement that provides for a . . . service" (p. 3). More specifically, a program is a grouping of organizational resources to accomplish a specific goal. Shadish, Cook, and Leviton (1991) assert that internal structure and external forces shape all programs. They describe the internal structure as the arrangement in which "staff, clients, resources, outcomes, administration, internal budget allocations, social norms, facilities, and internal organization [are combined to relate to] inputs to activities to outputs" (pp. 37–38). Fitzpatrick, Sanders, and Worthen (2004) suggest that the external forces that shape the program can include "local economic capacity, external funding agencies, prevailing political sentiments, pressures from powerful stakeholder groups, social mores, logistic or geographic constraints, and the like" (p. 54). Therefore, a program can be viewed as both an organization and a system with inputs, processes, and outcomes that support the organization's strategic goals and objectives.

Strategic planning is an evolutionary and transformational process that allows programs to be judged within the constraints faced by the organization. As programs are evaluated, the organization refines its strategic plan and adjusts programs as needed in order to continue its journey toward achieving its vision for the future. The strategic planning process thus provides the opportunity for program evaluations as part of the monitoring stage that tracks the trends, compares actual outcomes to intended (and unintended) outcomes, and provides justification for program change.

Fitzpatrick, Sanders, and Worthen (2004) define *program evaluation* as the identification, clarification, and application of defensible standards to determine the value or merit of the object of the evaluation in relation to those standards. They note:

> Evaluation uses inquiry and judgment methods, including (1) determining standards for judging quality and deciding whether those standards should be relative or absolute, (2) collecting relevant information, and (3) applying the standards to determine value, quality, utility, effectiveness, or significance. (p. 5)

There are at least three different types of use for program evaluations (Shadish, Cook, & Leviton, 1991):

- Instrumental: To support overt decision making
- Conceptual: To better understand a program or policy or the issues related to it
- Strategic: To persuade others or to use evaluation findings to gain particular outcomes.

Instrumental and strategic uses are especially relevant to program evaluation as a tool of the strategic planning process.

Rovai (2003) argues that institutions of higher education that offer programs at a distance are in a highly competitive marketplace where quality and service are strongly related to success. Consequently, schools offering distance education programs must compete with one another as well as with traditional programs in order to attract students. Schools must offer quality programs at a competitive price in order to be successful. Evaluation is an essential component of program improvement and renewal and long-term success. It provides valuable feedback to program managers concerning the effectiveness of their programs and to policymakers regarding their policy choices. "Even the best designed or adapted distance delivered course will likely require revision" (Willis, 1993, p. 70).

Palloff and Pratt (1999) identify several program issues as most significant to students who are enrolled in online degree programs. These issues, which should be addressed in a program evaluation, are: ease of access to the program (e.g., admittance to the program, enrollment process for courses); smooth, seamless delivery of courses (e.g., forewarning of hardware and software requirements, consistent navigational interface among courses, consistent and reliable offerings in the course schedule); availability of timely support (e.g., technical support, campus support services for learning, faculty support); and breadth and completeness of the program (e.g., the numbers and types of courses available).

A comprehensive evaluation of the effectiveness of distance education programs should be based on multiple sources of evidence and the convergence of different measures (Rovai, 2003). However, there has been a tendency in evaluations of distance education programs to be less rigorous and to rely on the use of limited self-reports and qualitative evaluations (Campbell, Lison, Borsook, Hoover, & Arnold, 1995). Additionally, some programs possess goals that cannot be measured or are irrelevant, have no apparent logic that connects program resources and activities to stated outcomes, and are inflexible to program modification for unstated political or ideological reasons (Jung & Schubert, 1983). Consequently, there is a need to determine whether a program can be evaluated for results prior to initiating a formal evaluation. In order for a program evaluation to be carried out successfully, it is important that a program be ready for evaluation. One way to determine its readiness is to have an evaluator conduct an evaluability assessment. The following section discusses this process.

EVALUABILITY ASSESSMENT

Developed by Joseph Wholey in 1979, the evaluability assessment is a tool that can help an evaluator determine whether a program meets the criteria for a meaningful evaluation to take place. According to Wholey (1979):

> Evaluability assessment explores the objectives, expectations, and information needs of program managers and policymakers; explores program reality; assesses the likelihood that program activities will achieve measurable progress toward program objectives; and assesses the extent to which evaluation information is likely to be used by program management. The products of evaluability assessment are: (1) a set of agreed-on program objectives, side effects, and performance indicators on which the program can realistically be held accountable; and (2) a set of evaluation/ management options which represent ways in which management can change program activities, objectives, or uses of information in ways likely to improve program performance. (p. xiii)

Accordingly, evaluability assessment is a process developed to determine whether a program has been planned and implemented well enough to be evaluated and to assist the planning of evaluations that can improve program performance (Wholey, 1994). Data collection, primarily by means of interviews and other qualitative techniques involving program administrators and major stakeholders, helps evaluators broaden their knowledge of the program and the ways in which it can be evaluated.

A six-step model in conducting an evaluability assessment was adapted from Smith (1989; see Figure 8.1). The steps are not meant to suggest that the process is fixed. Depending on the context and purpose, some steps can be modified or reordered. These steps, with brief explanations, are as follows:

Step 1: Determine purpose, secure commitment, and identify members of the evaluability assessment work team. Smith (1989) suggests the early formation of the work team, with the ideal team consisting of members from major stakeholder groups, program implementers, and administration. The goal of this team is to develop and produce the evaluability assessment.

Step 2: Identify and analyze program documentation and define the boundaries of the program to be examined. Also identify program goals and objectives. This step clarifies the purpose of the evaluability assessment. Included here are a review of documentation establishing or authorizing the program, grant applications, previous evaluations, audits, program brochures, and program Web sites with program descriptions and claims. Boundaries may vary based on factors such as geographic location or program objectives. Boundaries may also delimit the evaluability assessment to specific program components.

Step 3: Engage stakeholders in developing/clarifying program theory and logic, define evaluation questions, identify key performance indicators, and select appropriate data collection methods and tools. Also identify stakeholder needs, concerns, and differences in perceptions. Differences in these areas can indicate misperceptions of the program and intent, or a program that is not sufficiently meeting the needs of one or more stakeholder groups. Descriptions and comparisons of stakeholder perceptions are important for further understanding of the program. For example, stakeholders can be asked:

FIGURE 8.1. Evaluability Assessment Model

---

1 Create the evaluability assessment work team.

2 Identify and analyze program documentation, and define boundaries.

3 Engage stakeholders.

4 Determine plausibility of the program model.

5 Draw conclusions and make recommendations.

6 Plan specific steps for the use of evaluability assessment data.

- What was the reason for creating the program?
- Who is the program's target population? How is the program marketed?
- Do the students you serve differ from those you want to serve?
- What services are provided to students? How do they relate to the program's objectives?
- Are there professional development opportunities provided for the staff and faculty?
- What problems, if any, have been encountered in the implementation of the program?
- What is the program retention rate? Why do some students drop out?
- What information is needed to know that the program is working as intended?

According to Smith (1989), the major features of developing a program theory include analyzing assumptions and values, available resources, program activities, and objectives, and considering how these components relate to one another to produce outcomes. The important point in developing a program theory is to construct a reasonable depiction of how a program works so that the plausibility of the model can be assessed. Figure 8.2 depicts the logic of a hypothetical online program that can be used or adapted for use in an evaluability assessment. This evaluable program model identifies program components and subcomponents at the top and shows how program effects (i.e., outcomes) are related to each other and culminate in the program's ultimate goal effect of student achievement at the bottom of the model.

FIGURE 8.2. Evaluable Program Model

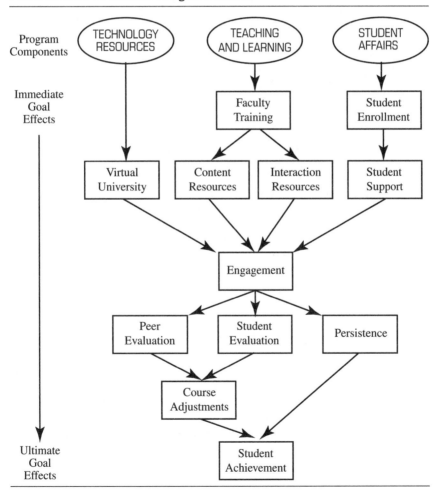

Table 8.1 identifies hypothetical key performance indicators associated with each measurable effect listed in this model. The performance indicators represent important variables that can be measured during the actual program evaluation to generate statistical data that can, in turn, be used to measure, among other things, the success of an institution when compared to its competition and relative to its past performance and established performance standards. The purpose of these indicators is to track trends over time, provide reliable data to support internal quality assurance systems, assess the health of the organization, support leadership by providing a focus for the organization, and reward outstanding performance. Thus, tracking key performance indicators becomes a part of the institution's performance management framework for its distance education programs. Key performance indicators also establish the frame of reference for the strategic planning cycle by specifying the primary numbers used to monitor institutional effectiveness. The ability of the work team to identify suitable variables as performance indicators for each program effect suggests that the program can be evaluated and monitored for results. However, it must be kept in mind that performance indicators are not fixed; indicators change as strategic goals and visions evolve for institutions.

Evaluators often select variables that are the easiest to measure when selecting performance indicators, e.g., course grades and completion rates. Although important, by themselves, they often represent immediate learner outcomes and do not address longer-term impacts of the learning, such as return on investment, productivity, or impact on the graduate's organizational culture. Moreover, they often fail to capture benefits, innovation, or unique value created via faculty learning (Forman, 2002). Consequently, it is important that evaluators include indicators of learning impacts such as alumni and employer feedback.

Each performance indicator also requires a benchmark or target in order to evaluate program performance against established standards. Accordingly, the program evaluator will be able to determine if the program exceeded, met, or failed to meet each of its targets. Generally, the rating of "exceeded its target" is awarded only when the measured performance indicator exceeds the benchmark by at least one standard deviation.

For established distance education programs, it is also useful for the evaluator to plan on analyzing multiyear trend data. This will enable the evaluator also to make a finding of improved, unchanged, or declined for each performance indicator, and to include line charts depicting trends in the final evaluation report.

In addition to distance education program performance indicators, the institution may also have institutional indicators that need to be included in the program evaluation. A typical indicator that falls into this category is faculty productivity, which is measured by the number of student credit hours per full-time equivalent instructional faculty. The institution should consider separate benchmarks for faculty who teach online and for those who teach traditional on-campus

TABLE 8.1. Key Performance Indicators

Effects	Performance Indicators
Virtual university	Reliability
	Availability
	Maintainability
	Ease of use/navigation
	User satisfaction
	Cost-effectiveness
Faculty training	Professional development
	Evaluation of teaching
Content resources	Adequacy
	Currency/accuracy
Interaction resources	Adequacy
Student enrollment	Number of contacts/prospects
	Number of enrollments
	Student quality
Support services	Usage
	Processing turnaround
	Client satisfaction
	Meeting client needs
	Staff satisfaction
	Effects on personal development
	Effects on academic performance
	Cost-effectiveness
Engagement	Student-student interactions
	Student-instructor interactions
	Student-system interactions
Peer evaluation	Peer ratings/recommendations
	Course relevance
Student evaluation	Student ratings/recommendations
	Program/course relevance
Course adjustments	Formative course changes
Persistence	Course completion rates
	Program completion rates
Student achievement	Key assignment grades
	Course grades
	Grade point average
	Alumni/employer feedback
	Job placement/advancement
	Certification exam results
	Parity with on-campus programs
	Achievement gap by race/ethnicity
	Achievement gap by handicap status
	Student gratification

courses, since some research suggests that teaching online can entail more faculty time than teaching an equivalent on-campus course (e.g., Lee & Wilner, 2002). Brown (1998), for example, estimates that online instruction requires roughly 40% to 50% more work on the teacher's part in comparison with traditional classroom delivery.

Step 4: Determine plausibility of the program model as depicted in the evaluable program model using data from program staff, documentation, and stakeholder interviews. Data are analyzed to determine the extent to which the program is properly implemented, sufficiently developed, and activities are appropriate to reasonably predict that desired outcomes will be met.

Step 5: Draw conclusions and make recommendations based on the data. One of two conclusions can be drawn:

- The program is ready for an evaluation. The evaluability assessment will suggest some of the parameters for the evaluation (e.g., standards and performance measures).
- The program is not ready for an evaluation. The program may not be ready for an evaluation due to fundamental planning and/or implementation issues. Smith (1989) identifies the following potential problem areas:
    Evaluators and intended users fail to agree on the goals, objectives, side effects, and standards to be used in evaluating the program.
    Program goals and objectives are found to be unrealistic given the resources that have been allocated and the program activities that have been implemented.
    Essential information on program performance is not available.
    Program administrators are unable or unwilling to change the program on the basis of evaluation information.

Step 6: Plan or recommend specific steps for the utilization of evaluability assessment data. Evaluability assessments can result in any of the following organizational decisions (Smith, 1989):

- Conducting a comprehensive evaluation of the program
- Changing the program
- Doing nothing/taking no further action
- Terminating the program
- Ignoring the evaluability assessment.

If the program is ready for evaluation, the evaluator must draw from the results of the evaluability assessment and plan for the evaluation. The following section identifies various program evaluation types and how they may be used in evaluations of distance education programs.

TYPES OF EVALUATION

Program evaluation is often described using Stufflebeam's CIPP model, consisting of the following four types of evaluation: context, input, process, and product evaluations (e.g., Reiser & Dempsey, 2007). These four types can be used alone or together in any evaluation.

The context evaluation judges the learning environment in which the educational program is implemented. This type of evaluation focuses on assessing needs, assets, and problems as it identifies factors that promote success and learning. A needs assessment is often conducted as part of a context evaluation. This evaluation is also used to develop or refine program goals and objectives. It answers the question, what must the program do?

Input evaluation assesses competing ways to achieve the goals developed or refined in the context evaluation, compares strategies of the competition to those of the program being evaluated, and estimates the ability of students to complete the program. The input evaluation guides program planning. It answers the question, how best should the program be implemented?

The process evaluation monitors the effectiveness of various program components and activities, as well as the instructional decisions made. Essentially, it examines how the program operates. It answers the question, how effectively and efficiently is the program operating?

Finally, product evaluation focuses on program results and helps determine the merit and worth of the program. It evaluates program outputs and outcomes and assesses the program's reach to the target audience. It answers the question, to what extent does the program succeed and make a difference?

The CIPP model is important because evaluation is ongoing and various components of this model address different aspects of the program in a systematic fashion. Another common way of classifying evaluations that combines various CIPP evaluation types is by formative and summative evaluations (Reiser & Dempsey, 2007), each of which is described below within the context of a distance education program evaluation.

Formative Evaluation

A formative evaluation is typically used to assess programs during the early stages of their development, and is comparable to the context, input, and process evaluations used in the CIPP model. It focuses on the needs of program clients (e.g., distance education students), the delivery of the program or technology, and the quality of its implementation (e.g., Rossi, Lipsey, & Freeman, 2003; Reiser & Dempsey, 2007). The focus, therefore, is on academic quality management. Formative evaluations often consist of assessing a developing program at a single site or as a pilot study prior to full implementation. Formative evaluations are also used with mature programs when the primary purpose of the evaluation is to assess program inputs (i.e., input evaluation), assess program processes (i.e., process evaluation), determine student needs (i.e., needs assessment), determine program cost-effectiveness (i.e., cost-effectiveness analysis), or determine whether an evaluation is feasible and how stakeholders can help shape its usefulness (i.e., evaluability assessment).

The focus of program evaluations is to respond to an agreed-upon set of evaluation questions. They are used to focus the evaluator's attention on the substantive areas and issues for evaluation and provide relatively constant reference points to help plan and guide the evaluation. Posavac and Carey (2002) suggest that responses to the following queries often help inform the development of evaluation questions:

- What program will be evaluated? What e-learning system is used to deliver the program?
- Who will use the results of the evaluation?
- What is the purpose of the evaluation?
- What issues have been raised, e.g., low persistence rates, poor student satisfaction, or low enrollment? How will the results be used?
- What decisions need to be made regarding the program, e.g., continuance, expansion, reducing costs?
- Who is going to conduct the program evaluation?
- How will the program evaluation be conducted?
- What method(s) should be used?

Formative evaluation questions that can be used for distance education programs include:

- What is the nature and scope of the problem that management has identified with the distance education program?
- How should the program or technology be changed to respond to the problem?
- How well is the program or technology delivered?
- What are the academic needs of students who enroll in distance education programs?
- To what extent are these needs being satisfied?
- How well are students satisfied with the program?
- How does student satisfaction compare with that of courses offered on-campus?
- Was the program equally effective for all participants? Why or why not?
- Are there characteristics that distinguish satisfied and dissatisfied students?
- Does the school apply this information to admission and recruiting policies and decisions?
- Is the program cost-effective?

Typical performance indicators commonly associated with formative evaluations are:

- Quality of students entering the program (e.g., SAT and GRE scores, prior academic achievement)
- Faculty qualifications
- Relevance (i.e., the extent to which the program corresponds to student perception of needs)
- Gratification (i.e., the extent to which the program enhances the students' self-esteem and sense of integrity)
- Currency of course materials
- Student evaluation of teaching
- Peer evaluation of teaching
- Timeliness of faculty and staff feedback
- Adequacy of support services
- Student reasons for refunds and enrollment termination
- Degree to which the institution responds to faculty needs
- Faculty satisfaction (e.g., with compensation, workload, training, and teaching load)
- Technology availability
- Learner reactions to the e-learning environment (e.g., general level of acceptance, ease of navigation)
- Quality of vendor support.

Summative Evaluation

A summative evaluation, in contrast, focuses on how well an implemented program works, and seeks to discover if the program makes a difference. That is, the emphasis is on determining the extent to which program objectives have been attained (e.g., Rossi, Lipsey, & Freeman, 2003; Reiser & Dempsey, 2007). Summative evaluation is comparable to a product evaluation using the CIPP model. Such evaluations examine what happens subsequent to the delivery of the program or technology. They can investigate whether the program or technology in the short term resulted in demonstrable effects on specifically defined target outcomes (i.e., outcome evaluations) or resulted in longer-term effects (i.e., impact evaluation), or it may determine the cost benefits of the program (i.e., cost-benefit analysis). Summative evaluations are often used for accountability purposes, to include program accreditation.

Summative evaluation questions that can be used for distance education programs include:

- What is the effectiveness of the program or technology?
     Were the objectives of the program met?
     Is the program cost-effective?

What are course and program completion rates?
What are the job placement rates of graduates?
How do graduates evaluate the program?
• What is the impact of the program or technology?
How do employers evaluate graduates?
What are the advanced professional study rates of graduates?
What are the career retention rates of graduates?
What professional recognition have graduates received?
How do graduates assess their program-related professional accomplishments?
Did the program have any unintended impacts?

Some performance indicators commonly associated with summative evaluations include:

• Quality of student effort (e.g., grade trends)
• Persistence (e.g., program completion rates)
• Impact (the extent to which the program reduced/eliminated student needs)
• Percentage of graduates who believe their instructional programs met their goals
• Attitudes of graduates concerning the program
• Changes (if any) in graduates' educational expectations
• Level of employer satisfaction
• Benefits of the learning to an employer
• Changes in graduates' job performance.

STANDARDS AND BENCHMARKS

In planning for a program evaluation, the institution identifies standards or goals for its educational programs, identifies associated benchmarks (i.e., expected student outcomes and program outputs), and evaluates whether the program achieves these benchmarks. Assessing the effectiveness of educational programs includes assessing multiple learning and program standards.

Table 8.2 provides examples of evaluation standards that might be used for an online educational leadership program. Evidence in the form of key performance indicators is then identified to assess these standards. Regardless of the evidence selected, it must be credible, which means that the evidence must be valid, reliable, and obtained from a representative sample of the target population. Nonetheless, evaluators must not equate evidence with truth. Rational decision making is based on both evidence and professional judgment. The danger is that evaluators and administrators may make decisions based solely on measurements because of the appearance of truth.

TABLE 8.2. Example Evaluation Standards for a Graduate Online Educational Leadership Program

Support Services Standards

1. Provide timely and helpful responses to applicant/student questions and requests
2. Achieve or exceed planned student headcounts while not lowering the quality of applicants and accepted students
3. Promote successful student persistence through student advising and successful resolution of complaints
4. Coordinate marketing and advertising strategies that reflect student outcomes and competencies
5. Provide faculty with training, support, and access to resources for developing and implementing technology-mediated instructional materials

Learning Standards

1. Plan, conduct, defend, and evaluate educational research
2. Possess and apply knowledge, skills, and dispositions to administer research-based programs and services within educational organizations
3. Develop and implement evidence-based educational programs and services to maximize student learning in educational organizations
4. Identify needed changes in educational organizations and direct change for the improvement of organizational effectiveness
5. Possess and apply knowledge of educational programs, policies, and practices to assure the appropriate implementation of educational services

Note: In other contexts support services and learning standards can be viewed as goals or instructional objectives.

Where appropriate, benchmarks are established to help evaluate each standard. For example, take the first support services standard from Table 8.2. A possible benchmark could be: At least 80% of students who complete the student survey will agree or strongly agree that the school provides timely and helpful responses to student questions and requests.

The Alfred P. Sloan Foundation Consortium identifies a quality framework for online programs and courses that consists of five pillars (Moore, 2002). These pillars are summarized as follows, and represent areas where standards and benchmarks should be established by the institution:

1. Learning effectiveness ensures that learners who complete an online program receive educations that represent the distinctive quality of the institution.
2. Access provides the means for students to complete their online programs based on three levels of support: academic (e.g., tutoring, advising, and library); administrative (e.g., financial aid and disability support); and technical (e.g., hardware reliability, uptime, and help desk).

3. Student satisfaction reflects the effectiveness of all aspects of the educational experience.
4. Faculty satisfaction means that instructors find the online teaching experience personally rewarding and professionally beneficial.
5. Cost-effectiveness enables institutions to offer their best educational value to learners by controlling costs so that tuition is affordable yet sufficient to meet development and maintenance costs, and to provide a return on investment in startup and infrastructure.

CONCLUSION

Educational leaders are expected to lead their institutions through continuous strategic renewal and transformational change to remain or become high-performing and highly competitive organizations that add value to all stakeholders in a balanced manner. The world in which these leaders find themselves today is rapidly changing as the result of:

- Evolving student needs and the demand for high-level skills
- The use of technology to deliver courses at a distance
- Higher tuitions and reduced public funding
- The pressure to increase institutional productivity despite altered funding circumstances
- Globalization and competition with other schools and programs
- The need to close achievement gaps without diminishing quality
- The trend toward increased public accountability for student learning.

The timeliness and nature of the response to a changing environment will largely determine the future success of institutions. Strategic planning and program evaluation are important tools that can lead organizations to a strategic renewal so they are able to adapt to change and thrive. Without periodic renewal, programs tend to be drawn toward disorganization and eventual demise (Katz & Kahn, 1978).

Strategic renewal is an evolutionary process associated with promoting, accommodating, and utilizing new knowledge and innovative behavior in order to bring about change in an organization's core competencies and/or a change in its product market domain (Burgelman, 1994). Successful strategic renewal overcomes the inertial forces of an institution's established strategy and closes the gap between its existing capabilities and the evolving basis of competitive advantage in the educational sector (e.g., Burgelman, 1994). To accomplish this goal, educational leaders must internalize information that diverges from their view of strategy and must use this information to shape new competencies and directions for the organization (Burgelman, 1994). The results of periodic program evaluations provide the impetus for this change.

CHAPTER 9

Institution and Program Accreditation

The previous chapter addresses program evaluation as an activity closely related to the institution's strategic planning process. It provides a means to determine the extent to which programs are supporting the institution's strategic goals and objectives. The results of program evaluations are used as inputs during the scanning and diagnosis phase of the next strategic planning cycle during which program adjustments can be made. Chapter 8 also highlights the importance of using evaluation findings to improve distance education programs and services and to document evidence for institution and program accreditation. The purpose of this chapter is to continue this discussion by:

- Describing the accreditation process
- Identifying evidence of quality distance education programs for accreditation purposes
- Identifying issues and red flags that should be of particular concern to distance education administrators who are preparing for reaffirmation of accreditation.

BACKGROUND

The Carnegie Classification System provides a broad set of standards for institutions wishing to reach the next level. Additionally, several publications rank colleges and universities based on implicit and sometimes explicit standards. One of the most popular is *U.S. News and World Report*'s annual ranking of the best colleges and universities. At its inception in 1983, standings were determined by reputation alone. In 1988, statistical data, such as acceptance rates, average freshman retention rates, and projected and actual graduation rates, were added as sources of information (Morse & Flanigan, 2004). However, such rankings are controversial and are often viewed as an evaluation of a few characteristics and heavily influenced by fame and wealth. However, at present, there are no alternatives to commercial rankings, and until university presidents refrain from completing reputational surveys and touting their institution's rankings, the present system is likely to continue.

Accrediting commissions, associations, and agencies add another layer of professional standards for institutions and programs that desire to be legitimized in a professional field or discipline. Altekruse and Wittmer (1991) describe accreditation as a "process whereby an association or agency grants public recognition to a school, institute, college, university, or specialized program of study that has met certain established qualifications or standards as determined through initial and periodic evaluations" (p. 53). Contreras (2007) reports that approximately one-fifth of degree-granting institutions operating legally in the United States are not accredited.

At present, there is no authoritative list of institutions/providers at the international level that is recognized by competent authorities to operate across borders. Each country has its own system, with varying standards of quality. In the United States, higher education accreditation is a voluntary and self-regulatory process. The U.S. Department of Education (2007) identifies two types of educational accreditation: The first is institutional, and the second is referred to as specialized or programmatic. Institutional accreditation applies to an entire institution, indicating that each of an institution's parts is contributing to the achievement of the institution's goals and objectives. The six regional accrediting commissions and associations and some national accrediting agencies perform institutional accreditation. The six regional commissions and associations and the areas they cover are:

- Middle States Commission on Higher Education (http://www.msche .org/)—Delaware, District of Columbia, Maryland, New Jersey, Pennsylvania, Puerto Rico, and Virgin Islands
- New England Association of Colleges and Schools (http://www.neasc .org/)—Connecticut, Maine, Massachusetts, New Hampshire, Rhode Island, and Vermont
- North Central Association of Colleges and Schools (http://www.ncacasi .org/)—Arizona, Arkansas, Colorado, Illinois, Indiana, Iowa, Kansas, Michigan, Minnesota, Missouri, Nebraska, New Mexico, North Dakota, Ohio, Oklahoma, South Dakota, West Virginia, Wisconsin, and Wyoming
- Northwest Association of Accredited Schools (http://www.boisestate.edu/ naas/)—Alaska, Idaho, Montana, Nevada, Oregon, Utah, and Washington
- Southern Association of Colleges and Schools (http://www.sacs.org/)—Alabama, Florida, Georgia, Kentucky, Louisiana, Mississippi, North Carolina, South Carolina, Tennessee, Texas, and Virginia
- Western Association of Schools and Colleges (http://www.wascWeb.org/)—California, Hawaii, and the Pacific Basin

These regional commissions and associations are the most important and influential for a broad-based institution of higher education in the United States.

Specialized or programmatic accreditation typically applies to specific programs, departments, or schools that are parts of an institution. For example, the American Psychological Association, Committee on Accreditation, is recognized by the U.S. Department of Education for the accreditation in the United States of doctoral programs in clinical, counseling, school, and combined professional-scientific psychology; predoctoral internship programs in professional psychology; and postdoctoral residency programs in professional psychology. Additionally, the

Accrediting Commission of the Distance Education and Training Council is recognized for the accreditation of postsecondary institutions in the United States that offer degree programs primarily by the distance education method up through the first professional degree level.

Although accreditation is a nongovernmental system, the U.S. Department of Education, as required by law, publishes a list of nationally recognized accrediting agencies that are reliable authorities regarding the quality of education or training. This list, located at http://www.ed.gov/admins/finaid/accred/index.html, is an important source of information to the educational community and to the public, as some institutions may claim accreditation from nonexistent agencies, from agencies they establish, or from agencies that claim to be legitimate but have no standing with the U.S. Department of Education (Loane, 2000). According to the Organisation for Economic Co-operation and Development (2004), "the emergence of nontrustworthy accreditation systems ('accreditation mills') . . . can provide misleading approval to educational providers, students, employers and the public" (p. 23). Students who attend institutions that are accredited through accreditation agencies not recognized by the U.S. Department of Education will not qualify for Title IV funding (e.g., Pell Grants, Stafford Loans, etc.) and may not be able to transfer college credits to an accredited institution.

ACCREDITATION PROCESS

According to the U.S. Department of Education (2007), the accreditation process consists of the following phases:

- Setting standards: The accrediting agency, in collaboration with educational institutions, establishes the standards. Although each accrediting agency establishes its own standards, these standards address similar areas (i.e., expected student achievement, curriculum, faculty, services and academic support for students, and financial capacity).
- Self-study: The institution or program seeking accreditation conducts an in-depth self-evaluation, with involvement by the faculty, program graduates, and employers of those graduates. The self-study measures institution/ program performance against the standards established by the accrediting agency and its own claims and standards. During this phase of the process, the institution or program communicates the results to appropriate stakeholders and uses the results to improve learning outcomes and program outputs.
- On-site evaluation: A team selected by the accrediting agency visits the institution or program to determine if established standards are met. In some situations, an off-site team does the majority of its evaluation at a distance,

focusing on self-study materials that the institution makes available on the Internet. An on-site team checks areas of interest and prepares a written report of its findings, noting areas of noncompliance, if applicable.

• Publication: Upon being satisfied that the standards are met, the accrediting agency grants accreditation or pre-accreditation status and lists the institution or program in an official publication with other similarly accredited or pre-accredited institutions or programs.

• Monitoring: The accrediting agency monitors each accredited institution or program throughout the period of accreditation granted to verify that it continues to meet standards.

• Reevaluation: The accrediting agency periodically reevaluates each institution or program that it lists to ascertain whether reaffirmation of its accredited or pre-accredited status is warranted.

U.S. regional accrediting associations and commissions have been moving away from a primary focus on inputs and a series of "must statements" toward a focus on requiring institutions to focus on student learning outcomes and institutional effectiveness as part of their self-study and review processes. Analyzing learning outcomes requires a conceptual approach that can distinguish among institution, program, and student units of analysis and different kinds of academic results, e.g., cognitive learning, career success, and satisfaction (Ewell, 2001). Consequently, the accreditation process requires institutions and programs to demonstrate acceptable levels of performance across various perspectives.

When the student is the unit of analysis, specific evidence selected by the institution can take various forms, but must include, at a minimum, direct evidence of student attainment. For example, direct evidence can include faculty-designed comprehensive or capstone assignments, licensure examination results, and portfolios of student work over time. Indirect evidence can include self-reports of learning, results of focus groups, and student satisfaction surveys. When the unit of analysis is the program instead of the student, program performance is analyzed in terms of program outputs (instead of learning outcomes), such as graduation rates and program persistence rates, and productivity or efficiency, such as cost-effectiveness. The overall program evaluation consists of the results of both the student and the program as the unit of analysis.

Specific elements of design that can be used to establish standards for student learning include:

(a) comprehensiveness, or the degree to which the assessment system is capable of providing evidence about the full range of student learning outcomes established by the institution or program; (b) multiple judgment, or the extent to which multiple sources of evidence are used in a mutually reinforcing way to examine outcomes; (c) multiple dimensions, or the degree to which different facets of student performance with respect to established learning outcomes can be investigated so that patterns of strength and weakness can be identified (and addressed); and (d) direct evidence, or the extent to which the approach relies upon direct measures of student attainment instead of self-reports about learning or proxy indicators of attainment like graduation rates or graduate placement. (Ewell, 2001, p. 19)

Comparing the performance of an institution or program against established standards set by an external body, accreditation certifies that the objectives an institution seeks are relevant and that resources are available to reach those objectives (Dill, Massy, Williams, & Cook, 1996). Thus, accreditation is a type of program evaluation that uses mostly expertise-oriented and objectives-oriented evaluation approaches. The goals of the accreditation process are school improvement and quality assurance by promoting continuing review and self-improvement by the institutions themselves. Accreditation assures the educational community and the general public that an institution or a program has clearly defined and appropriate objectives and maintains conditions under which student achievement that satisfies institutional and program goals can reasonably be expected. The challenge to institutions seeking accreditation is to systematically gather, manage, maintain, and monitor the various sources of evidence needed to follow through with the implementation, benchmarking, evaluation, and improvement of programs and the institution.

However, a note of caution is in order. In this era of emphasis on public accountability in education, it is relatively easy to identify a set of outcomes-assessment performance measures associated with high-stakes decisions for institutional or program accreditation. In this regard, one is reminded of the following theory put forward by Donald T. Campbell (1976):

The more any quantitative social indicator is used for social decision making, the more subject it will be to corruption pressures and the more apt it will be to distort and corrupt the social processes it is intended to monitor. (p. 27)

The danger is that the greater the importance placed on assessment data, the more likely the data will become corrupted. The solution is not to forgo public accountability using assessment data, but to ensure that assessment data are only one element of an overall assessment strategy used for high-stakes accreditation purposes.

DISTANCE EDUCATION

Distance education programs can affect the institution's educational goals, intended student population, curriculum, and modes or venues of instruction, and can thus have an impact on both the institution and its accreditation status. Because of distance education's global reach, market forces are increasing the importance of an institution's reputation and accreditation status. Knight (2005) writes:

Major investments are being made in marketing and branding campaigns to get name recognition and to increase enrollments. Some type of accreditation is part of the campaign, assuring prospective students that the programs and awards are of high standing. This is introducing a commercial dimension to accreditation practices and the desire for institutions or providers to have as many accreditation labels or stars as possible. (p. 3)

The quality of distance education programs influences both the accreditation status of the institution as whole as well as individual programs for which accreditation is sought. Additionally,

the high probability that cross-border and for-profit provision is not covered by national systems for quality assurance, accreditation and recognition of qualifications may increase the risk that students/learners are victim of rogue providers ("degree mills"), offering low-quality educational experiences and qualifications of limited validity. (Organisation for Economic Co-operation and Development, 2004, p. 23)

The Council for Higher Education Accreditation (CHEA) is the primary national voice for voluntary accreditation and quality assurance to the U.S. Congress and the U.S. Department of Education. According to the CHEA Institute for Research and Study of Accreditation and Quality Assurance, recognized accrediting commissions, associations, and agencies routinely review the following seven key areas of institutional activity when they examine the quality of distance learning programs:

1. Institutional mission: Does offering distance learning make sense in this institution?
2. Institutional organizational structure: Is the institution suitably structured to offer quality distance learning?
3. Institutional resources: Does the institution sustain adequate financing to offer quality distance learning?
4. Curriculum and instruction: Does the institution have appropriate curricula and design of instruction to offer quality distance learning?
5. Faculty support: Are faculty members competent to engage in offering distance learning, and do they have adequate resources, facilities, and equipment?
6. Student support: Do students have needed counseling, advising, equipment, facilities, and instructional materials to pursue distance learning?
7. Student learning outcomes: Does the institution routinely evaluate the quality of distance learning based on evidence of student achievement? (CHEA, 2002, p. 7)

Evidence of Quality

Appendix C describes evidence of quality for distance learning programs in each of the above seven areas. This information is derived primarily from the following sources. The U.S. Department of Education (USDOE, 2006) identifies evidence of quality in distance education programs drawn from interviews with members of the accrediting community. The Southern Association of Colleges and Schools (SACS, 2000, 2006) identifies standards and best practices that are directly related to distance education programs and that are broadly consistent with those published by the other five regional commissions and associations. In particular, *Best Practices for Electronically Offered Degree and Certificate Programs* (SACS, 2000) represents a joint document prepared by the regional accrediting associations and the Western Cooperative for Educational Telecommunications. Additionally, the CHEA Institute for Research and Study of Accreditation and Quality Assurance (CHEA, 2002) provides examples of distance education standards obtained from various accrediting organizations. Finally, pertinent standards developed by the Institute for Higher Education Policy (IHEP, 2000) are also listed.

The standards listed are representative of generally accepted accreditation standards that are relevant for distance education programs. However, the list is not comprehensive, and program administrators need to consult the specific standards used by the accreditation agency or agencies that have jurisdiction for their institution and programs. Moreover, all accrediting agencies do not employ identical review practices to ensure quality in distance learning. Standards, policies, and guidelines vary by agency and the type of institution or program that is reviewed.

Many examples of exemplary distance education programs exist in the professional literature. For example, two of the seven standards listed above deal with faculty support and student support. Cavanaugh (2002) reports that support to the distance education faculty and students at the University of Central Florida is noteworthy. The university requires all online instructors to complete a distance education professional development program, for which they receive a stipend or a laptop computer. They are also allowed release time and extra compensation for course development, and are assisted in course design and delivery by trained staff. To support online students, the university has a full range of student support services online, including 24/7 technical support.

Issues and Red Flags

Eaton (2001) writes, "whatever our opinions may be about distance learning and its future, there is no disputing the evidence that some elements of the distance learning experience are significantly different from a site-based educational experience" (p. 13). She goes on to note that some of the more significant differences include curricula development, computer-mediated classrooms, separation in time of communication between teachers and students, and online support services.

Institutional researchers and program evaluators must take account of these differences and evaluate their impact on student outcomes. Strategic planners must then take the results and ensure that the institution's strategic plan responds with appropriate strategies, activities, and programs that ensure institutional effectiveness and equity in educational outcomes between traditional face-to-face programs and those delivered at a distance. Quality assurance depends on demonstration of quality against standards that are understood and accepted by all stakeholders.

The USDOE (2006) lists several red flags associated with the quality of distance education programs that point to programmatic and accreditation problems. These red flags are as follows:

- New programs are launched on the basis of perceived need, but without any research indicating that there is a market for them.
- Faculty members engage in distance education course development, while carrying a full-time teaching load.
- Large numbers of students are enrolled in sections of online courses with insufficient faculty for effective faculty-student interaction.
- There is little discussion board activity in online courses.
- The majority of student postings lack substance and show little evidence of reflection or critical thinking.
- Student evaluation of teaching is poor.
- There is rapid adjunct faculty turnover.
- Course materials are outdated.
- Faculty members are given primary responsibility for solving students' technical problems.
- Students don't know whom to contact if they have questions or problems.
- Student persistence is low.

Eaton (2001) also identifies three issues regarding quality that are of particular interest to state and federal governments:

- Accountability of state and federal funds delivered in a distance learning environment (i.e., avoidance of fraud and abuse)
- Ability of traditional accreditation procedures to ensure quality in a distance learning environment
- Adequacy of self-regulation in higher education as distance learning expands.

Government officials, according to Eaton (2001), have legitimate concerns about the impact of distance learning programs. Consequently, institutions have an obligation to acknowledge the implications of distance learning for common understandings with government officials about public funding and quality. Additionally, a program offered in whole or part by telecommunications is Title IV–eligible regarding federal student aid only if the offering institution is not a foreign institution and is evaluated to have the capability to effectively deliver distance education programs by a recognized accrediting agency or association that has evaluation of those programs within the scope of its recognition.

CONCLUSION

Learners need to be protected from the risks of low-quality education and credentials of limited validity. Moreover, the complexity of national qualifications and their lack of comparability across national borders increase the difficulties for qualified professionals and for credential evaluators in the recognition process (Organisation for Economic Co-Operation and Development, 2004). Consequently, it is important that each institution assume responsibility to award easily readable and transparent qualifications.

Accreditation agencies remain unsettled about how to deal with substantive differences between for-profit and not-for-profit institutions with distinctly different missions (Hawthorne, 1995). However, one outcome is clear. The emergence of for-profit institutions with clear and specific missions regarding job training as part of the mix of higher education has resulted in accreditation agencies' holding traditional higher education more accountable for the employability and job performance of their graduates.

Acquiring legitimacy requires conforming to "broad institutional scripts" that, in turn, influence actions (Ogawa & Bossert, 1995, p. 321). Scripts "are observable, recurrent activities and patterns of interaction characteristic of a particular setting" (Barley & Tolbert, 1997, p. 98). In higher education, the accreditation process is an example of a highly scripted process for acquiring and retaining legitimacy from recognized sources. Relevant scripts for institutions of higher education that engage in distance learning include:

- Consistency of distance education initiatives with the mission and vision of the institution
- The presence of evaluative mechanisms to ensure that programs and courses offered at a distance have the same requirements and meet the same learning outcomes as traditionally offered programs and courses
- Periodic assessments of student persistence and student and faculty satisfaction
- Equivalence of faculty teaching loads in distance and traditional learning environments, since teaching at a distance often takes more time if effectively implemented
- Quality assurance for distance education programs and courses, to include quality of faculty used to teach at a distance and their equivalence with on-campus faculty who teach in traditional programs
- Adequacy of student support services at a distance, including financial aid, academic advisement, placement, counseling, tutoring, and technical help
- Appropriate and adequate learning resources that are available to all students
- Adequacy of student-student and student-teacher interactions

- Adequacy of human and financial resources for faculty and staff training and distance education program and course development
- Strong accountability of state and federal student aid funds
- Adherence to the 50% rule by Title IV–eligible institutions by adequate differentiation between online and correspondence courses.

The focus of higher education should be the pursuit of quality learning outcomes, and not the pursuit of prestige.

CHAPTER 10

Course Evaluation

Chism (1999) writes that the culture of higher education teaching has developed a strong norm of privacy, which inhibits the growth of what [Ernest] Boyer terms "the scholarship of teaching"—that is, the thoughtful, problem-solving, discipline-based approach to teaching that involves "continual reasoning about instructional choices, awareness of the solutions that other scholars have made to key problems in facilitating student learning in the field, and active, ongoing research about the effects of instructor actions on student learning" (p. 6).

Course evaluation is an important aspect of distance education program evaluation, accreditation, and improvement, and the pursuit of the scholarship of teaching. These evaluations typically include four steps: selection of the standards or objectives and related performance indicators, setting the level of planned performance (i.e., the benchmark or target), collecting data and comparing actual performance to the benchmark, and making a value judgment regarding the course (Reiser & Dempsey, 2007). Course evaluations are most often used for summative purposes to obtain evidence to support merit pay, promotion, and tenure decisions, as well as inputs to program evaluations. When used for high-stakes decisions regarding faculty members, the focus of the evaluation is on assessing teaching effectiveness. However, formative purposes are also essential to maintaining and improving the quality of teaching and learning.

The desired outcomes of teaching courses at a distance and face-to-face are the same: student mastery of instructional objectives. What differs is how these outcomes are achieved. The successful distance education teacher becomes conversant with new technology and develops new instructional styles, moving from creating instruction to managing resources and students and disseminating views (Strain, 1987). Therefore, teaching and its evaluation differs based on the instructional medium.

The purpose of this chapter is to highlight salient considerations when attempting to evaluate the quality of online courses. It describes important standards from the research literature that can be used to evaluate online courses and examines the scheduling, sources, and receivers of salient evaluative feedback in order to optimize the summative and formative values associated with course evaluations.

BACKGROUND

Based upon research conducted at the National Center for Postsecondary Improvement, Massy (2005) reports seven quality principles to which postsecondary programs should adhere in order to facilitate program improvement. These principles can be juxtaposed to the course level as follows:

1. A quality course is one in which desirable learning outcomes are achieved.
2. Professional development and self-evaluation should inform instruction.
3. Student and academic services should attend to the learning needs of students.
4. Consultation with colleagues, along with peer review of practice, should inform instruction.
5. Data from evaluations should drive course design.
6. Standards and benchmarks should help define course quality.
7. Instructors should continuously assess the adequacy of the course design to accomplish desired learning outcomes and modify the design if deemed necessary.

These principles highlight the importance of learning outcomes, self- and peer evaluation, data-driven decision making, and selecting standards and establishing benchmarks within an organizational culture that values continuous improvement.

Standards

The professional literature (e.g., Bonk, Wisher, & Lee, 2003; Harroff & Valentine, 2006; Kearsley & Blomeyer, 2004; Phipps & Merisotis, 2000; Roberts, Irani, Telg, & Lundy, 2005; Stephenson, 2001) identify online teaching standards that can be used for course evaluations. This research suggests that an effective online course instructor:

- Is a subject matter expert
- Demonstrates technical competency using the online medium
- Selects technological tools based on desired learning outcomes rather than mere availability
- Communicates course objectives and expected learning outcomes to all students
- Periodically reviews instructional objectives for appropriateness
- Selects course materials that support independent learning
- Reviews course materials to ensure program relevance
- Creates active and authentic learning activities that engage all students
- Provides students with methods of both finding and evaluating supplemental learning resources
- Keeps students interested and motivated
- Shows enthusiasm
- Communicates high expectations
- Promotes diverse, rich, and interactive experiences
- Establishes teacher presence and maintains effective student-instructor interaction

- Promotes student-student interaction in establishing social and cognitive presence
- Provides timely and meaningful feedback
- Encourages students to be critical and reflective
- Shows respect and concern for the welfare of students
- Respects diversity and different ways of learning
- Elicits critical thinking and high levels of learning, such as analysis, synthesis, and evaluation
- Elicits agreement from students to deadlines for course deliverables and subsequent faculty feedback
- Uses diverse methods of evaluating educational effectiveness against specific standards
- Encourages independent learning
- Uses course materials that support cultural diversity
- Accommodates the special needs of students.

Additionally, the same professional research literature identifies the following program standards that directly influence course effectiveness. This research suggests that an effective online program:

- Provides electronic security to protect course access and archive information
- Uses a reliable and capable learning management system (LMS)
- Ensures availability of online student support services and library resources
- Provides rich program information to students (e.g., technical requirements, tuition, fees, and proctoring requirements)
- Provides technical training and assistance to students and faculty members
- Provides ample professional development opportunities for faculty members in designing and teaching online courses.

While Husmann and Miller (2001) report that "administrators perceive quality to be based almost exclusively in the performance of the faculty" (¶ 17), a holistic evaluation of all indicators that define a quality course includes services outside the instructor's responsibility. As an example, an unreliable course delivery system can influence the attainment of important learning outcomes regardless of how well the instructor designs and presents the course; thus, student learning and satisfaction can be diminished independent of faculty performance. Information technology (IT) support, program coordinators, instructional team members, and other administrative services all contribute to course quality and bear varying degrees of responsibility for achieving or failing to achieve specific benchmarks.

Similar to instructors not being the sole determinant of course quality, students are not the sole source of evaluative feedback. Course evaluation should be based on information collected from multiple sources, such as student evaluation of teaching (SET), peer review, teaching portfolios, virtual classroom observations, and self-evaluation (Seldin, 2007).

Student Evaluation of Teaching

Administrators view teacher evaluations based on student ratings as valid, but faculty members tend to question this source of assessment data (Aleomoni, 1984). Nonetheless, SETs are used more than any other method to evaluate teaching performance (Seldin, 2007). However, there are risks in placing too much emphasis on SETs for course evaluations. As James (2001) asserts:

> Students are well-equipped to judge the quality of certain aspects of higher education and we should trust their intuitions on these matters. Generally speaking, students are in a reasonable position to judge the more tangible, short-term components of the experience and to judge aspects of the process of higher education. . . . But the student expectation-quality relationship is not altogether this straightforward. . . . There are deeper dimensions to quality in higher education . . . [that] are usually less tangible, less intuitive and require a longer-term view. Students are not necessarily in the best position to judge these aspects. . . . (p. 8)

Thus, important sources of feedback regarding course quality may also include instructors, their peers and supervisors, and IT personnel. Chism (1999) suggests that students are in the best position to report on the day-to-day functioning and activities of a course and to provide feedback on their own learning experiences, interpersonal rapport of teachers with students, and teacher concern for student progress.

Although SETs are generally viewed as valid and reliable, they are criticized when ratings reflect factors other than the quality of student learning. There is a potential for bias or abuse if students are asked to evaluate aspects of teaching that they are not well equipped to judge, if there is an overreliance on SETs in course evaluation, or if too much weight is placed on relatively minor differences in ratings that do not account for the measurement error that exists in survey data. When SETs are used well, they can be helpful in supporting the agendas for which they are intended. When abused, trust is lost, impact is negative, and something potentially valuable becomes damaging.

Supervisor and Peer Review of Teaching

In order to promote the scholarship of teaching, individual courses as well as entire programs should be evaluated for formative as well as summative purposes. However, such dual purposes for faculty evaluations have the potential to introduce conflict. On the one hand, formative evaluation promotes and supports faculty development; on the other hand, summative evaluation yields information upon which decisions regarding promotion, rank, and tenure are made (Seldin, 2007). According to Mills and Hyle (1999):

> When these approaches are combined in one review, faculty members must choose between providing honest, reflective self-criticism or minimizing weaknesses while emphasizing (even exaggerating) their contributions when reviewing their performance with their chair, who is expected to use information from the review to justify a summative decision reported to higher levels in the institution. (p. 353)

However, supervisors and peers are in a much better position than students to provide feedback on course goals and objectives, course organization and content, course design, and the instructor's subject-matter expertise (Chism, 1999). Malik (1996) adds assessment of disciplinary competence, currency of course materials, and relevance to related disciplines to this list. Consequently, supervisor and peer reviews are important components of a complete, balanced, and fair evaluation of teaching effectiveness.

Hutchings (1996) argues for peer evaluation by noting that most postsecondary faculty do not learn to teach on their own or through a formal teacher education program; they learn to teach through a professional socialization process that includes imitation, mentoring, and responding to feedback from others. Consequently, peer evaluation has the added benefit of nurturing collegiality and supporting the scholarship of teaching.

However, the validity and reliability of peer ratings of teaching are not as well established as they are for SETs. Additionally,

> [Peer] reviewers should make sure that they are appropriate judges. If there are conflicts of interest, . . . personality conflicts between the reviewer and the colleague being reviewed, . . . or if there are other compelling reasons why the reviewer cannot do a thorough and fair job, that reviewer should request to be excused from the review. (Chism, 1999, p. 33)

Institutions using peer review to evaluate teaching effectiveness should follow sound procedures in selecting and training reviewers; establish guidelines, criteria, and standards for the reviews; and collect data to assess the validity and reliability of the reviews (Chism, 1999). The risk in using peer evaluations without careful planning is the possibility of a clash between the institutional culture of collegiality and accountability on the one hand and valid peer evaluations on the other, particularly if such evaluations are to be used for summative purposes.

Parker Palmer (1998) suggests that a holistic approach to peer review be adopted based on multiple observations and collegial conversations, as well as self-reflections, that result in "a communal effort to stretch each other and make better sense of the world" (p. 103). Such a vision of formative evaluation is closely linked to Ernest Boyer's view of the scholarship of teaching.

MULTISTAGE COURSE EVALUATION MODEL

The above background includes research-based standards for effective online instructors and programs. Additionally, Appendix C describes evidence of quality distance learning programs used by accreditation associations and agencies. Together, these standards can be used for evaluating the quality of online courses. In addition to a purely summative purpose, such evaluations have great potential to improve the quality of courses (i.e., a formative purpose) if data are collected and evaluations are conducted at a time when they are of greatest value, gathered from the most knowledgeable sources, and relayed to the person or organization who values the information (or should value it) the most. Standards can be examined by asking oneself the following five questions:

1. Which group of students (i.e., those who are enrolled, those who will enroll at a later term, or those who will enroll in other courses that use the present course as a prerequisite) do I want to benefit from analyzing this standard?
2. With the target benefit group from question 1 established, when is the optimal time to gather information?
3. From whom should I gather such information?
4. What are the performance indicators and benchmarks (if needed) for each standard?
5. To whom should I provide evaluation results?

Multiple answers to all five questions for a given standard are possible, suggesting that course evaluation is a complex activity requiring numerous types of information, assessments, sources, and receivers.

In addition to standards, performance indicators and benchmarks are often required, especially if the purpose of the evaluation is summative. Selecting appropriate and useful performance indicators and benchmarks is a fairly straightforward process, but often involves refinement and collaboration with others. As an example, take the following standard: The online instructor provides timely and meaningful feedback. One possible performance indicator is student perception. A benchmark could be: At least 80% of students who complete the end-of-course student survey will agree or strongly agree (on a five-point Likert Scale) that the instructor provides timely and meaningful feedback.

A multistage course evaluation model (see Figure 10.1) is described in the subsections to follow that address course evaluation along a temporal path, i.e., start of the term, middle of the term, and end of the term, where "term" is used generically to represent the duration of a course. The discussion is not meant to be exhaustive in that not all of the standards from the literature are addressed. Instead, the standards discussed are meant to illustrate the notion that valuable feedback is available at various times during the term.

FIGURE 10.1. Multistage Course Evaluation Model

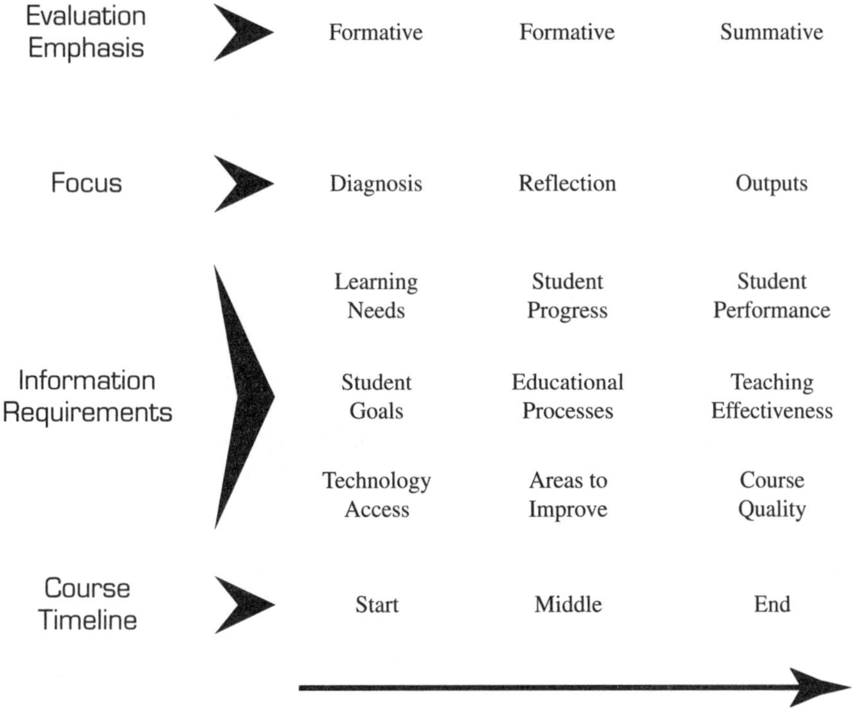

Evaluation Emphasis	Formative	Formative	Summative
Focus	Diagnosis	Reflection	Outputs
Information Requirements	Learning Needs	Student Progress	Student Performance
	Student Goals	Educational Processes	Teaching Effectiveness
	Technology Access	Areas to Improve	Course Quality
Course Timeline	Start	Middle	End

Start of the Term

In the broadest sense, course evaluation is an examination of any component that affects a course's quality, thereby producing results that can be used to judge quality for course improvement (i.e., the formative goal) or to judge quality for high-stakes decision making (i.e., the summative goal). At the start of the term, the emphasis is on a formative evaluation that typically assesses inputs, such as level of student prerequisite competencies, student learning needs, and student access to adequate technology. Input evaluations, therefore, ask questions about the re-sources and competencies that are needed for students to succeed in the course in order to inform adjustments in how the course is presented.

Less-prepared students may feel excluded from the educational process that comprise the course and therefore have lower expectations than the rest of the class (Chism, 1999) as well as reduced motivation to succeed. Therefore, asking students for diagnostic feedback early in a course is an important formative step toward improving teaching and learning because it allows the instructor to assess student readiness, communicate high but attainable expectations, and make adjustments to the course based on student feedback.

A standard associated with a quality course is the stimulation of interest in the students by the instructor. Interest in any course is a function of the relationship between the course's objectives, outcomes, and activities, and the individual student's educational goals. The instructor can engender interest by actively highlighting the strength of this relationship. To do this, the instructor should solicit feedback from students outlining their respective goals early in the term so that explicit connections with the course can be made throughout the term. For example, some students who enroll in a statistics course as part of an educational leadership program may not see the value of statistics if they do not intend to become active researchers. However, the instructor can address the need for educational leaders to be critical consumers of educational research and program evaluations, which require statistical knowledge and skills.

From a structural perspective, an online course is not effective if technical impediments exist. Students should also be queried to determine if they have access to various technologies that are minimally required for the current course design as well as skills in using these technologies. Such technologies include both hardware and software. There is little point in attaching elaborate video files to the course content if some students use slow-speed Internet connections, as this is a recipe for incomplete learning, frustration, dissatisfaction, and potential attrition. Also, if there are large variations in student geography spanning multiple time zones, there is little point in attempting to incorporate synchronous activities that require an alignment of schedules. Information that can precipitate corrective action (e.g., avoiding large downloadable files or live chat sessions) by the instructor should be gathered as early as possible.

Similarly, specialized software (e.g., a statistical package) that is essential for the current course (e.g., a statistics course) needs to be accessible. As such software may not be required for other courses, students may not be appropriately aware of this special requirement. Feedback would alert the instructor that potential delays in course performances are likely if student access to special software is delayed. The instructor should attempt to determine the appropriate level of accessibility present so that the schedule for deliverables can be agreed. In addition, any feedback regarding purchasing or software installation or licensing difficulties should be forwarded to the appropriate student services personnel (e.g., the bookstore or IT technical support) for resolution.

If students are new to online learning or the LMS, feedback should also determine if technical training has been completed or if concerns or questions still exist. In addition, if the course requires the use of any specialized LMS tools with which users may be unfamiliar, feedback items should query proficiency regarding specific competencies. To deal with insufficient skills, feedback should identify whether students know how to access technical assistance. Identified deficiencies in knowledge and skills will require immediate training, either provided by the instructor or by IT personnel. In addition, such feedback may alert IT personnel to improve training programs for future students.

Quality online courses provide clearly written objectives and expected learning outcomes, which are typically available at the beginning of the term in the syllabus. Feedback gathered within the first few days of the course can determine whether students are uncertain regarding what the course intends to accomplish both on its own and as part of a larger program, and what the student should be able to do or know upon course completion. Conceptual difficulties can be dealt with by the instructor early and appropriately. In addition, a clear understanding of objectives and outcomes can facilitate the student's understanding of the appropriateness of learning activities and assessments and can foster motivation and engagement.

Another potential source of ambiguity that can lead to student dissatisfaction is in defining *timely feedback*. That is, what is "timely" to one person may not be timely to another. Instructors can, of course, proactively define feedback deadlines (e.g., graded papers will be returned to students within 2 weeks after submission) that may help persuade the student to define *timeliness* in the instructor's terms; however, this is not always reasonable. If students are expected to submit papers every 3 weeks, returning graded papers 2 weeks after submission affords the student little time to use the instructor's constructive criticism to improve student learning as reflected in subsequent submissions. Additionally, the assignment will not be fresh in the student's mind upon receiving delayed feedback.

Although it is advisable for instructors to offer deadlines for faculty feedback, it is also recommended that students provide feedback regarding the appropriateness of these deadlines. Defining *timeliness* is a negotiation based upon course requirements, instructor workload, and student expectations from previous experiences. When creating deadlines associated with student deliverables and faculty feedback, it is often helpful for the instructor to consider submission due dates in light of other known demands, such as scheduled conferences, committee meetings, or the requirements of other courses taught—these considerations can thwart schedule conflicts before they are allowed to occur.

Middle of the Term

The middle of the term provides another formative opportunity to assess how well the current course is running and make adjustments prior to the end of the term. At mid-course, an informal approach could be used with a discussion forum created for students to provide constructive comments. Minimally, students should be queried regarding progress in satisfying their goals and the functioning of various educational processes, such as delivery system reliability, the adequacy of technical assistance, and the functioning of threaded online discussions. The instructor should enable anonymous postings to this forum in order to encourage candid comments. Students should also be encouraged to communicate directly with the instructor if their comments are of a sensitive or private nature.

One standard of a quality online course is an instructor who provides timely and constructive feedback. Students should be queried to determine whether instructor feedback thus far in the term has been effective in helping students to reach course-related learning objectives and outcomes. Based on student feedback suggesting changes, the instructor can either modify the nature of future feedback or clarify existing limitations, particularly if such limitations are relevant to important learning outcomes.

An instructor may limit feedback when fostering independent learning, another standard of a quality online course. For example, an instructor may provide feedback such as "reread the introductory section in Chapter 3 of your assigned text, as you still do not fully understand the difference between [concept 1] and [concept 2]. Contact me if you still do not understand." While the instructor could have identified the distinction between the two concepts explicitly, an important learning outcome is being targeted (i.e., student self-directedness) by not doing so. A student, however, may not perceive such feedback as constructive. If this is the case, the instructor should help the student understand the learning purpose of this type of feedback. In addition, feedback that directs the student to access and synthesize other sources of online information (e.g., library databases, related Web sites) not only promotes independent learning but also attends to other standards: helping students to learn methods of accessing additional information and promoting higher levels of learning. Because student dissatisfaction can occur if expectations are not realized, such information can assist the instructor in helping the student foster new and more appropriate expectations for feedback.

In addition to feedback from students, peer review and self-analysis are also important factors related to course improvement.

> If we want to grow in our practice, we have two primary places to go: to the inner ground from which good teaching comes and to the community of fellow teachers from whom we can learn more about ourselves and our craft. (Palmer, 1998, p. 141)

Because LMSs provide a written record of dialogue, peer review and self-analysis of instruction can occur anytime, even long after a course ends. However, such analyses near the middle of the term can provide an important formative role to improve current course quality. An interesting advantage to the "invisible" peer review during a course is that the peer observer does not contaminate the evaluation situation by his or her presence as can be the case in a face-to-face class when an evaluator attends a class meeting and affects instructor and student short-term behaviors. Such assessments should focus not only on determining whether instructor feedback is timely and constructive but also if the instructor shows respect and concern for students, stimulates interest, shows enthusiasm, and accommodates cultural diversity and, perhaps, special needs. Such feedback can influence an instructor's practice in future interactions and should be provided to the instructor as quickly as possible.

End of the Term, and Later

After a course is completed (or nearly completed), feedback is collected primarily for summative purposes. End-of-term data collection should focus on assessing student performance, teaching effectiveness, and course quality. For example, feedback can help inform merit pay, promotion, and tenure decisions. It can also be used to support decisions regarding the course and/or program. However, as with all summative evaluations that have high-stakes consequences, each standard evaluated must be attributed to the responsible agent.

SETs are commonly associated with end-of-course evaluations completed by students to assess teaching effectiveness. However, as has already been discussed, course quality is influenced by factors that are outside the instructor's influence but can erroneously be consumed in an aggregate assessment of instructor quality. As an example, reliable technology has already been identified as a criterion associated with a quality online course. Gathering student feedback regarding this quality indicator is not only appropriate but essential. But it is IT, not the instructor, who should receive such feedback for formative and/or summative purposes. Instructors do not maintain the servers or instructional platforms used for online courses; therefore, negative student feedback regarding the reliability of these technologies should not be used to evaluate instructor quality.

Neumann (2000) recommends the development of a teaching effectiveness rating interpretation guide for use with SETs because of the uncertainties associated with potential bias introduced by the method of course delivery and other potential biasing factors, such as grade leniency, student motivation, and content difficulty. He suggests the development of a guide for administrators who make high-stakes decisions regarding faculty that takes into account different teaching contexts and emphasizes interpretation based on a range of scores rather than on a mean score.

Summary

In the multistage course evaluation model proposed above, the quality of any agent's performance is justly evaluated at a number of times during the course. Following a previous example, at the beginning of the term, students should provide their educational goals to the instructor so that interest in the course's objectives, outcomes, and activities can be fostered. Similarly, at the middle of the term, peer evaluations should examine if interest is being fostered with feedback provided to the instructor. At this point, the instructor should be armed with the requisite knowledge to correct deficient practices if they exist. Thus, end-of-term evaluations conducted by students and peers that reflect a continuing lack of instructor interest and enthusiasm suggests an inability to adjust despite possessing the requisite information to inform and improve practice.

A similar argument can be made for other standards. Course quality is improved by administrators who compensate for the additional time demands of online teaching. Often, teaching online requires more time than face-to-face courses due to the mechanics of dealing with a text-based communication, providing timely responses 7 days a week, and constructing feedback in greater detail by often accessing additional sources of information. At the beginning of the term, instructors (and, in particular, full-time faculty) should provide feedback regarding how well their supervisors allotted the necessary time to develop their online courses; near the middle of the term, a similar assessment is needed regarding how well their supervisors considered the time demands of online teaching when assigning other duties. These two evaluations should provide reasonable feedback from instructors regarding their supervisors' ability to recognize and compensate for online teaching demands. Thus, an end-of-term evaluation of supervisors by instructors regarding this criterion provides fair summative information to improve supervisory practice based upon previous instructor feedback.

A quality course must also support the objectives of the larger program in which it resides. As educational programs often incorporate a scaffolding strategy in which advanced courses build upon foundational knowledge and skills learned in prerequisite courses, standards associated with prerequisite courses must be evaluated when advanced courses are completed. Such evaluations would include a review of the prerequisite course's objectives and outcomes, materials, and performance expectations. The instructor of an advanced course would provide formative feedback to the program coordinator and/or the prerequisite course's instructor.

CONCLUSION

Research provides us with a rich description of those standards that characterize a high-quality online course. These standards highlight the responsibilities of numerous institutional members that include not only the instructor but also IT personnel, program coordinators, and other student and academic support administrators. Without question, a quality online course is the result of a team effort.

The danger is that course evaluation as implemented at specific institutions may place too much emphasis on supporting summative purposes and too little emphasis on formative purposes. A comprehensive course evaluation system should embrace both high-stakes decision making regarding the course and the instructor as well as developing faculty, improving the course, and nurturing the scholarship of teaching. Parker Palmer (1998) criticizes institutional culture that keeps teaching privatized. He claims that one price we pay for such privatization is evaluation practices that are distanced, demoralizing, and even disreputable (p. 142). Simplistic questionnaires used in SET or questionnaires that ask the wrong questions "are not simply the result of administrative malfeasance, as faculty sometimes complain. They are the outcome of a faculty culture that offers no alternative" (p. 143). Consequently, "good talk about good teaching is unlikely to happen if presidents . . . , deans and department chairs, and others who have influence without position, do not expect it and invite it into being" (Palmer, 1998, p. 156).

In order to increase course improvement opportunities, there are some logical considerations that should be considered when determining when is the best time to evaluate courses. In particular, identifying the student group that will benefit from feedback is imperative, as evaluative information can be used to help students who are currently enrolled in the course under examination, those who will enroll in the next term, or those who will enroll much later, either in the same course or in an advanced course. Evaluative feedback can be collected from instructional team members, students, peers, supervisors, and IT personnel.

For summative purposes, standards can be evaluated as part of a performance appraisal system. While students are best qualified to evaluate the teaching process from the perspective of learners, peers are best qualified to evaluate the content of a course from the perspective of the discipline. Consequently, the appraisal system should incorporate multiple sources of evaluation that include SET and peer review. Because performance appraisals have high-stakes consequences (i.e., they affect professional advancement), each criterion evaluated must be attributed to the responsible agent.

The multistage course evaluation model presented above may seem cumbersome due to the multiple measurement points recommended and multiple sources and receivers of information. However, the major benefit of information technology is rooted in its ability to efficiently manage data acquisition and dissemination. Thus, people must buy into this strategy and create the requisite capabilities for this holistic course evaluation strategy. The availability of easy-to-complete evaluations with quick-to-disseminate feedback focused on relevant quality indicators will help build a culture of continuous improvement that facilitates assessing and assuring the quality of online courses and improves student achievement.

CHAPTER 11

Summary and Conclusion

Educating and training students at a distance is a major and growing element of the mission of many colleges and universities as they respond to the needs of students beyond their traditional constituencies. Arthur Levine (1997) believes that higher education is at a crossroads:

> There is an underlying belief that colleges and universities are making precisely the same mistake that the railroads made. The railroads believed they were in the railroad business; they focused on making bigger and better railroads. The problem is that they were actually in the transportation industry and, as a result, were derailed by the airlines. Similarly, it can be said that higher education is making the mistake of thinking it is in the campus business, when in reality it is in the very lucrative education business. (p. 17)

This expanded role of higher education is sustained by the enhanced capacity for efficient and widespread use of technology for delivering programs and courses. Distance education delivered mostly asynchronously via the Internet is the most common distance education mode used in higher education today. This anytime, anywhere delivery of online education and its power to bring people together for collaborative and reflective learning are widely recognized virtues of asynchronous learning networks.

CONCEPTS OF DISTANCE LEARNING

The concepts and theories presented in this book represent a philosophy of teaching and learning that helps readers better understand the principles of distance education. Common threads of perspective will be apparent to assist individuals in formulating a philosophical foundation for online learning with implications for instructional systems design. The first concept discussed is constructivism.

Constructivism

The philosophy of learning that permeates distance education is constructivism. It is based on the premise that each individual constructs knowledge through his or her interactions with the environment, including other learners. Thus, from the constructivist viewpoint, knowledge is not purely objective but is socially constructed in part, the learner is an active processor of information and creator of personal knowledge, and the instructor's major role is that of facilitator of learning.

Adult Teaching and Learning

College and university students are adults who possess unique needs, motivations, goals, and self-concepts. Most current theories of adult teaching and learning are based on the work of Malcolm Knowles (1988), who popularized the term *andragogy* to describe the learner-centered art of helping adults learn. Andragogy is a learner-centered approach characterized by active learning and self-directedness that draws from the principles of constructivism. It assists adults in moving from dependency to self-directedness as it draws from their life experiences in order to help them solve problems and apply new knowledge.

Computer-Mediated Communication

Online learning relies on computer-mediated communication (CMC), which represents how people communicate using computers. CMC supports the interactivity and collaborative work that is valued in a constructivist environment. In asynchronous learning networks, CMC's strong points include opportunities for reflective thought prior to participating in a discussion and post-participation review/access to written discussions. The weakness most often cited in the professional literature is the reduction of nonverbal cues, such as encouraging gestures, during the communication process. Consequently, CMC tends to be less friendly. Moreover, there are increased opportunities for miscommunication when using CMC, especially in a multicultural learning environment.

Sense of Community

Sense of community is also an important aspect of distance education that supports the constructivist approach to learning. Community-building also helps reduce or prevent feelings of isolation and alienation that often contribute to distance education student attrition. Sense of community in an educational setting includes social community and learning community (Rovai, Wighting, & Lucking, 2004). Social community represents the feelings of the learning community members regarding their cohesion, connectedness, mutual trust, safety, interdependence, and sense of belonging. Learning community, on the other hand, consists of the feelings of community members regarding the degree to which they share group norms and values and the extent to which their educational goals and expectations are satisfied by group membership. The online instructor fosters a sense of community by creating a safe environment where students are not threatened when they express their ideas, promoting socialization, communicating respect for diverse perspectives and backgrounds, providing timely feedback that gives direction and keeps information flowing, responding to the educational needs of students, and maintaining an online presence.

Presence

Presence is a sense of "being there" and is important to building a strong sense of classroom community. Garrison, Cleveland-Innes, and Fung (2004) describe a "community of inquiry" (p. 63) model that highlights three important presences that are necessary for a meaningful online educational experience: social, cognitive, and teacher. *Social presence* refers to the copresence of students and teacher to create a climate that supports productive CMC to accomplish shared educational objectives. *Cognitive presence* refers to an individual student's constructivist learning via CMC and, hence, level of content engagement within the course. Finally, *teacher presence* refers to the instructor's presence, which promotes interaction among all members of the learning community and provides feedback and direction. Because the online learning environment does not support these various presences by scheduled, physical proximity, the online instructor must continually assess presence within the learning community and respond as needed to any perceived weaknesses.

Self-Directed and Autonomous Learning

Self-directed learning is an approach to learning in which students take the initiative to determine their learning needs, formulate their own learning goals, identify resources for learning, adopt suitable learning strategies, and evaluate their learning outcomes. *Learner autonomy* can be defined as the characteristic of the person who independently exhibits agency (i.e., initiative) in learning activities where independence is the characteristic of the person who controls his or her own actions. The main benefits of self-directed and autonomous learning are typically seen as fostering lifelong learning by allowing students greater abilities to control their own learning process, create their learning agendas, develop their learning strategies, and establish a learning pace. Educators must support the building of necessary cognitive processes within learners that further the development of their self-directedness and autonomy. These processes include helping students value learning as a means to desired outcomes, understand that the accomplishment of suitably chosen learning goals can lead to desired outcomes, and assume responsibility for one's own learning.

Social Equity

The goal of social equity is to ensure that no individual or groups of individuals are subject to discriminatory practices based on factors such as race, national origin, religious practices, age, ethnicity, disabilities, and gender. Social equity is promoted by self-directed and autonomous learning that permits every individual to choose a life trajectory by developing in personally meaningful ways without being hindered by discrimination. Social impediments to learning can occur when students of diverse backgrounds experience dissonance between (a) derived meanings and intended meanings, and (b) culturally influenced preferred communicative patterns and those perceived as required or appropriate. Both of these factors influence the effectiveness and efficiency of communication. Online instructors must be diligent in strengthening text-related modalities, reducing the cultural effects of misconstrued meanings, and encouraging all forms of respectful participation so that all members of the learning community have equal opportunities to learn.

GENDER

Research evidence suggests that females and males differ on at least two dimensions that can influence learning, learner satisfaction, and sense of community in the virtual classroom. Communication pattern is the first dimension. Researchers (e.g., Belenky, Clinchy, Goldberger, & Tarule, 1996) posit that most females and some males communicate using a connected voice that emphasizes socialization, caring, cooperation, consensus, and the indirect resolution of conflict. Most males and some females, on the other hand, have a more independent voice that emphasizes self-sufficiency, autonomy, and competition.

Cognitive style, the second dimension, may also influence one's communication pattern. Research (e.g., Merriam & Caffarella, 1999) provides evidence that field dependent individuals, who tend to be females, are socially oriented, externally directed, more pragmatic, and tend to perceive the field as a whole. In contrast, males tend to be field independent. A person who perceives items as more or less separate from the surrounding field leans toward a field independent cognitive style. They tend to be individualistic, internally directed, more competitive, and are able to focus on relevant details and not be distracted by unnecessary details.

Learners tend to engage in heightened stereotypical behavior in the relatively less personal environment of CMC and online learning. Such behavior, left unchecked, could give rise to interpersonal conflict, resulting in negative feelings, including intimidation, distrust, anger, loss of a community spirit, and decreased learning and learner satisfaction. It is therefore incumbent for the online instructor to explore and reflect on the ways in which gender affects ways of interacting and communicating and to develop skills in, and critical awareness of, the possibilities and limitations of CMC. Belenky, Clinchy, Goldberger, and Tarule (1996) suggest that the preferred methods of knowing and learning for many students may be cooperative rather than competitive and active group learning rather than passive lecture.

CULTURE

The distance education student base is highly diverse as a result of the increased cross-border mobility of students and providers and the massification of higher education. If distance education is going to reduce academic inequities, online educators must pay close attention to the specific needs of the clients they serve. Schools should provide all students with strategies to succeed in spite of culturally related differences. Consequently, infusing a multicultural approach to online education by creating an inclusive classroom and institutional culture is an important element of effective online teaching and learning. Such an approach is possible only if there is mutual respect among teachers and students. The real challenge for online instructors is to resist becoming impersonal and mechanical in one's approach to teaching and to avoid the view that "one size fits all."

To be effective in a multicultural learning environment, teachers must first learn to become culturally responsive and aware of differences. One goal is to create a strong sense of community among learners rather than evoking a tendency toward cultural separatism. Multicultural education is grounded in issues of equity and social justice in which all students reach their full potential as learners and as socially aware and active individuals. Consequently, online instructors must be aware of the dispositional and situational challenges that frequently confront minority students, e.g., racial stereotyping, and become proactive in reducing these barriers to learning.

STRATEGIC PLANNING

Distance education requires careful planning in order to achieve its potential and meet the needs of its diverse student population. In order for colleges and universities to survive in a competitive market, they need to be productive and distinguish themselves from their peers, and strategic planning is a means to these ends. Strategic planning is a flexible process by which an organization envisions its future and develops the necessary strategies, programs, and activities to achieve that future, attending to issues that can influence the quality of educational outcomes and academic equity, e.g., gender equity and cultural or ethnic equity.

Fornaciari, Forte, and Mathews (1999) propose distance education planning strategies based on "institution size, tuition cost, and reputation" (p. 709). They suggest that large regional universities with low national reputations should adopt cost-leadership strategies based on the goal of achieving a lower cost position than the competition to attract out-of-state students by charging them in-state tuition rates. Small institutions with strong national reputations can pursue differentiation strategies by offering highly selective distance degree programs. Institutions that do not have the resources to be full-fledged competitors in the broader marketplace often adopt focus strategies. Consequently, they avoid competition and target a specific market or niche instead of competing in the mass marketplace.

PROGRAM AND COURSE DESIGN

There are many different approaches to distance education, ranging from fully online asynchronous courses to synchronous online courses conducted in 3-D virtual worlds, and from exclusively textual material to portable audio and video instructional content. Programs and courses can be designed with various class sizes, content delivery, classroom environments, and campus time in mind. Online courses range in size from a single student to hundreds of students. The four most common sizes of online classes can be categorized as independent studies, tutorials, seminars, and audiences, each of which has its own advantages and disadvantages. Online courses also use a variety of online and offline technologies to deliver course content, such as text, presentation graphics, audio and video, videoconferencing, simulations, and virtual worlds. There are also four basic online environments categorized by type of opportunities for discussion: none, audio or videoconferencing, synchronous online chat, and asynchronous online discussion.

Although a significant growth in distance education over the past decade has been with online courses, there is a growing interest in combining online and face-to-face instruction into a blended learning model. A blended approach enables instructors to combine the advantages of online class learning with the benefits of face-to-face interaction; furthermore, the reduced seat time of blended learning is attractive as a cost savings approach for institutions that are coping with shrinking budgets and reduced classroom space.

Once the overall online program and course models are selected, the task then shifts to the actual design and development of the instruction. Although individual courses can be effectively taught online by a few motivated faculty, successful online programs also require the proper planning, commitment, and support of key administrators. In general, when developing online instruction, the process is more efficient and effective when a systems design model is followed and a team works on the project. E-mail, Web pages, word processors (e.g., Microsoft Word), and presentation software (e.g., Microsoft PowerPoint) are common tools that are used extensively in online learning. Some of the newer tools that have enriched the online learning experience include learning management systems, blogs, wikis, podcasting, and virtual worlds.

ASSESSMENT OF STUDENT LEARNING

Overreliance on traditional tests that emphasize factual recall is not consistent with the nature of learning that occurs in adult constructivist learning environments, where collaboration, inquiry, and authentic assessments are valued. Consequently, there is a move away from traditional, selected-response tests and toward performance and constructed-response assessments. Performance assessments are based on observation and evaluation of student-created products, projects, and performances. They require students to perform a task or demonstrate a skill rather than simply select a response. Cooperative work is also possible and recommended as part of an overall distance education assessment strategy. The inclination of online instructors to rely exclusively on assessments that involve independent work should be avoided; such a single-minded strategy violates the principle of employing diverse types of assessments.

Assessment should be viewed as an integral part of learning and must be perceived by all students as grounded in authentic (i.e., real-world) experiences. Unless students are required to engage in authentic tasks and address complex real-world issues, they will not develop the skills of intercultural competence and global thinking. Moreover, teachers of students with diverse cultural backgrounds need to open classrooms to more than one approach to intellectual work.

The unique characteristics of the distance education medium can create challenges to the process of student assessment, particularly when assessments are used for summative purposes. Identity security and academic honesty for assessments in distance education courses are about the same as they are for a take-home assignment in the traditional classroom. Options for key assignments include postponement of immediate assessment in favor of: (a) addition of a telephone conversation in which students have the opportunity to defend or explain their submitted work, (b) proctored testing at decentralized locations, and (c) proctored testing at centralized on-campus residencies. Proctored testing is particularly relevant when testing is for high-stakes purposes. Additionally, online services such as Turnitin at http://www.turnitin.com can be used to help detect plagiarism in submitted papers.

ONLINE DISCUSSIONS

Learning in computer-mediated virtual classrooms requires a focus on the social construction of knowledge. Online instructors need to create safe environments for learners to express themselves, share their ideas, and ask questions. Maintaining interaction is more challenging in online learning environments than in face-to-face learning contexts because of time and space separations.

Learners are unlikely to participate actively in productive discussions if they perceive interpersonal interaction as a marginalized or supplemental activity (Anderson, 2004). Good interaction is design-driven and carefully planned before the start of the course in order to establish and maintain presence and promote a balance between learner-instructor and learner-learner interactions. Online instructors must plan a course in ways that encourage learners to be interactive, think harder about their learning, and promote critical thinking.

Productive online discussions typically do not occur spontaneously, and require a skilled moderator to be effective. The major purpose of moderating online discussions is to establish teacher presence in the virtual classroom and, by doing so, to promote both social presence, and cognitive presence. However, in establishing teacher presence, the instructor must nurture the development of a community of inquiry in which he or she moves away from center stage by promoting collaboration and cooperation.

Although the moderator has the responsibility to guide the discussion procedurally, he or she should not lead the discussion down a predetermined path. The moderator's roles are that of group-building and maintenance and are oriented toward the functioning of the group as a group. At various times, the moderator challenges, widens horizons, and becomes the devil's advocate. The situation generally dictates the role the moderator chooses to adopt at a specific time. Skill in performing these roles is useful in maintaining critical group discussion and in promoting a sense of community.

PROGRAM EVALUATION

Evaluation is an essential component of resource allocation decision making, program improvement and renewal, long-term success, and realization of the school's strategic vision of itself. Educational administrators cannot fully understand the overall impact of program improvement efforts without program evaluation data, which offer decision makers evidence in determining what works best for distance education. Moreover, without periodic renewal, programs are less able to respond to the changing needs of their clients. The results of periodic program evaluations provide the impetus for necessary change.

Evaluations should be based on multiple sources of evidence and the convergence of different measures. To promote distance education quality assurance, evaluations should address both program processes, e.g., quality of student-student and student-instructor interactions; and program outputs and outcomes, e.g., student persistence rates, alumni and employer satisfaction, and licensure test results. Palloff and Pratt (1999) suggest that the following program issues are most significant to students enrolled in online degree programs: ease of access to the program (e.g., admittance to the program, enrollment process for courses); smooth, seamless delivery of courses (e.g., forewarning of hardware and software requirements, consistent navigational interface among courses, consistent and reliable offerings in the course schedule); availability of timely support (e.g., technical support, campus support services for learning, faculty support); and breadth and completeness of the program (e.g., the numbers and types of courses available).

INSTITUTION AND PROGRAM ACCREDITATION

Accreditation is a type of evaluation and conformity assessment used to determine compliance of institutions and/or programs with professional quality standards and the requirements designated by the accrediting agency. The Council for Higher Education Accreditation (CHEA) is the primary national voice for voluntary accreditation and quality assurance to the U.S. Congress and the U.S. Department of Education. According to CHEA (2002), recognized accrediting agencies routinely review the following seven key areas of institutional activity when examining the quality of distance learning programs: institutional mission, institutional organizational structure, institutional resources, curriculum and instruction, faculty support, student support, and student learning outcomes.

COURSE EVALUATION

Course evaluation is an important aspect of distance education program evaluation and quality assurance. A comprehensive course evaluation system should embrace both high-stakes decision making regarding the course and the instructor (i.e., the summative purpose) as well as developing faculty, improving the course, and nurturing the scholarship of teaching (i.e., the formative purpose). Although the emphasis at many institutions is to rely on student evaluations of teaching (SETs) for course evaluation, it is important that a multimethod approach be used that includes a variety of sources, such as SET, peer and supervisor review, teaching portfolios, virtual classroom observations, and self-evaluation.

Unlike traditional classroom teaching, online teaching is a team effort and is only as good as its weakest link. In particular, effective teaching depends not only on the teacher but also on a good production staff, instructional team, and technical support staff. Although many elements of online and traditional teaching are the same, there are also substantive differences, as the online instructor is primarily a facilitator of learning and not necessarily the primary source of information, as is often the case in a traditional classroom. Consequently, evaluation of teaching effectiveness should not employ the same data collection questionnaires for online and face-to-face courses. Since the construct of teaching effectiveness differs between traditional and online environments, the instruments used to measure teaching effectives in these two environments must also differ if they are construct- and content-valid.

Neumann (2000) recommends the development of a teaching effectiveness rating interpretation guide because of the uncertainties associated with potential bias introduced by the method of course delivery and other potential biasing factors, such as grade leniency, student motivation, and content difficulty. Moreover, because teaching online is a team effort, care must be exercised to ensure that course evaluations used for faculty summative purposes are not contaminated by variables outside the instructor's ability to control.

CONCLUSION

Numerous factors are combining to change the nature of higher education. They include globalization and the massification of higher education, resulting in an increasingly diversified student population with equally diversified academic needs; advances in information technology and the concurrent growth of technology-based distance education; the need for a more educated workforce; rising student and public expectations; a decrease in government financial support, coupled with escalating tuition costs; and an increasing demand for accountability and measurable outcomes. In response, the higher education landscape is changing as corporate universities and for-profit institutions are expanding to fill the gap left by traditional institutions, which historically are slow to change or embrace innovation as a result of their organizational culture of shared governance and years of tradition. Arthur Levine (1997) suggests that "high technology and entertainment companies are viewing noncampus-based education as an opportunity" (p. 17). Added to this mix are foreign universities that are placing greater emphasis on strategic marketing and recruiting international students.

For-profit higher education "has demonstrated cost-efficient and consumer-oriented ways of developing and delivering training programs" (Morey, 2001, p. 310) that take advantage of emerging technologies and changing market mechanisms. The expansion of corporate-owned, for-profit institutions results in increased differentiation in higher education between the for-profit and the not-for-profit sectors and places competitive pressures on vulnerable not-for-profit institutions that lack large endowments and cannot finance themselves entirely through tuition. For-profit institutions are out to harness the powers of free enterprise to fix what some claim to be a failed higher education sector that is stuck in the past by lowering costs, increasing productivity, and providing differentiated products to match the greater variety of educational needs and interests inherent in a more diverse student population. Arthur Levine calls this differentiation phenomenon "a Boutiqueing" of higher education (1997, p. 3).

Hawthorne (1995) suggests that the for-profit sector provides education to make money, while traditional colleges and universities accept money to provide an education. Indeed, there are cultural differences between for-profits and not-for-profits, but they may not be as straightforward as Hawthorne suggests. Lechuga (2006) identifies positive aspects of the for-profit sector as well as its disruptive potential for the academic values of traditional colleges and universities as the for-profit sector is shaking up the status quo in battles with accreditors, state regulators, and others representing traditional interests.

For-profits are typically better equipped to respond quickly to both threats and opportunities as the result of their culture of hierarchical governance, pursuit of profit, and emphasis on seeking competitive advantage. Morey (2001) suggests many adults who enroll in for-profit institutions recognize that they are not receiving a degree from a brand-name university, but the convenience, differentiated products, and ability to reduce time to degree completion attract them and more quickly satisfy their primary objective of entering a career. Consequently, these institutions pose a credible challenge to traditional schools in recruiting new students, especially in online programs.

The for-profit and not-for-profit sectors are not homogeneous, as differences exist between institutions within each of these two sectors. There are also basic differences in the institutional values between these two sectors that heavily influence organization culture and account for differences between for-profit and not-for-profit institutions. Figure 11.1 identifies an idealized set of organizational values and effects that influence institutions in each sector. It is important to realize that these sector differences are not absolute and that the two sets of values and effects depicted in Figure 11.1 are at opposite ends of a continuum, with each institution falling somewhere along the continuum. However, institutions tend to be drawn to the end of the continuum that is characteristic of their sector.

An examination of the subcultures within not-for-profit institutions reveals a variety of institutional forms and frictions between teaching and research and between administrators and faculty who share institutional governance. Although teaching is clearly the focus in for-profits, these institutions encompass varying degrees of tension between their academic and business sides, but the focus of this tension is on academic freedom versus academic standardization. Although varying levels of tension exist in both sectors between mission and financial results, the for-profit sector places the emphasis on financial results whereas the not-for-profit institution is more likely to place the emphasis on mission.

Consumerism

In the highly competitive environment for market share, many colleges and universities are embracing consumerism and assuming the role of educational vendors as they pursue a demand-led approach to student recruitment where education is largely viewed as a commodity that is shaped by consumer demand. Students are increasingly viewed as customers, and institutions are marketing higher education directly to them via mass-marketing media, such as billboards, the Internet, and television. Richard Chait, professor of higher education at Harvard University, observes that the competition for students as customers has caused the majority of schools to bombard students with color brochures and the promise of amenities such as state-of-the-art weight rooms and entertainment centers (O'Meara, 2001). Much of this marketing strategy implies that customer satisfaction is of paramount importance, and one result of this strategy is to intensify competitive pressures among institutions.

The consumer approach to student recruitment is becoming more prevalent than the traditional provider approach where enrollment management balances

FIGURE 11.1. Values and Ultimate Goal Effects for For-Profit and Not-for-Profit Sectors

For-Profit Sector	Traditional Not-for-Profit Sector

Hierarchical governance
Tight control of the workforce
Product standardization
Efficiency
Market-oriented decisions
Pursuit of profit
Seeking competitive advantage
Customer orientation

Shared governance
Academic freedom
University and community service
Promoting the public good
Pursuit of truth
Basic research
Scholarship
Student orientation

Profit
Educating students

Enhancing the possibilities
of life for its students
and for society at large

the quality of the applicant's academic credentials, professional standards for the intended program of study, and the demands and needs of society. Even some elite universities are altering their recruiting strategies as they compete with each other for the top students, which they need to maintain their elite status. As higher education responds to market forces, Chait suggests that a greater divide will emerge between the have and have-not institutions (O'Meara, 2001). Contreras (2007) suggests that

> Americans sometimes speak of the market as though we were speaking of the Bible, or perhaps the New York Yankees—something that, although imperfect, is by its nature an object of veneration. In fact, the presence of a thriving industry [in the United States] that sells fake and substandard college degrees to thousands of Americans every year points out the problem: Just because something can be sold to many willing buyers does not make it a good thing. Diploma-mill degrees are the pornography of higher education, and like pornography will always have a market. (p. B16)

Institutions with the most prestige and strongest brand name will have greater access to capital, and those without such resources will find their share of the market dwindling unless they adapt successfully to a changing environment. The danger is that in responding to diminished funding support and increased competition, the ethos of academic altruism will give way to academic capitalism (Slaughter & Leslie, 1997).

> Academic capitalism is not simply a matter of entrepreneurial colleges and universities seeking to generate more revenues in tight financial times. It's a matter of these not-for-profit institutions behaving more like private enterprises, as the relationship between public and private entities shifts. (Rhoades, 2006, p. 385)

However, academic capitalism is not an unopposed trend in not-for-profit institutions. Organized challenges to rebalance the academy exist (e.g., Rhoades, 2006). Many stakeholders are challenging the trend of higher education to adopt big business practices and are critiquing what academic capitalism does to the traditional areas of teaching, scholarship, and service. Other stakeholders are celebrating the entrepreneurial efforts of higher education and consider these efforts to be a natural outcome of modernity (e.g., Breneman, 2005).

Contreras (2007) reports that the American Council of Trustees and Alumni (ACTA), a generally conservative organization that advocates educational reform, criticizes the present higher education accreditation process and recommends that states and the market assume primary responsibility for academic quality control. Thus, there are additional pressures to move higher education toward academic capitalism, with the belief that the free choice of educational customers should dictate educational structure and products. Under this rubric, institutions of higher education aim to maximize income, while potential students act as individuals, searching for the lowest price and what they perceive to be the best match between higher education and their educational goals. Unfortunately, some students may also be seeking the easiest and quickest path to a college degree while others may not be astute enough to discern diploma mills from reputable institutions.

The drift toward academic capitalism is coming about more through default than by strategic intention and planning in not-for-profit schools, as it is often the result of numerous small decisions made by administrators at various levels concerned with keeping their institutions viable in a competitive market. Although schools in the past have competed with each other in recruiting students, what makes the situation different today is the global reach of distance education programs, increased competition for funding, and the expectations of students who are accomplished information age consumers and are able to select a program across a large and diverse higher education marketplace. Consequently, more market-susceptible institutions are taking such actions as eliminating non-self-supporting departments, increasing activities that generate revenues, outsourcing campus services that might be provided by others at less cost, and adjusting or creating programs that respond to student interests and desires in order to attract more student customers.

Consumerism, in its pure form, assumes that the consumer student knows best what must be learned and how best it should be taught, notwithstanding the fact that the student, by definition, is not the expert in either area, although it can be argued that students do know some of the things they need to learn to be successful in their chosen field. Additionally, the economic model that is typically aligned with consumerism values market-oriented decision making, efficiency, product standardization, and tight control of the workforce in order to achieve cost-effectiveness and productivity gains. Applied to an academic institution, tight control of the workforce equates to constraining academic freedom. These values are in sharp contrast to the traditional values of higher education as depicted in Figure 11.1.

An emphasis on consumerism can also relegate student evaluation of teaching to a customer satisfaction survey, which can be destructive to authentic teaching and learning if not used properly. A business model may be more appropriate for student support services, but may not be the best model for academic services in the competitive distance education marketplace. The risk is that higher education institutions will become retailers of instructional commodities and will take care of some of their customers by tailoring academic rigor and standards to their customers' demands. Moreover, attempting to satisfy some students may become synonymous with lowering the degree of challenge, refraining from intellectually stretching students beyond their comfort zones during the educational process, awarding higher grades, and placing more emphasis on entertaining rather than educating students. Student satisfaction is an important pillar of a quality program, but it must be balanced with other pillars of distance education quality as identified by the Sloan Consortium: learning effectiveness, cost-effectiveness, access, and faculty satisfaction (Moore, 2002). One might also add benefit to society to this list.

Certainly, the finances of all colleges and universities should be managed in accordance with professional business practices. However, the economic models that apply to corporations fail to account for the economics of a traditional college or university education based on an organizational culture that values faculty independence in teaching and research, university and community service, shared governance, promoting the public good, and the sharing, rather than hoarding, of knowledge (Austin, 1990). Accrediting agencies still possess these core values, but there is growing criticism of higher education as well as its accreditation system, e.g., ACTA (see above), resulting in a growing debate over how to change accreditation. These pressures for change are largely based on a growing demand for increased higher education accountability, reduced funding and rising costs and pressures to find more cost-effective solutions, and the changing structure and delivery of higher education. Consequently, there are pressures to move accreditation standards toward the consumer model.

In a consumer-oriented environment that embraces academic capitalism, fewer professors are likely to make life commitments to specific institutions and are more likely to view themselves as free-market agents who sell their services to the highest bidder. In support of this view, for-profit institutions, in particular, rely heavily on an adjunct professorate. Faculty members in such an environment are likely to focus on being subject-matter experts with less motivation and incentives to pursue scholarship and service activities, unless they accrue competitive or monetary advantages, as the emphasis is on the pursuit of profit and productivity as measured by the educational commodities that are sold. Moreover, the strongest institutions are likely to become producers and wholesalers of packaged world-class courses presented by nationally distinguished faculty members, while others become the retailers of such courses with slimmer margins and greater dependency as many of their faculty members become course facilitators (O'Meara, 2001). In such an academic culture, there is a real danger that dedication to ideas and ideals and the less tangible institutional outputs that benefit society at large, such as service to the community, pursuit of truth, and the discovery of knowledge for its own sake, will fade as the emphasis shifts to produce educational commodities that can be sold for profit.

Higher education is traditionally viewed as an investment in human capital. The benefits of higher education cannot be fully known or realized during the short term. Consequently, what Robert Birnbaum (2001) refers to as "a trust market, in which people do not know exactly what they are buying [in higher education] and may not discover its [true] value for years" (p. 216), will likely become increasingly irrelevant as colleges move toward the corporate economic model and accrediting agencies insist on evaluating programs based on measurable outputs and shorter-term outcomes. Bok (2003) cautions:

> No university can measure the value of its research output or determine reliably how much its students are learning. . . . For this reason, efforts to adapt the corporate model by trying to measure performance . . . are much more difficult and dangerous for universities than they are for commercial enterprises. (p. 30)

Consequently, there is a risk that the needs of institutions to expand enrollments and meet financial goals by adopting the business model will take precedence over serving the public good. Grace Roosevelt (2006) also argues that the commercialization of higher education and the corresponding decline of liberal education and relentless pursuit of relativism and indifference to civic responsibility will limit the range of political discourse. Historically, postsecondary institutions and churches have provided venues in which the profit motive can be openly questioned. But with today's new emphasis on consumerism in higher education, Roosevelt suggests that many schools are less likely to expose students to visions of social justice and equality that challenge the ethics of an unfettered market system.

Additionally, Press and Washburn (2000) report evidence of corporations exerting increasingly more control over some research universities by funding multimillion-dollar projects in return for exclusive access to the results of the research and by creating industry-endowed chairs that serve corporate interests. Chait

(O'Meara, 2001) reports that more than 20% of all voluntary support to higher education now comes from corporate sponsorship. He claims that some corporations are sponsoring courses in which students conduct market research or related work for the client. As a consequence of such activities, Press and Washburn argue that universities, "once wary beneficiaries of corporate largess, have become eager co-capitalists, embracing market values as never before" (p. 41). Giroux (2001) writes that "as large amounts of corporate capital flow into universities, those areas of study that do not translate into substantial profits get marginalized, underfunded, or eliminated" (p. 4). Thus, corporate funding can raise issues such as conflict of interest and its influence on the curriculum.

Increasingly, modern society is viewing higher education as a private good instead of a public good with the benefits accruing to its customers in the form of higher future wages. Consumerism and the utilitarian value of higher education, e.g., increased prestige and opportunities for better employment, should not trump educating students, especially if it does not foster an environment conducive to nurturing intellectual inquiry and development, providing a liberal education, and infusing civic engagement in academic life. Accordingly, Engell and Dangerfield (2005) conclude,

> education pursued exclusively as an instrumental economic good will attenuate education as an associative intellectual and social good, erode it as a civic good in a free society, diminish it as a moral good, and ultimately destroy it as a final good in which knowledge is sought regardless of its perceived usefulness. (quoted by Singell, 2006, p. 68)

Organizational Change

Gappa, Austin, and Trice (2007) contend that it is time for a radical rethinking of the academic approach to higher education. One may ask, how do colleges and universities manage the pressures for change fueled by the competitive distance education marketplace and the expansion of consumerism without seriously compromising their traditional values? The key is for educational leaders to simultaneously manage four interconnected aspects of organizational change in the academic setting: institutional values and culture, people, the budget, and technology. Gallant (2000) suggests that an important element of technological innovation and adoption is the ability of an institution to "communicate a vision of how and why changes are being planned and implemented, as well as ensure that changes are being driven by learning and teaching issues rather than by the imperatives of economic rationalism or the silicon veneer of technological determinism" (p. 73).

Leadership challenges are seldom solved by a cookbook approach. This is particularly true in higher education because of the complex, multilayered problems often encountered and the system of shared governance. A participatory leadership approach is necessary to pursue organizational change that encompasses committee participation and involvement by varied campus groups and institutional stakeholders. Organizational resistance to change increases in response to changes that threaten the core values and culture of the institution. Accordingly, leaders should be aware of institutional culture and seek organizational changes that account for and respect that culture within the context of the institutional mission.

In addition to preserving the traditional values of higher education identified previously, areas that need to be addressed include the extent of institutional commitment to distance education, ways that virtual campuses might foster collegial academic communities, ways to remove lingering inequities regarding access and who earns postsecondary degrees, the measurement of "value-added" outcomes resulting from the college or university distance education experience, and the organization of academic work in ways that achieve institutional and faculty goals and priorities. Gappa, Austin, and Trice (2007) suggest that administrators and faculty members must maintain flexibility as they reassess the right of every faculty member to be treated fairly, the right of faculty members to freely express their views when such views are appropriately and responsibly expressed, the ability of faculty members to construct work arrangements to maximize their contributions, opportunities that enable faculty to broaden their knowledge and skills, and opportunities for faculty members to feel that they belong to a mutually respectful community of colleagues (pp. 140–141).

Some tenured faculty, who are heavily invested in traditional education, are likely to view organizational change fueled by the expansion of distance education programs and the growing trend toward academic capitalism as a threat to their traditional roles (Beaudoin, 1990) and historical institutional values. They may also rebel against collective curriculum authorship, producing instructional materials that others will use (Rumble, 1989), increased workload demands arising from teaching at a distance, or inadequate instructional support structures and faculty development programs. Some faculty may even fear being exposed as poor teachers in a medium that broadcasts and records their work (Wilkes & Burnham, 1991). Students, on the other hand, resist distance education when they perceive that they are being offered a second-rate educational service, when they fear technology, when they are not adequately supported by the university, or when they perceive that their status as a minority group member is marginalized by a less personal, standardized approach to education.

Goffee and Jones (1998) provide a framework of organizational culture and its influence on organizational change. They argue that sociability and solidarity are important in understanding organizational culture. Sociability refers to the level of collegiality in an organization. The greater the degree of collegiality, the greater the morale and creativity an organization typically possesses. Solidarity refers to the ability to pursue shared goals efficiently. Solidarity generates dedication, as well as relatively swift organizational change. Accordingly, it is clear that efforts to promote organizational change must consider the importance of both individuals and institutional culture. Gallant (2000) suggests that rewards and incentives are especially important for the early adopters of innovation and change, as they can serve as a model for others.

The increased competition among distance education providers outlined above also suggests the increased importance of strategic planning as institutions pursue change in a rational and systematic fashion as they address their internal strengths and weaknesses as well as the opportunities and threats they face. Not-for-profit institutions need to develop quality assurance, strategic enrollment management, and evaluation processes that are intended to enhance strategic advantages in the competition for students if they are to compete successfully with for-profits and with each other. In doing so, they can draw from their traditional values and become more entrepreneurial by actions such as copyrighting and producing educational materials, e.g., distance education course packages, and by innovative fund-raising and capital campaigns. Traditional institutions can also challenge for-profits head-on by undertaking for-profit ventures, such as those taken on by the University of Maryland's University College, which receives considerable public monies from the U.S. Department of Defense for contractual educational services.

For-profit institutions, on the other hand, need to address their critics by finding ways to increase faculty involvement in curricular decisions, reduce tensions between the academic and business sides of their institutions, and move from a "one-size-fits-all" to a multicultural approach to education. In essence, they need to find ways to move toward the traditional higher education model while making a reasonable profit and satisfying their investors.

Quality assurance can be achieved in online teaching and learning, provided that approaches are employed that build on the strengths of technology and compensate for its weaknesses. Online learning's high-tech media may provide the illusion that knowledge can be produced, packaged, consumed, and exchanged online, but the professional literature on constructivism and adult learning makes a strong case that it is in fluid, dynamic, and highly social contexts where meaningful learning and creative problem solving are most likely to occur (e.g., Hardaker & Smith, 2002; Trentin, 2002; Wenger, 1998).

Distance learning must be backed by an organizational commitment to quality and institutional effectiveness in all aspects of the learning environment. Commercial interests must not take precedence over quality assurance. Program evaluation and accreditation have important overlapping roles to play in this area. An important goal of evaluation is to identify factors that decrease costs and improve overall learning and organizational impact. The economic key is to spread development and revision costs over large numbers of learners, and to drive down ongoing costs. The academic key is to improve the quality of learning outcomes. The entrepreneurial key is for colleges and universities to adapt to function in a market-driven educational environment that leverages technology in order to best serve student clients on an education-on-demand basis using a variety of delivery options without abandoning traditional institutional values, while producing graduates who have the necessary skills, knowledge, and attitudes to succeed in a globalized economy. Institutions that respond effectively will thrive, and those that do not will decline.

Example Extract from a Strategic Plan

STRATEGIC GOAL 1: Develop a learner-centered distance education environment that promotes the learning and personal development of students.	
Objective 1: Establish guidelines and procedures for developing and delivering distance education courses.	
Benchmark: By the year ____, guidelines and procedures will be developed and approved by Academic Council	*Sources:* Report from the Director of the Center for Teaching and Learning
and 90% of participating faculty will indicate satisfaction with such guidelines and procedures.	*Sources:* Report from the Faculty Senate, survey of faculty
Objective 2: Identify the school's market for distance education course and program offerings and develop and implement a marketing plan to successfully reach these markets.	
Benchmark: Marketing plan will be developed and approved by the Provost.	*Sources:* Report from the Director of University Marketing
Objective 3: Expand distance education program enrollment.	
Benchmark: By the year ____, 20% of university students will be enrolled in online or blended courses.	*Sources:* Report from the Director of Institutional Research
Objective 4: Establish international links for the collaborative development and delivery of distance education courses.	
Benchmark: By the year ____, at least two new international partnerships will be developed.	*Sources:* Report from the Executive Director for International Programs and Initiatives
Objective 5: Provide faculty with sufficient training, instructional design/development, production, and technical support to create and deliver online and blended courses.	
Benchmark: By the year ____, 80% of faculty will have participated in one or more activities designed to enhance teaching and assessment of student learning.	*Sources:* Report from the Director of the Center for Teaching and Learning
Objective 6: Ensure that all distance education students have access to library and student support services that are equivalent to those available for on-campus students.	
Benchmark: By the year ____, full equivalency will be achieved	*Sources:* Reports from the Vice President of Student Affairs and the Dean of the University Library
and at least 80% of students will indicate satisfaction with the distance services provided.	and report from the Director of Institutional Research, survey of distance education students

Analytic Participation Rubric

	Grade of C or Below	Grade of B	Grade of A
Social Presence	Accesses forums once a week or less. Contributions are sporadic. Many postings are directed to the instructor. Postings sometimes reflect sharpness or lack of sensitivity for the feelings, beliefs, or cultural backgrounds of others.	Accesses forums twice each week. Posts at least one message each week. Avoids numerous "thank you" or "I agree" postings. Most postings are directed to other learners. Manifests sociability, sensitivity, discernment, concern, kindness, gentleness, and self-control. Shows evidence of respect for cultural diversity.	Accesses forums three or more times each week. Posts two or more messages each week. Avoids numerous "thank you" or "I agree" postings. Postings are mostly directed to other learners. Always demonstrates appropriate professional behavior. Always shows evidence of respect for cultural diversity and the views of others.
Cognitive Presence	Rarely provides constructive feedback. Postings tend to consist of opinions or facts and sometimes are off-task. There is little evidence of analytical or critical thinking. Seldom are details or examples provided. Seldom engages in peer teaching.	Sometimes stimulates discussion. Postings are on-task but sometimes show a lack of adequate analytical skills and critical thinking. Learners draw from their existing knowledge and experiences. Often provides supporting details or examples. Engages in peer teaching.	Stimulates discussion. Postings are clear, original, and relevant. Reasoning shows well-developed analytical skills and critical thinking. Encourages others. Always provides supporting details or examples. Engages in peer teaching.
Writing Skills	Postings often contain errors in spelling and/or grammar. Many postings appear to be hastily written. Word choice is not always accurate.	Most postings are well written and demonstrate accurate spelling and grammar, good organization, careful editing, conciseness, and clarity.	All postings are well written and demonstrate accurate spelling and grammar, good organization, careful editing, conciseness, and clarity.

APPENDIX C

Evidence of Quality Distance Learning Programs

1. Institutional Mission
- Distance education program content, purposes, organization, and enrollment history must be consistent with the institution's role and mission (CHEA, 2002).

2. Institutional Organizational Structure
- Distance learning programs offered by an institution must be appropriately integrated into the institution's administrative structures, as well as its planning and oversight mechanisms (CHEA, 2002).
- Institutional evaluation of electronically offered programs must take place in the context of the institution's regular evaluation of all academic programs (CHEA, 2002).

3. Institutional Resources
- The institution's budgets and policy statements must reflect its commitment to the students for whom the electronically offered programs are designed (CHEA, 2002).
- Distance learning programs must not adversely affect the institution's administrative effectiveness, result in faculty overload, or cause financial stress or instability (CHEA, 2002).
- Faculty members are provided with professional incentives for innovative practices to encourage the development of distance learning courses (IHEP, 2000).
- There are institutional rewards for the effective teaching of distance learning courses (IHEP, 2000).
- A technology plan is in place to ensure quality standards (IHEP, 2000).
- Electronic security measures are in place to ensure the integrity and validity of information (IHEP, 2000).
- Support for building and maintaining the distance education infrastructure is addressed by a centralized system (IHEP, 2000).
- Long-range planning, budgeting, and policy development processes reflect the facilities, staffing, equipment, and other resources essential to the viability and effectiveness of the distance education program (SACS, 2006).
- Intent to increase the number of distance education programs and students is explicitly stated in planning documents and by institutional leaders (USDOE, 2006).

- Strategic plan includes specific growth targets with budgets (USDOE, 2006).
- Five-year technology plan addresses the institution's goals for distance education (USDOE, 2006).
- Strategy is present for identifying, hiring, and training faculty needed for new programs and for those that are expected to grow (USDOE, 2006).
- Revenue derived from distance education programs is invested to sustain and strengthen the institution's capacity to provide quality distance education programs and services (USDOE, 2006).
- Results are used to make decisions about resource allocation (USDOE, 2006).

4. Curriculum and Instruction

- School has researched the industry, has reviewed curricula of programs offered by mainstream schools, and has adopted mainstream texts (USDOE, 2006).
- Academically qualified persons participate fully in decisions concerning program curricula and program oversight (SACS, 2006).
- Distance learning course development is approved through a broad peer-review process (IHEP, 2000).
- Guidelines exist regarding minimum standards for course development, design, and delivery (IHEP, 2000).
- Course design is managed by teams comprised of faculty, content experts, instructional designers, technical experts, and evaluation personnel (IHEP, 2000).
- Course descriptions and learning objectives are clearly stated in syllabi, and assessments are mapped to learning objectives (USDOE, 2006).
- During course development, the various learning styles of students are considered (IHEP, 2000).
- Courses are designed with a consistent structure, easily discernable to students of varying learning styles (IHEP, 2000).
- Courses are designed with benchmarks and clear deadlines or recommended schedules (USDOE, 2006).
- Courses include timely and appropriate faculty-student and student-student interaction (IHEP, 2000; SACS, 2006; USDOE, 2006).
- Feedback to students is provided in a manner that is constructive and non-threatening (IHEP, 2000).
- Faculty retains responsibility for program rigor and quality of instruction (SACS, 2006; USDOE, 2006).
- Technology is appropriate for program objectives, and expectations are clearly communicated to students (SACS, 2006).
- Courses are separated into self-contained segments (modules) that can be used to assess student mastery before moving forward in the course or program (IHEP, 2000).
- Materials, programs, and courses are current (SACS, 2006).

- Specific expectations are set for students with respect to a minimum amount of time per week for study and homework assignments (IHEP, 2000).
- Faculty are required to grade and return all assignments within a certain time period (IHEP, 2000).
- Distance education policies are clear regarding ownership of materials, faculty compensation, copyright issues, and use of revenue (SACS, 2006).
- Admission and recruitment consider the capability of students to succeed (SACS, 2006).
- On-campus and distance education programs are equivalent (SACS, 2006).
- Integrity of student work and the credibility of degrees and credits are ensured (SACS, 2006).
- The importance of appropriate interaction (synchronous or asynchronous) between instructor and students and among students is reflected in the design of the program and its courses, and in the technical facilities and services provided (SACS, 2000).

5. Faculty Support

- In the development of an electronically offered program, the institution and its participating faculty have considered issues of workload, compensation, ownership of intellectual property resulting from the program, and the implications of program participation for the faculty member's professional evaluation processes (SACS, 2000).
- Faculty support services are appropriate (SACS, 2006; USDOE, 2006).
- Faculty members have access to specialized resources and technical support for course development and delivery (IHEP, 2000; USDOE, 2006).
- Peer mentoring resources are available to faculty members teaching distance courses (IHEP, 2000).
- Faculty members receive appropriate training that goes beyond software training and includes distance education pedagogy, with specific emphasis on instructional strategies to foster interaction, to convey concepts, and to assess student learning (SACS, 2006; USDOE, 2006).
- Faculty members are assisted in the transition from classroom teaching to distance instruction, and are assessed in the process (IHEP, 2000).
- Distance instructor training continues throughout the progression of the online class (IHEP, 2000).
- Adjunct faculty have access to training and support comparable to that provided the regular faculty (USDOE, 2006).
- Course evaluations are used to improve faculty training and development (USDOE, 2006).

6. Student Support

- The institution has a commitment—administrative, financial, and technical—to the continuation of the program for a period sufficient to enable all admitted students to complete a degree or certificate in a publicized timeframe (SACS, 2000).

- Prior to admitting a student to the program, the institution (SACS, 2000):
    Informs the student concerning required access to technologies and required technical competence
    Assists the student in understanding independent learning expectations and the nature and potential challenges of learning in the program's technology based environment
- Admitted students have the appropriate equipment and personal characteristics, such as being self-directed and having good time management skills (USDOE, 2006).
- Processes are in place to document weaknesses and improvements in services to students as a result of assessments (USDOE, 2006).
- Students receive written information about the program (IHEP, 2000).
- Students can obtain assistance to help them use electronically accessed data successfully (IHEP, 2000).
- All students have easy access to technical assistance throughout the duration of the course/program (IHEP, 2000).
- Students have access to the range of services appropriate to support the programs (SACS, 2006; USDOE, 2006).
- Students receive timely services and information (USDOE, 2006).
- Students receive information and hands-on training to aid them in securing material through electronic databases, interlibrary loans, government archives, news services, etc. (IHEP, 2000; USDOE, 2006).
- There are adequate procedures for resolving student complaints (IHEP, 2000; SACS, 2006).
- Advertising, recruiting, and admissions information accurately represent the programs, requirements, and services available to students (SACS, 2006).
- Students are able to use the technology employed, have the equipment necessary to succeed, and are provided with assistance in using the technology employed (SACS, 2006).

7. Student Learning Outcomes

- Institutions must assess student achievement in the distance learning programs in both general skills (communication, comprehension, analysis, etc.) and skills specific to the field of study (CHEA, 2002).
- When examinations are employed (paper, online, demonstrations of competency, etc.), they take place in circumstances that include firm student identification (SACS, 2000).
- Sufficient opportunities are present for students to acquire comparable levels of knowledge and competencies as in similar programs or courses offered in more traditional ways (CHEA, 2002).

- Documented procedures ensure that security of personal information is protected in the conduct of assessments and evaluations and in the dissemination of results (SACS, 2000).
- Completion, placement, and licensing exam pass rates must be assessed for the distance learning program and must be found to be comparable to site-based programs (CHEA, 2002).
- The program's educational effectiveness is measured using several methods (IHEP, 2000; SACS, 2000), such as:

    The extent to which student learning matches intended outcomes

    The extent to which student intent is met

    Student retention rates, including variations over time

    Student satisfaction, as measured by regular surveys

    Measures of the extent to which library and learning resources are used appropriately by the program's students

    Measures of student competence in fundamental skills such as communication, comprehension, and analysis

    Cost-effectiveness of the program to its students, as compared to campus-based alternatives

- Specific standards are in place to compare and improve learning outcomes (IHEP, 2000).
- Course evaluations are used to improve courses (USDOE, 2006).
- Referrals are made to an academic advisor or tutor, or to some other resource, if students don't perform as required (USDOE, 2006).
- Intended learning outcomes are regularly reviewed to ensure clarity, utility, and appropriateness (IHEP, 2000).

Glossary

Accreditation. An evaluation process in which an external group examines a school or program to ensure that it is meeting professional standards established by experts in the field.

Active learning. A learner-centered approach to learning where the learner actively participates in the learning process through interaction with the environment.

Andragogy. The learner-centered art of teaching adults.

Assessment. The process that schools use to measure student learning in terms of student skills, knowledge, and/or attitudes.

Assessment decisions. The decisions made by teachers regarding student achievement using data gathered from assessment tools.

Assessment events. Situations in which learners are assessed.

Assessment processes. The strategies used by teachers to evaluate student achievement.

Assessment tools. The instruments or assessment tasks in which teachers gather information to assess students.

Asynchronous discussion. Communication that permits a time separation between the transmission and reception of information. As an example, one person can make a message available to another person without knowing when the message will actually be read.

Asynchronous learning network (ALN). An Internet-based network of people with computers learning together using mostly asynchronous communication tools, e.g., e-mail, discussion boards.

Audio conferencing. An electronic conferencing tool in which participants chat using synchronous voice communications, e.g., Internet, phone.

Authentic assessment. Resembles a "real-life" task as closely as possible and often refers to testing under natural, actual conditions rather than in a clinical or artificial environment.

Benchmark. A predetermined value used to determine whether a standard or objective has been achieved.

Blended courses or programs. Distance education courses (or programs) that include both face-to-face and online components. Also called *hybrid* by some educators.

Blog. Short for "Web log"; an electronic communication tool that consists of a public HTML page representing an individual's journal. A blog can be read by anyone accessing the World Wide Web.

Case study. A scenario-based approach to learning.

CIPP Model. A comprehensive framework for guiding program evaluations. It consists of context, input, process, and product evaluations.

Collaborative learning. A learning strategy that involves the less-structured and less-prescriptive variety of interactive group work to support the learning of all group members.

Computer-mediated communication. The synchronous or asynchronous interactions between individuals using computer-based, networked telecommunications systems, e.g., e-mail.

Constructivism. A philosophy of learning based on the social construction of knowledge and understanding.

Cooperative learning. A learning strategy that involves the systematic and prescriptive variety of interactive group work to support the learning of all group members.

Cost-effectiveness. The extent to which program outcomes equal or surpass the results of competitors' programs at the same cost.

Credibility. The property of a measure that suggests it is valid, reliable, and obtained from a representative sample of the target population.

Criteria. See **Standards**.

Criterion-referenced assessments. Used to assess a student's level of proficiency in or mastery of the standards. This is accomplished by comparing a student's performance to a criterion. Such information tells one whether a student needs more or less work regarding the standards, but it says nothing about the student's performance relative to that of other students.

Critical thinking. Disciplined thinking in which the thinker imposes rigorous standards on the thinking process in order to produce a well-founded judgment.

Discussion board. An electronic conferencing tool that permits asynchronous threaded discussions. Either text-based or voice-based boards are possible, although the vast majority of boards are text-based. A discussion board can be open to all students enrolled in a course, or multiple group boards can be created. Learning management systems typically include this tool.

Discussion forum. A subelement of a discussion board. Each discussion board consists of one or more forums where threaded discussions take place. For example, an instructor might create weekly discussion forums throughout the academic term in order to manage discussions.

Disinhibition. An individual's CMC behavior that violates accepted social norms and is characterized by a reduction in consideration for self-presentation and critical judgment of others.

Distributed learning. A blend of traditional face-to-face and computer-mediated learning resources that permit a mix of on-campus and off-campus learning.

E-mail. Short for "electronic mail"; a communication tool that allows transmission of messages by an individual via the Internet to one or more recipients for viewing, replying, or archiving.

Evaluability assessment. A systematic method used to determine whether a program can be evaluated for results.

Evaluation. A general term referring to the appraisal of the characteristics or relative value of a person, program, organization, or thing based on assessments and other sources of information.

Facilitator. The individual, usually the instructor, who administers the discussion board or chat room, identifies discussion topics, supervises the moderator, and helps a group interact. Often, the facilitator is also the moderator.

Flaming. A verbal attack on an individual using hostile and insulting language, usually posted on a computer-mediated discussion board.

Formative evaluation. A judgment regarding an ongoing, changing process or product for diagnosis and improvement.

Globalization. The worldwide trend toward a more interdependent global society. In a higher education context, Altbach (2002) describes globalization as "trends in higher education that have cross-national implications [that] include mass higher education; a global marketplace for students, faculty, and highly educated personnel; and the global reach of the new Internet-based technologies, among others" (p. 29).

Groupware. A broad category of both computer software and group process that permits group members to collaborate with each other. It includes electronic communication tools, e.g., instant messaging systems; electronic conferencing tools, e.g., discussion boards; and collaborative management tools, e.g., learning management systems.

Hyperlink. An element of an HTML page that links to either a different location on that same page or links to a different HTML page on the Web.

HyperText Markup Language (HTML). The computer programming language that defines the structure and layout of Web pages so that Web browsers, e.g., Microsoft Internet Explorer, know how to display the pages.

HyperText Transfer Protocol (HTTP). The protocol that governs the exchange of information on the World Wide Web.

Instant messaging (IM). A synchronous text-based electronic communication tool that is made private by limiting participants and providing alerts when participants are present and available for communication. Some tools, such as Pronto, allow both text-based and audio chat.

Instructional systems design (ISD). The systematic process of designing education and training that includes analysis, development, implementation, and evaluation.

Instructor immediacy. A set of instructor behaviors to enhance teaching presence and reduce the social distance between instructor and students by verbal and nonverbal actions such as eye contact, smiles, and nods.

Interaction. Two-way communication between objects, such as individuals and groups, as well as an exchange between an individual and technology.

Internet. A network of computers that can exchange information using numerous protocols.

iTunes U. A method of getting recorded audio and video content, e.g., presentations, performances, lectures, demonstrations, debates, tours, and archival footage, to students. Colleges and universities create their own iTunes U sites, faculty post content they create, and students download what they need for playback on their computer or MP3 player, e.g., an iPod.

Learning Management System (LMS). A vendor-supplied collaborative management tool designed to organize all aspects of course delivery that include one-way dissemination of information, two-way discussion, and tracking of student progress, e.g., Angel, Blackboard, Lotus Notes, and WebCT. Modules are also available that provide additional communication tools, such as instant messaging and live voice chat.

Learning outcome. A type of outcome that is described in terms of student attainment across cognitive, affective, and psychomotor domains of learning.

Moderator. The individual who leads/regulates the discussion in a discussion board or chat room, opens/closes threads, summarizes the discussion, and offers closing thoughts. The moderator can be the instructor/facilitator, an assistant instructor, or a student designated by the facilitator.

Multiuser domain (MUD) or a MUD that is object-oriented (MOO). A synchronous electronic conferencing tool that allows participants to share a virtual world consisting of spaces or rooms that contain objects. Individuals can interact with each other and with objects and can communicate with each other using synchronous chat.

Needs assessment. A systematic process to determine the extent of the needs of a population in a specific area for the purpose of developing or refining a program that responds to those needs. Includes market research analysis.

Norm-referenced assessments. Used to assess a student's performance in comparison to a norm or average of performance. Norm-referenced tests are often reported in terms of percentiles or percentile rankings. A norm-referenced assessment says nothing about the level of mastery of the standards.

Open learning. An approach to learning that gives students flexibility over what, when, where, at what pace, and how they learn.

Outcome. A change that happens to a student as a result of his or her attendance at a higher education institution and/or participation in a specific program.

Peer evaluation. An evaluation by students of the work produced by other students or an evaluation by faculty members of the teaching practices of other faculty members.

Performance assessments. Assessments that are based on observation and evaluation of student-created products, projects, and performances. It requires students to perform a task or demonstrate a skill rather than simply select a response.

Performance indicator. A measure that describes how well a program is achieving its objectives. Indicators tell what to measure to determine the degree to which an objective or criterion has been achieved.

Podcasting. An electronic communication tool similar to RSS except that the feeds are digital media files and are available for playback on computers and MP3 players such as iPods. Individuals can subscribe to feeds by submitting the feed address to an aggregator, e.g., iTunes, and when new files become available, they are automatically downloaded to the user's computer.

Portable Document Format (PDF). The de facto standard for electronic document delivery, created and read by Adobe Acrobat software. PDF files are electronic copies that look and print (including text, graphics, and photos) identically to the original hardcopy version.

Presence. The sense of being close to others, e.g., teaching presence or social presence, in a physical or virtual environment, or closely attending to cognition, i.e., cognitive presence.

Problem-based learning (PBL). An active learning strategy in which small collaborative groups are given challenging, open-ended problems to solve with limited scaffolding.

Program evaluation. A formal, systematic study to determine how well a program is performing.

Reliability. The extent to which a measure yields consistent results.

Representativeness. How accurately a sample represents the population from which it is drawn.

Rich Site Summary (RSS). An electronic communication tool that provides syndicated documents containing information registered with a publisher and made available for inclusion on any number of subscribing Web sites in order to update frequently changing content, e.g., blogs, podcasts, and running news feed.

Rubric. A set of guidelines for rating student work that describes what is being assessed and how it should be assessed by describing various levels of quality. A rubric is also frequently used as an instructional tool to promote self-assessment.

Social equity. Achieved when diverse individuals have the same status in a certain respect, such as opportunities for achievement in a social learning environment. The goal of social equity is to eliminate unequal treatment of individuals based on factors such as race, national origin, religious practices, age, ethnicity, disabilities, and gender.

Social justice. Concerned with fair and equitable treatment given to all individuals. Within an educational context, this means all individuals receive a just share of the educational benefits of society.

Stakeholders. Individuals or groups that have an interest or stake in the organization's future.

Standards. Principles or criteria used in program and course evaluations and accreditations that represent the ideal and are used to judge the value or quality of a program or course.

Strategic planning. A cyclical process by which an organization envisions its future, develops the necessary strategies, programs, and activities to achieve that future, and determines how success is to be measured and evaluated.

Summative evaluation. A judgment regarding the results or outcomes of a program or other unit, e.g., a course; used for high-stakes decision making, e.g., evidence for grades, promotion, placement, certification, accountability, continued funding, etc.

SWOT analysis. An abbreviation used to denote analysis of an organization's internal Strengths and Weaknesses and external Opportunities and Threats.

Synchronous discussion or real-time conferencing. Communication that permits real-time interaction, either text-based or audio.

Teacher immediacy. A concept that encompasses those teacher communication behaviors that enhance closeness with another through verbal and nonverbal cues, e.g., smiles, head nods, and eye contact.

Transformative learning. Learning that is not merely assimilative but results in a paradigm shift or perspective transformation.

Validity. The extent to which a measure accurately reflects the concept that it purports to measure, nothing less and nothing more.

Videoconferencing or video teleconferencing (VTC). An electronic conferencing tool in which participants communicate using synchronous video and voice communications, e.g., CU-SeeMe and Microsoft NetMeeting.

Virtual whiteboard. A computer simulation of a dry-erase or dry-wipe board that is used as an electronic conferencing tool. It is most often used in conjunction with other conferencing tools and applications, e.g., virtual meetings, chat, and instant messaging.

Virtual world. A computer-based conferencing tool that simulates a real environment in which individuals, depicted by avatars, can interact with each other using text or voice. Virtual worlds are mostly used for multiuser computer gaming or socializing, e.g., *The Sims Online* and *Second Life*.

Web cam. A camera that uses the World Wide Web to share pictures or videos.

Web page. An HTML page available on the World Wide Web.

WebQuest. An online problem-based activity in which most or all of the information used by students is online. The six-part WebQuest (introduction, task, resources, process, evaluation, and conclusion) promotes critical thinking.

Web site. The World Wide Web location of a Web page.

Wiki. Named for the Hawaiian word meaning quick, a Web site that allows visitors to add, delete, or modify information contained on a Web page quickly. Typically, a wiki allows linking to other pages and is a useful tool for collaborative authoring.

World Wide Web. A system of information sharing that uses HTTP to access information from different computers connected to the Internet. Also referred to as "the Web" or "cyberspace."

References

Alavi, M., & Dufner, D. (2005). Technology-mediated collaborative learning: A research perspective. In S. R. Hiltz & R. Goldman (Eds.), *Learning together online: Research on asynchronous learning networks* (pp. 191–213). Mahwah, NJ: Erlbaum.

Aleomoni, L. M. (1984). The dynamics of faculty evaluation. In P. Seldin (Ed.), *Changing practices in faculty evaluation: A critical assessment and recommendations for improvement* (pp. 75–79). San Francisco: Jossey-Bass.

Allen, I. E., & Seaman, J. (2003). *Sizing the opportunity: The quality and extent of online education in the United States, 2002–2003.* Wellesley, MA: The Sloan Consortium. Retrieved August 4, 2007, from http://www.sloan-c.org/resources/sizing_opportunity .pdf

Allen, I. E., & Seaman, J. (2006). *Making the grade: Online education in the United States, 2006.* Needham, MA: Sloan Consortium.

Allport, G. W. (1954). *The nature of prejudice.* Cambridge, MA: Addison-Wesley.

Alstete, J. W. (1995). *Benchmarking in higher education: Adapting best practices to improve quality.* ASHE-ERIC Higher Education Reports, No. 5. Washington, DC: George Washington Graduate School of Education and Human Development.

Altbach, P. G. (2002). Perspectives on international higher education. *Change, 34*(3), 29–31.

Altekruse, M., & Wittmer, J. (1991). Accreditation in counselor education. In F. Bradley (Ed.), *Credentialing in counseling* (pp. 53–62). Alexandria, VA: American Counseling Association.

American Federation of Teachers (2000). *Distance education, guidelines for good practice.* Retrieved July 30, 2007, from http://www.aft.org/pubs-reports/higher_ed/distance .pdf

American Psychological Association. (2001). *Publication manual of the American Psychological Association* (5th ed.). Washington, DC: Author.

Anderson, D. M., & Haddad, C. J. (2005). Gender, voice, and learning in online course environments. *Journal of Asynchronous Learning Networks, 9*(1), 3–14.

Anderson, J. A. (1988). Cognitive styles and multicultural populations. *Journal of Teacher Education, 39*(1), 2–9.

Anderson, S. B., Ball, S., Murphy, R. T., et al. (1975). *Encyclopedia of educational evaluation: Concepts and techniques for evaluating education and training programs.* San Francisco: Jossey-Bass.

Anderson, T. (2004). Teaching in an online learning context. In T. Anderson & F. Elloumi (Eds.), *Theory and practice of online learning* (pp. 273–294). Athabasca, Canada: Athabasca University.

Angelo, T. A., & Cross, K. P. (1993). *Classroom assessment techniques* (2nd ed.). San Francisco: Jossey-Bass.

Ashby, C. M. (2002). *Distance education: Growth in distance education programs and impli-*

cations for federal education policy. United States General Accounting Office Report GAO-02-1125T. Washington, DC: Government Printing Office.

Association of American Colleges and Universities. (2002). *Greater expectations: A new vision for learning as a nation goes to college.* National Panel Report. Washington, DC: Author.

Astin, A. (1997). *What matters in college? Four critical years revisited.* San Francisco: Jossey Bass.

Ausburn, L. (2004). Gender and learning strategy differences in nontraditional adult students' design preferences in hybrid distance courses. *Journal of Interactive Online Learning, 3*(2). Retrieved July 30, 2007, from http://www.ncolr.org/jiol/issues/PDF/3.2.6.pdf

Austin, A. E. (1990). Faculty cultures, faculty values. In W. G. Tierney (Ed.), *Assessing academic climates and cultures* (pp. 61–74). San Francisco: Jossey-Bass.

Baker, J. D. (2004). An investigation of relationships among instructor immediacy and affective and cognitive learning in the online classroom. *Internet & Higher Education, 7*(1), 1–13.

Bandura, A. (1997). *Self-efficacy: The exercise of control.* New York: W. H. Freeman.

Bangert, A. W. (2004). The seven principles of good practice: A framework for evaluating on-line teaching. *Internet and Higher Education, 7*(3), 217–232.

Banks, J. A. (1996). The historical reconstruction of knowledge about race: Implications for transformative teaching. In J. A. Banks (Ed.), *Multicultural education, transformative knowledge, and action: Historical and contemporary perspectives* (pp. 64–87). New York: Teachers College Press.

Banks, J. A., & Banks, C. A. M. (Eds.). (2004). *Handbook of research on multicultural education* (2nd ed.). San Francisco: Jossey-Bass.

Barkley, E. F., Cross, K. P., & Major, C. H. (2005). *Collaborative learning techniques: A handbook for college faculty.* San Francisco: Jossey-Bass.

Barley, S., & Tolbert, P. (1997). Institutionalization and structuration: Studying the links between action and institution. *Organization Studies, 18*(1), 93–117.

Bassoppo-Moyo, T. C. (2006). Evaluating elearning: A front-end, process and post hoc approach [Electronic version]. *International Journal of Instructional Media, 33*(1), 7–22.

Battiste, M., & Henderson, J. Y. (2000). *Protecting indigenous knowledge and heritage: A global challenge.* Saskatoon, Canada: Purich.

Baxter-Magolda, M. B. (1992). *Knowing and reasoning in college: Gender-related patterns in students' intellectual development.* San Francisco: Jossey-Bass.

Beaudoin, M. (1990). The instructor's changing role in distance education. *American Journal of Distance Education, 4*(2), 21–29.

Beaudoin, M. F. (2002). Distance education leadership: An essential role for the new century. *Journal of Leadership Studies, 8*(3), 131–144.

Belenky, M., Clinchy, B, Goldberger, N., & Tarule, J. (1996). *Women's ways of knowing: The development of self, voice, and mind* (10th anniversary ed.). New York: HarperCollins.

Benjamin, R., & Carroll, S. J. (1997). *Breaking the social contract: The fiscal crisis in California higher education.* Santa Monica, CA: Rand Corporation, Council for Aid to Education. (ERIC Reproduction Service No. EJ414807)

Benne, K., & Sheats, P. (1978). Functional roles of group members. In L. P. Bradford (Ed.), *Group development* (2nd ed., pp. 52–61). La Jolla, CA: University Associates.

Bennett, C. I. (2006). *Comprehensive multicultural education: Theory and practice* (6th ed.). Needham Heights, MA: Allyn & Bacon.

Berge, Z. L., & Muilenburg, L. (2006). *Obstacles faced at various stages of capability regarding distance education in institutions of higher education: Survey results.* Retrieved July 30, 2007, from http://www.emoderators.com/barriers/hghred_stgs.shtml

Bergman, E., & Johnson, E. (1995). Toward accessible human-computer interaction. In J. Nielsen (Ed.), *Advances in human-computer interaction: Vol. 5.* Norwood, NJ: Ablex.

Bernard, R. M., Abrami, P. C., Lou, Y., Borokhovski, E., Wade, A., Wozney, L., Wallet, P. A., Fiset, M., & Huang, B. (2004). How does distance education compare to classroom instruction? A meta-analysis of the empirical literature. *Review of Educational Research, 74*(3), 379–439.

Berry, L. L. (2004). *Marketing services: Competing through quality.* New York: Free Press.

Biggs, J. (2001). Assessment of student learning: Where did we go wrong? [Electronic version]. *Assessment Update, 13*(6), 6–11.

Birnbaum, R. (2001). *Management fads in higher education: Where they come from, what they do, why they fail.* San Francisco: Jossey-Bass.

Black, E. J. (1992). Faculty support for university distance education [Electronic version]. *Journal of Distance Education, 7*(2), 5–30.

Blignaut, S., & Trollip, S. R. (2003). Developing a taxonomy of faculty participation in asynchronous learning environments—An exploratory investigation [Electronic version]. *Computers & Education, 41*(2), 149–172.

Blimling, G. S., & Whitt, E. J. (1998). Creating and using principles of good practice for student affairs. *About Campus, 3*(1), 10–15.

Bok, D. (2003). *Universities in the marketplace.* Princeton, NJ: Princeton University Press.

Bonk, C. J., Wisher, R. A., & Lee, J.-Y. (2003). Moderating learner-centered e-learning: Problems and solutions, benefits and implications. In T. S. Roberts (Ed.), *Online collaborative learning: Theory and practice* (pp. 54–85). Hershey, PA: Idea Group.

Breneman, D. (2005). Entrepreneurship in higher education. In B. Pusser (Ed.), *Arenas of entrepreneurship: Where nonprofit and for-profit institutions compete* (pp. 3–10). San Francisco: Jossey-Bass.

Brookhart, S. M., & Nitko, A. J. (2007). *Assessment and grading in classrooms.* Upper Saddle River, NJ: Pearson.

Brown, B. M. (1998). Digital classrooms: Some myths about developing new educational programs using the Internet. *T.H.E. Journal, 26*(5), 56–59.

Brown, D. J. (2001). Hybrid courses are best. *Syllabus, 15*(1), 22.

Bruffee, K. A. (1995). Sharing our toys: Cooperative learning versus collaborative learning [Electronic version]. *Change, 27*(1), 12–18.

Bryson, J. M. (2004). *Strategic planning for public and nonprofit organizations* (3rd ed.). San Francisco: Jossey-Bass.

Burgelman, R. A. (1994). Fading memories: A process theory of strategic business exit in dynamic environments. *Administrative Science Quarterly, 39*(1), 24–56.

Camp, R. C. (1989). Benchmarking: The search for best practices that lead to superior performance. *Quality Progress, 22*(1), 61–68.

Campbell, D. T. (1976). *Assessing the impact of planned social change,* Paper #8, Occasional Paper Series. Hanover, NH: Dartmouth College. Retrieved July 30, 2007, from http://www.wmich.edu/evalctr/pubs/ops/ops08.html

Campbell, J. O., Lison, C. A., Borsook, T. K., Hoover, J. A., & Arnold, P. (1995). Using computer and video technologies to develop interpersonal skills. *Computers in Human Behavior, 11*(2), 223–239.

Carr, S. (2000, February 11). As distance education comes of age, the challenge is keeping the students. *Chronicle of Higher Education, 46*(23), A39. Retrieved July 30, 2007, from http://chronicle.com/weekly/v46/i23/23a00101.htm

Cavanaugh, C. (2002). Distance education quality: Success factors for resources, practices and results. In R. Discenza, C. Howard, & K. Schenk (Eds.), *The design & management of effective distance learning programs* (pp. 171–189). Hershey, PA: Idea Group.

Chene, A. (1983). The concept of autonomy in adult education: A philosophical discussion. *Adult Education Quarterly, 34*(1), 38–47.

Chesler, M., Lewis, A. E., & Crowfoot, J. E. (2005). *Challenging racism in higher education: Promoting justice.* Lanham, MD: Rowman & Littlefield.

Chism, N. V. (1999). *Peer review of teaching.* Bolton, MA: Anker.

Chronicle of Higher Education. (2004, September 3). Forum: How can colleges prove they're doing their jobs? *The Chronicle of Higher Education, 51*(2), B6. Retrieved July 30, 2007, from http://chronicle.com/weekly/v51/i02/02b00601.htm

Clay-Warner, J., & Marsh, K. (2000). Implementing computer mediated communication in the college classroom. *Journal of Educational Computing Research, 23*(3), 257–274.

Cohen, E. G. (1994). *Designing groupwork: Strategies for the heterogeneous classroom* (2nd ed.). New York: Teachers College Press.

Cole, E. B., & McQuin, S. C. (Eds). (1992). *Explorations in feminist ethics: Theory and practice.* Bloomington: Indiana University Press.

Colis, B., & Moonen, J. (2001). *Flexible learning in a digital world: Experiences and expectations.* London: Kogan-Page.

Collison, G., Elbaum, B., Haavind, S., & Tinker, R. (2000). *Facilitating online learning: Effective strategies for moderators.* Madison, WI: Atwood Publishing.

Confessore, G. J. (1991). Human behavior as a construct for assessing Guglielmino's self-directed learning readiness scale: Pragmatism revisited. In H. B. Long & Associates (Eds.), *Self-directed learning: Consensus and conflict* (pp. 123–146). Norman, OK: Oklahoma Research Center for Continuing Professional and Higher Education of the University of Oklahoma.

Contreras, A. (2007, August 10). Point of view: How not to fix accreditation. *The Chronicle of Higher Education, 53*(49), B16. Retrieved August 8, 2007, from http://chronicle.com/weekly/v53/i49/49b01601.htm?=attw

Cooper, J., & Weaver, K. D. (2003). *Gender and computers: Understanding the digital divide.* Mahwah, NJ: Erlbaum.

Copeland, L., & Griggs, L. (1985). *Going international: How to make friends and deal effectively in the global marketplace.* New York: Random House.

Cose, E. (1997). *Color-blind: Seeing beyond race in a race-obsessed world.* New York: HarperCollins.

Council for Higher Education Accreditation (CHEA), Institute for Research and Study of Accreditation and Quality Assurance. (2002). *Accreditation and assuring quality in distance learning* (CHEA Monograph Series 2002, Number 1). Washington, DC: Author.

Crawford, M., & MacLeod, M. (1990). Gender in the college classroom: An assessment of the "chilly climate" for women. *Sex Roles, 23*(3–4), 101–122.

Cross, K. P. (1992). *Adults as learners: Increasing participation and facilitating learning.* San Francisco: Jossey-Bass.

Dahl, S. (2007). Turnitin®: The student perspective on using plagiarism detection software [Electronic version]. *Active Learning in Higher Education, 8*(2), 173–191.

Davis, S. N. (1999). Creating a collaborative classroom. In S. N. Davis, M. Crawford, & J. Sebrechts (Eds.), *Coming into her own: Educational success in girls and women* (pp. 123–138). San Francisco: Jossey-Bass.

Dede, C. (1996). Distance learning to distributed learning: Making the transition. *Learning & Leading with Technology, 23*(7), 25–30.

Dewey, J. (1916). *Democracy and education.* New York: Macmillan.

Diaz, D. P. (1999). CD/Web hybrid: Delivering multimedia to the online learner. *Journal of Educational Multimedia and Hypermedia, 8*(1), 89–98. Retrieved February 27, 2007, from http://home.earthlink.net/~davidpdiaz/LTS/html_docs/cdhybrid.htm

Dill, D., Massy, W., Williams, P., & Cook, C. (1996). Accreditation and academic quality assurance: Can we get there from here? *Change, 28*(5), 16–24.

DiMaggio, P., & Hargittai, E. (2001). *From the "digital divide" to "digital inequality": Studying Internet use as penetration increases.* Working Paper Series number 15. Princeton, NJ: Princeton University Center for Arts and Cultural Policy Studies.

Duggan, F. (2006). Plagiarism: Prevention, practice and policy [Electronic version]. *Assessment & Evaluation in Higher Education, 31*(2), 151–154.

Dunlap, J. C. (2005). Workload reduction in online courses: Getting some shuteye. *Performance Improvement, 44*(5), 18–25.

Eaton, J. S. (2001). *Distance learning: Academic and political challenges for higher education accreditation.* CHEA Monograph Series 2001, No. 1. Washington, DC: Council for Higher Education Accreditation. Retrieved July 30, 2007, from http://www.chea.org/pdf/mono_1_dist_learning_2001.pdf

Engell, J., & Dangerfield, A. (2005). *Saving higher education in the age of money.* Charlottesville, VA: University of Virginia Press.

Ewell, P. T. (2001). *Accreditation and student learning outcomes: A proposed point of departure.* CHEA occasional paper. Washington, DC: National Center for Higher Education Management Systems.

Fabos, B., & Young, M. D. (1999). Telecommunication in the classroom: Rhetoric versus reality. *Review of Educational Research, 69*(3), 217–259.

Fahy, P. J. (2002). Use of linguistic qualifiers and intensifiers in a computer conference. *American Journal of Distance Education, 16*(1), 5–22.

Fairlie, R. W. (2004). Race and the digital divide. *Contributions to economic analysis & policy, 3*(1), Article 15. Retrieved July 30, 2007, from http://www.bepress.com/bejeap/contributions/vol3/iss1/art15

Falicov, C. J. (1996). Mexican families. In M. McGoldrick, J. Giordano, & J. K. Pearce (Eds.), *Ethnicity and family therapy* (pp. 169–182). New York: Guilford Press.

Farrell, E. F. (2005, February 4). Among freshmen, a growing digital divide. *The Chronicle of Higher Education, 51*(22), A32. Retrieved July 30, 2007, from http://chronicle.com/weekly/v51/i22/22a03201.htm

Fitzpatrick, J. L., Sanders, J. R., & Worthen, B. R. (2004). *Program evaluation: Alternative approaches and practical guidelines* (3rd ed.). Boston: Pearson.

Foley, J. (2006, May 23). *Race an appropriate admission criterion, guest lecturer says.*

Charlottesville, VA: The Cavalier Daily. Retrieved July 30, 2007, from http://www .cavalierdaily.com/CVArticle_print.asp?ID=19753&pid1151

Forman, D. (2002) Benefits, costs and the value of e-learning programs. In A. Rossett (Ed.), *The ASTD e-learning handbook* (pp. 398–413). New York: McGraw-Hill.

Fornaciari, C., Forte, M., & Mathews, C. (1999). Distance education strategy: How can your school compete? *Journal of Management Education, 23*(6), 703–718.

Foskett, N. (2002). Marketing. In T. Bush & L. Bell (Eds.), *The principles and practice of educational management* (pp. 241–257). London: Chapman.

Fox, T. (1990). *The social uses of writing: Politics and pedagogy.* Norwood, NJ: Ablex.

Freed, G. (1996). Captioning video clips on the world wide Web. *First Monday, 1*(3). Retrieved August 4, 2007, from http://www.firstmonday.dk/issues/issue3/freed/index .html

Gallant, G. M. (2000). Professional development for Web-based teaching: Overcoming innocence and resistance. *New Directions for Adult and Continuing Education, 88*(1), 69–78.

Gallien, L. B., Jr., & Peterson, M. S. (2004). *Instructing and mentoring the African American college student: Strategies for success in higher education.* Needham Heights, MA: Allyn & Bacon.

Gallimore, R., & Tharp, R. (2005). Teaching mind in society: Teaching, schooling, and literate discourse. In L. Moll (Ed.), *Vygotsky and education* (pp. 175–205). New York: Cambridge University Press.

Gappa, J. M., Austin, A. E., & Trice, A. G. (2007). *Rethinking faculty work: Higher education's strategic imperative.* San Francisco: Jossey-Bass.

Garrison, D. R. (2003). Cognitive presence for effective asynchronous online learning: The role of reflective inquiry, self-direction and metacognition. In J. Bourne & J. C. Moore (Eds.), *Elements of quality online education: Practice and direction, Vol. 4* (pp. 47–58). Needham, MA: Sloan.

Garrison, D. R., Anderson, T., & Archer, W. (2000). Critical inquiry in a text-based environment: Computer conferencing in higher education. *Internet & Higher Education, 2*(2–3), 1–19.

Garrison, D. R., Anderson, T., & Archer, W. (2001). Critical thinking, cognitive presence, and computer conferencing in distance education. *American Journal of Distance Education, 15*(1), 7–23.

Garrison, D. R., Cleveland-Innes, M., & Fung, T. (2004). Student role adjustment in online communities of inquiry: Model and instrument validation [Electronic version]. *Journal of Asynchronous Learning Networks, 8*(2), 61–74.

Gay, G. (2002). Preparing for culturally responsive teaching. *Journal of Teacher Education, 53*(2), 106–116.

Gefen, D., & Straub, D. W. (1997). Gender differences in the perception and use of e-mail: An extension to the technology acceptance model. *MIS Quarterly, 21*(4), 389–400.

Gerber, S., Scott, L., Clements, D. H., & Sarama, J. (2005). Instructor influence on reasoned argument in discussion boards. *Educational Technology Research and Development, 53*(2), 25–39.

Gilligan, C. (1993). *In a different voice: Psychological theory and women's development.* Cambridge, MA: Harvard University Press.

Giroux, H. A. (2001). Introduction. In H. A. Giroux & K. Myrsiades (Eds.), *Beyond the corporate university: Culture and pedagogy in the new millennium* (pp. 1–12). Lanham, MD: Rowman & Littlefield.

Goffee, R., & Jones, G. (1998). *The character of a corporation.* New York: Harper Business.

Grace, K. S. (1996). *The board's role in strategic planning.* Washington, DC: National Center for Nonprofit Boards.

Gunawardena, C. N. (1990). Integrating telecommunication systems to reach distance learners [Electronic version]. *American Journal of Distance Education, 3*(2), 35–43.

Gunn, C., McSporran, M., Macleod, H., & French, S. (2003). Dominant or different? Gender issues in computer supported learning [Electronic version]. *Journal of Asynchronous Learning Networks, 7*(1), 14–30.

Gunter, K. (1995). *Authority is not a luxury: "Courageous Dialogue" in the feminist classroom.* Retrieved July 30, 2007, from http://www.lib.wmc.edu/pub/researcher/issyeXI-2/gunter.html

Hall, E. T., & Hall, M. R. (1990). *Understanding cultural differences.* New York: Intercultural Press.

Hardaker, G., & Smith, D. (2002). E-learning communities, virtual markets and knowledge creation. *European Business Review, 14*(5), 342–350.

Harroff, P. A., & Valentine, T. (2006). Dimensions of program quality in Web-based adult education [Electronic version]. *American Journal of Distance Education, 20*(1), 7–22.

Hawthorne, E. M. (1995). Proprietary schools and community colleges: The next chapter. *New Directions for Community Colleges, 23*(3), 93–98.

Hax, A. C., & Majluf, N. S. (1996). *The strategy concept and process: A pragmatic approach.* Upper Saddle River, NJ: Prentice Hall.

Herring, S. C. (1996a). Posting in a different voice: Gender and ethics in computer-mediated communication. In C. Ess (Ed.), *Philosophical perspectives on computer-mediated communication* (pp. 115–145). Albany, NY: SUNY Press.

Herring, S. C. (1996b). Bringing familiar baggage to the new frontier: Gender differences in computer-mediated communication. In V. J. Vitanza (Ed.), *CyberReader* (pp. 144–154). Needham Heights, MA: Allyn & Bacon.

Herring, S. C. (2000). Gender differences in CMC: Findings and implications. *CPSR Newsletter, 18*(1), 3–11.

Hewett, J. (2003). How habitual online practices affect the development of asynchronous discussion threads. *Journal of Educational Computing Research, 28*(1), 31–45.

Hewstone, M., & Brown, R. J. (1986). Contact is not enough: An intergroup perspective on the Contact Hypothesis. In M. Hewstone & R. J. Brown (Eds.), *Contact and conflict in intergroup encounters* (pp. 1–44). Oxford: Blackwell.

Hillman, D. C., Willis, D. I., & Gunawardena, C. N. (1994). Learner-interface interaction in distance education: An extension of contemporary models and strategies for practitioners. *American Journal of Distance Education, 8*(2), 30–42.

Hiltz, S. R., & Turoff, M. (1993). *The network nation: Human communication via computer* (Revised ed.). Reading, MA: Addison-Wesley.

Hislop, G., & Ellis, H. (2004). A study of faculty effort in online teaching. *Internet and Higher Education, 7*(1), 15–32.

Hofstede, G. (2004). *Cultures and organizations: Software of the mind* (2nd ed.). New York: McGraw-Hill.

Hrastinski, S. (2006). The relationship between adopting a synchronous medium and participation in online group work: An explorative study. *Interactive Learning Environments, 14*(2), 137–152.

Husmann, D. E., & Miller, M. T. (2001). Improving distance education: Perceptions of program administrators [Electronic version]. *Online Journal of Distance Learning Administration, 4*(3). Retrieved June 15, 2007, from http://www.westga.edu/~distance/ojdla/fall43/husmann43.html

Hutchings, M. (2002). Computer mediated communication: Impact on learning. In S. Fallows & R. Bhanot (Eds.), *Educational development through information and communications technology* (pp. 87–99). London: Kogan Page.

Hutchings, P. (1996). The peer review of teaching: Progress, issues and prospects. *Innovative Higher Education, 20*(4), 221–234.

Ibarra, R. A. (2001). *Beyond affirmative action: Reframing the context of higher education.* Madison, WI: University of Wisconsin Press.

Illeris, K. (2003). Towards a contemporary and comprehensive theory of learning. *International Journal of Lifelong Education, 22,* 396–406.

Institute for Higher Education Policy (IHEP). (2000, April). *Quality on the line: Benchmarks for success in Internet-based distance education.* Washington, DC: Author.

Jackson, L. A., Ervin, K. S., Gardner, P. D., & Schmitt, N. (2001). Gender and the Internet: Women communicating and men searching. *Sex Roles, 44*(5), 363–379.

James, R. (2001, September). *Students' changing expectations of higher education and the consequences of mismatches with the reality* [Electronic version]. Paper for the OECD-IMHE Conference: Management Responses to Changing Student Expectations. Retrieved July 14, 2007, from http://www.cshe.unimelb.edu.au/people/staff_pages/James/James-OECD_IMHE.pdf

Joinson, A. (2006). Causes and implications of disinhibited behavior on the Internet. In J. Gackenbach (Ed.), *Psychology and the Internet: Intrapersonal, interpersonal, and transpersonal Implications* (2nd ed., pp. 43–60). New York: Academic Press.

Joint Committee on Standards for Educational Evaluation. (1994). *The program evaluation standards* (2nd ed.). Thousand Oaks, CA: Sage.

Jung, S. M., & Schubert, J. G. (1983). Evaluability assessment: A two-year retrospective. *Educational Evaluation and Policy Analysis, 5*(4), 435–444.

Kantrowitz, B. (1996). Men, women, computers. In V. J. Vitanza (Ed.), *CyberReader* (pp. 134–140). Needham Heights, MA: Allyn & Bacon.

Kanuka, H., & Anderson, T. (1998). Online social interchange, discord, and knowledge construction [Electronic version]. *Journal of Distance Education, 13*(1), 57–74.

Katz, D., & Kahn, R. L. (1978). *The social psychology of organizations* (2nd ed.). New York: Wiley.

Kearsley, G., & Blomeyer, R. (2004). Preparing K–12 teachers to teach online. *Educational Technology, 44*(1), 49–52.

Keller, G. (1997). Examining what works in strategic planning. In M. W. Peterson, D. D. Dill, & L. A. Mets (Eds.), *Planning and management for a changing environment: A handbook on redesigning postsecondary institutions* (pp. 158–170). San Francisco: Jossey-Bass.

Kemp, W. C. (2002). Persistence of adult learners in distance education [Electronic version]. *American Journal of Distance Education, 16*(2), 65–81.

Kiesler, S., Siegel, J., & McGuire, T. (1984). Social psychological aspects of computer-mediated communication. *American Psychologist, 39*(10), 1123–1134.

Knight, J. (2005). The international race for accreditation. *International Higher Education*, *40*(Summer), 2–3.

Knowles, M. S. (1988). *The modern practice of adult education: From pedagogy to andragogy* (Revised ed.). New York: Cambridge Books.

Knowles, M. S., Holton, E. F., III, & Swanson, R. A. (2005). *The adult learner: The definitive classic in adult education and human resource development* (6th ed.). Woburn, MA: Butterworth-Heinemann.

Kosecoff, J., & Fink, A. (1982). *Evaluation basics: A practitioner's manual*. Newbury Park, CA: Sage.

Kotler, P., & Fox, K. A. (1995). *Strategic marketing for educational institutions*. New York: Prentice-Hall.

Kramarae, C. (2003). Gender equity online, when there is no door to knock on. In M. G. Moore & W. G. Anderson (Eds.), *Handbook of distance education* (pp. 261–272). Mahwah, NJ: Erlbaum.

Kreijns, K., Kirschner, P. A., & Jochems, W. (2002). The sociability of computer-supported collaborative learning environments [Electronic version]. *Educational Technology & Society*, *5*(1), 8–22.

Kulhavy, R. W., & Stock, W. A. (1989). Feedback in written instruction: The place of response certitude. *Educational Psychology Review*, *1*(4), 279–308.

Labi, A. (2005, December 16). Two agencies announce quality controls. *The Chronicle of Higher Education*, *52*(17), A41. Retrieved July 30, 2007, from http://chronicle.com/weekly/v52/i17/17a04101.htm

Lacey, C. H., Saleh, A., & Gorman, R. (1998, October). *Teaching nine to five: A study of the teaching styles of male and female professors*. Paper presented at the Annual Women in Educational Leadership Conference, Lincoln, NE.

Lagier, J. (2003). Distance learning and the minority student: Special needs and opportunities. *Internet and Higher Education*, *6*(2), 179–184.

Lechuga, V. M. (2006). *The changing landscape of the academic profession: The culture of faculty at for-profit colleges and universities*. New York: Routledge/Falmer.

Lee, A. C. K. (2003). Undergraduate students' gender differences in IT skills and attitudes. *Journal of Computer Assisted Learning*, *19*(4), 488–500.

Lee, C. D. (1998). Culturally responsive pedagogy and performance-based assessment. *Journal of Negro Education*, *7*(3), 268–279.

Lee, J., & Wilner, A. (2002). The promise and the reality of distance education. *National Education Association Higher Education Research Center Update*, *8*(3), 1–4.

Lefcourt, H. M. (2003). Humor as a moderator in life stress in adults. In C. E. Schaefer (Ed.), *Play therapy with adults* (pp. 144–165). Hoboken, NJ: John Wiley & Sons.

Levine, A. (1997). How the academic profession is changing. *Daedalus*, *126*(4), 1–20.

Lewis, B., Massey, C., & Smith, R. (2001). *The tower under siege: Technology, power, and education*. Montreal: McGill-Queen's University Press.

Lim, C. K. (2001). Computer self-efficacy, academic self-concept, and other predictors of satisfaction and future participation of adult distance learners [Electronic version]. *American Journal of Distance Education*, *15*(2), 41–51.

Lindemann, E. (2001). *A rhetoric for writing teachers* (4th ed.). New York: Oxford University Press.

Lipman, M. (2003). *Thinking in education* (2nd ed.). Cambridge, UK: Cambridge University Press.

Loane, S. (2000). *Distance education and accreditation. ERIC digest.* Washington, DC: ERIC Clearinghouse on Higher Education. (ERIC Document Reproduction No. ED464525)

Long, H. B. (1989). Self-directed learning: Emerging theory and practice. In H. B. Long & Associates (Eds.), *Self-directed learning: Emerging theory and practice* (pp. 1–11). Norman, OK: Oklahoma Research Center for Continuing Professional and Higher Education of the University of Oklahoma.

Long, H. B. (1998). Theoretical and practical implications of selected paradigms of self-directed learning. In H. B. Long & Associates (Eds.), *Developing paradigms for self-directed learning* (pp. 1–14). Norman, OK: Public Managers Center, College of Education, University of Oklahoma.

Lou, Y., Abrami, P. C., & d'Apollonia, S. (2001). Small group and individual learning with technology: A meta-analysis. *Review of Educational Research, 71*(3), 449–521.

Lyons, R. E. (2003). *Success strategies for adjunct faculty.* Needham Heights, MA: Allyn & Bacon.

Macdonald, J. (2004). Developing competent e-learners: The role of assessment [Electronic version]. *Assessment & Evaluation in Higher Education, 29*(2), 215–226.

Macdonald, R., & Carroll, J. (2006). Plagiarism—a complex issue requiring a holistic in-stitutional approach. *Assessment and Evaluation in Higher Education, 31*(2), 233–245.

MacKnight, C. B. (2000). Teaching critical thinking through online discussion. *Educause Quarterly, 23*(4), 38–41.

Malik, D. J. (1996). Peer review of teaching: External review of course content. *Innovative Higher Education, 20*(4), 277–286.

Marable, M. (1992). *Black America.* Westfield, NJ: Open Media.

Martin, R. A., Puhlik-Doris, P., Larsen, G., Gray, J., & Weir, K. (2003). Individual differ-ences in uses of humor and their relation to psychological well-being: Development of the humor styles questionnaire. *Journal of Research in Personality, 37*(1), 48–75.

Martyn, M. (2003). The hybrid online model: Good practice. *Educause Quarterly, 26*(1), 18–23.

Maslach, C. (2003). Job burnout: New directions in research and intervention. *Current Directions in Psychological Science, 12*(5), 189–192.

Maslach, C., & Jackson, S. (1986). *Maslach burnout inventory manual.* Palo Alto, CA: Con-sulting Psychologists Press.

Massy, W. F. (2005). Academic audit for accountability and improvement. In J. C. Burke & Associates (Eds.), *Achieving accountability in higher education: Balancing public, academic, and market demands* (pp. 173–197). San Francisco: Jossey-Bass.

Matthews, R. S., Cooper, J. L., Davidson, N., & Hawkes, P. (1995). Building bridges be-tween cooperative and collaborative learning. *Change, 27*(4), 35–40.

McKeachie, W. J., & Svinicki, M. (2006). *McKeachie's teaching tips: Strategies, research, and theory for college and university teachers* (12th ed.). Boston: Houghton Mifflin.

McKeever, L. (2006). Online plagiarism detection services—savior or scourge? [Electronic version]. *Assessment & Evaluation in Higher Education, 31*(2), 155–165.

McLuhan, M. (1962). *The Gutenberg galaxy.* Toronto: University of Toronto Press.

McLuhan, M. (1964). *Understanding media: The extensions of man.* New York: McGraw-Hill.

McMillan, D. W., & Chavis, D. M. (1986). Sense of community: A definition and theory. *Journal of Community Psychology, 14*(1), 6–23.

Meister, J. C. (1998). *Corporate universities—Lessons in building a world-class workforce.* New York: McGraw Hill.

Mendoza, M. (2001). *The global digital divide: Exploring the relation between core national computing and national capacity and progress in human development over the last decade.* Unpublished doctoral dissertation, Tulane University.

Merriam, S. B., & Caffarella, R. S. (1999). *Learning in adulthood: A comprehensive guide* (2nd ed.). San Francisco: Jossey-Bass.

Mezirow, J. (1991). *Transformative dimensions of adult learning.* San Francisco: Jossey-Bass.

Mills, M., & Hyle, A. (1999). Faculty evaluation: A prickly pear. *Higher Education, 38,* 351–371.

Minorities in higher education: Twenty-second annual status report. (2006). Washington, DC: American Council on Education.

Mintzberg, H. (1994). *The rise and fall of strategic planning: Reconceiving roles for planning, plans, planners.* New York: Free Press.

Moore, J. C. (Ed.). (2002). *Elements of quality: The Sloan-C framework.* Needham, MA: Sloan Center for Online Education.

Moore, M. G. (1989). Editorial: Three types of interaction [Electronic version]. *American Journal of Distance Education, 3*(2), 1–6.

Moore, M. G., & Kearsley, G. (2005). *Distance education: A systems view* (2nd ed.). Belmont, CA: Wadsworth.

Morey, A. (2001). The growth of for-profit higher education. *Journal of Teacher Education, 52*(4), 300–311.

Morse, K. (2003). Does one size fit all? Exploring asynchronous learning in a multicultural environment [Electronic version]. *Journal of Asynchronous Learning Networks, 7*(1), 37–55.

Morse, R. J., & Flanigan, S. (2004, May). *America's best college rankings: A look back and a look ahead at plans for 2004: U.S. News and World Report.* Paper presented at the meeting of the Association of Institutional Researchers, Boston, MA.

Mupinga, D. M., Nora, R. T., & Yaw, D. C. (2006). The learning styles, expectations, and needs of online students. *College Teaching, 54*(1), 185–189.

National Center for Educational Statistics. (2006). *Adult Education Participation in 2004–05.* Retrieved February 6, 2007, from http://nces.ed.gov/pubs2006/adulted/tables/table_16.asp?referrer=report

Neumann, R. (2000). Communicating student evaluation of teaching results: Rating interpretation guides (RIGs). *Assessment & Evaluation in Higher Education, 25*(2), 121–134.

Neumann, Y., Finaly-Neumann, E., & Reichel, A. (1990). Determinants and consequences of students' burnout in universities. *Journal of Higher Education, 61*(1), 20–31.

Nielsen, J. (2000). *Designing Web usability: The practice of simplicity.* Indianapolis, IN: New Riders.

Noddings, N. (2003). *Caring: A feminine approach to ethics & moral education* (2nd ed.). Berkeley: University of California Press.

Nova, N. (2003). *Socio-cognitive functions of space in collaborative settings: A literature review about space, cognition and collaboration.* Retrieved March 14, 2007, from http://tecfa.unige.ch/~nova/CRAFT_report1.pdf

Oblinger, D. G. (1997). High tech takes the high road: New players in higher education. *Educational Record, 78*(1), 30–37.

Oblinger, D. G., Barone, C. A., & Hawkins, B. L. (2001). *Distributed education and its challenges: An overview.* American Council on Education (ACE) and Educause. Retrieved July 30, 2007, from http://www.acenet.edu/bookstore/pdf/distributed-learning/distributed-learning-01.pdf

Oddi, L. F. (1987). Perspectives on self-directed learning. *Adult Education Quarterly, 38*(1), 21–31.

Ogawa, R., & Bossert, S. (1995). Leadership as an organizational quality. *Educational Administration Quarterly, 31*(2), 224–243.

Olcott, D., Jr., & Wright, S. J. (1995). An institutional support framework for increasing faculty participation in postsecondary distance education [Electronic version]. *American Journal of Distance Education, 9*(3), 5–17.

O'Meara, K. (2001). The impact of consumerism, capitalism, and for-profit competition on American higher education. *International Higher Education* (Winter). Chestnut Hill, MA: Boston College. Retrieved August 22, 2007, from http://www.bc.edu/bc_org/avp/soe/cihe/newsletter/News22/text002.htm

Organisation for Economic Co-Operation and Development. (2004). *Quality and recognition in higher education: The cross-border challenge.* Paris: Author.

Ory, J., Bullock, C. D., & Burnaska, K. K. (1997). Gender similarity in the use of and attitudes about ALN in a university setting [Electronic version]. *Journal of Asynchronous Learning Networks, 1*(1), 39–51.

Palloff, R., & Pratt, K. (1999). *Building learning communities in cyberspace.* San Francisco: Jossey-Bass.

Palmer, J. (1994). *Taking humour seriously.* London: Routledge.

Palmer, P. J. (1998). *The courage to teach: Exploring the inner landscape of a teacher's life.* San Francisco: Jossey-Bass.

Pardey, D. (1991). *Marketing for schools.* London: Kogan Page.

Paulsen, M. F. (1995). *The online report on pedagogical techniques for computer-mediated communication.* Retrieved February 26, 2007, from http://www.nettskolen.com/forskning/19/cmcped.html

Pew Internet & American Life Project. (2006a). *Internet penetration and impact.* Washington, DC: Author. Retrieved February 6, 2007, from http://www.pewInternet.org/pdfs/PIP_Internet_Impact.pdf

Pew Internet & American Life Project (2006b). *Demographics of Internet users.* Washington, DC: Author. Retrieved July 30, 2007, from http://www.pewInternet.org/trends.asp

Phinney, J. S. (1996). When we talk about American ethnic groups, what do we mean? *American Psychologist, 51*(9), 918–927.

Phipps, R., & Merisotis, J. (2000). Quality on the line: Benchmarks for success in Internet-based distance education. Washington, DC: The Institute for Higher Education Policy. Retrieved June 14, 2007, from http://www.ihep.com/Pubs/PDF/Quality.pdf

Pieper, S. L., Fulcher, K. H., Morrow, A. K., & Thelk, A. D. (2002). Assessment and measurement: Exactly right for student learning [Electronic version]. *Assessment Update, 14*(4), 4–14.

Ponton, M. K., & Carr, P. B. (2000). Understanding and promoting autonomy in self-directed learning. *Current Research in Social Psychology, 5*(19). Retrieved March 15, 2007, from http://www.uiowa.edu/~grpproc/crisp/crisp.5.19.htm

Posavac, E. J., & Carey, R. G. (2002). *Program evaluation: Methods and case studies* (6th ed.). Englewood Cliffs, NJ: Prentice-Hall.

Postmes, T., Spears, R., & Lea, M. (1998). Breaching or building social boundaries? SIDE-effects of computer-mediated communication. *Communication Research, 25*(6), 689–715.

Postmes, T., Spears, R., Sakhel, K., & De Groot, D. (2001). Social influences in computer-mediated communication: The effects of anonymity on group behavior. *Personality and Social Psychology Bulletin, 27,* 1242–1254.

Prensky, M. (2001). Digital natives, digital immigrants. *On the Horizon, 9*(5), 1–6.

Press, E., & Washburn, J. (2000). The kept university. *The Atlantic Monthly, 285*(3), 39–54.

Proust, M. (1960). *Time regained* (S. Hudson, Trans.). London: Chatto & Windus. (Original work published 1927).

Reiser, R. A., & Dempsey, J. V. (2007). *Trends and issues in instructional design* (2nd ed.). Upper Saddle River, NJ: Pearson Education.

Resnick, L. B., & Klopfer, L. E. (1989). Toward the thinking curriculum: An overview. In L. B. Resnick & L. E. Klopfer (Eds.), *Toward the thinking curriculum: Current cognitive research—1989 ASCD yearbook* (pp. 1–18). Alexandria, VA: Association for Supervision and Curriculum Development.

Rhoades, G. (2006). The higher education we choose: A question of balance. *Review of Higher Education, 29*(3), 381–404.

Roberts, T. G., Irani, T. A., Telg, R. W., & Lundy, L. K. (2005). The development of an instrument to evaluate distance education courses using student attitudes [Electronic version]. *American Journal of Distance Education, 19*(1), 51–64.

Roosevelt, G. (2006). The triumph of the market and the decline of liberal education: Implications for civic life. *Teachers College Record, 108*(7), 1404–1423.

Rossi, P. H., Lipsey, M. W., & Freeman, H. E. (2003). *Evaluation: A systematic approach* (7th ed.). Newbury Park, CA: Sage.

Rovai, A. P. (2000). Online and traditional assessments: What is the difference? *The Internet and Higher Education, 3*(2000), 141–151.

Rovai, A. P. (2001). Building classroom community at a distance: A case study. *Educational Technology Research and Development, 49*(4), 35–50.

Rovai, A. P. (2002). Building sense of community at a distance. *International Review of Research in Open and Distance Learning, 3*(1), 1–16.

Rovai, A. P. (2003). A practical framework for evaluating online distance education programs. *Internet & Higher Education, 6*(2), 109–124.

Rovai, A. P. (2007). Facilitating online discussions effectively. *Internet & Higher Education, 10*(1), 77–88.

Rovai, A. P., Gallien, L. B., Jr., & Stiff-Williams, H. R. (Eds.). (2007). *Closing the African American achievement gap in higher education.* New York: Teachers College Press.

Rovai, A. P., & Ponton, M. K. (2005). An examination of sense of classroom community and learning among African American and Caucasian graduate students. *Journal of Asynchronous Learning Networks, 9*(3), 77–92.

Rovai, A. P., Wighting, M. J., & Lucking, R. (2004). The classroom and school community inventory: Development, refinement, and validation of a self-report measure for educational research. *Internet & Higher Education, 7*(4), 263–280.

Rowley, D. J., Lujan, H. D., & Dolence, M. G. (1997). *Strategic change in colleges and universities.* San Francisco: Jossey-Bass.

Royal, M. A., & Rossi, R. J. (1997). *Schools as communities.* Eugene, OR: ERIC Clearinghouse on Educational Management. (ERIC Document Reproduction Service No. ED405641)

Salmon, G. (2004). *E-moderating. The key to teaching and learning online* (2nd ed.). London: RoutledgeFalmer.

Schroeder, C. (1999). Forging educational partnerships that advance student learning. In G. S. Blimling & E. J. Whitt (Eds.), *Good practice in student affairs: Principles to foster student learning* (pp. 133–156). San Francisco: Jossey-Bass.

Seldin, P. (Ed.). (2007). *Changing practices in evaluating teaching: A practical guide to improved faculty performance and promotion/tenure decisions.* San Francisco: Jossey-Bass.

Shadish, W. R., Cook, T. D., & Leviton, L. C. (1991). *Foundations of program evaluation.* Newbury Park, CA: Sage.

Sharan, Y., & Sharan, S. (1992). *Expanding cooperative learning through group investigation.* New York: Teachers College Press.

Sharp, A. (2004). The other dimension of caring thinking. *Critical & Creative Thinking, 12*(1), 9–14.

Shashaani, L. (1994). Gender-differences in computer experience and its influence on computer attitudes. *Journal of Educational Computing Research, 11*(4), 347–367.

Shea, P., Fredericksen, E., Pickett, A., Pelz, W., & Swan, K. (2001). Measures of learning effectiveness in the SUNY learning network. In J. Bourne & J. C. Moore (Eds.), *Online education, Volume 2: Learning effectiveness, faculty satisfaction and cost effectiveness* (pp. 31–54). Needham, MA: Sloan.

Sheldon, K. M., & Elliot, A. J. (1998). Not all personal goals are personal: Comparing autonomous and controlled reasons for goals as predictors of effort and attainment. *Personality and Social Psychology Bulletin, 24*(5), 546–557.

Singell, L. (2006). Saving higher education in the age of money. *Academe, 92*(1), 67–68.

Slaughter, S., & Leslie, L. L. (1997). *Academic capitalism: Politics, policies and the entrepreneurial university.* Baltimore, MD: Johns Hopkins University Press.

Slavin, R. E. (1989). Research on cooperative learning: An international perspective [Electronic version]. *Scandinavian Journal of Educational Research, 33*(4), 231–243.

Smerdon, B., Cronen, S., Lanahan, L., Anderson, J., Iannotti, N., Angeles, J., & Greene, B. (2000). *Teachers' tools for the 21st century: A report on teachers' use of technology.* Washington, DC: U.S. Department of Education, National Center for Education Statistics. Retrieved July 30, 2007, from http://nces.ed.gov/pubsearch/pubsinfo.asp?pubid=2000102

Smith, M. F. (1989). *Evaluability assessment: A practical approach.* Clemson: Kluwer Academic.

Solorzano, D. G., & Yosso, T. J. (2001). From racial stereotyping and deficit discourse toward a critical race theory in teacher education. *Multicultural Education, 9*(1), 2–8.

Southern Association of Colleges and Schools (SACS), Commission on Colleges. (2000, December). *Best practices for electronically offered degree and certificate programs.* Decatur, GA: Author.

Southern Association of Colleges and Schools (SACS), Commission on Colleges. (2006, December). *Distance education policy statement.* Decatur, GA: Author.

Spotts, T. H., Bowman, M. A., & Mertz, C. (1997). Gender and use of instructional technologies: A study of university faculty. *Higher Education, 34*(4), 421–436.

Stahl, G. (2006). *Group cognition: Computer support for building collaborative knowledge.* Cambridge, MA: MIT Press.

Stanley-Spaeth, B. (2000). *Taming Talos: Cyberfeminist pedagogy in classical studies.* Retrieved September 16, 2007, from http://www.tulane.edu/~spaeth/talosabstract.htm

Stansfield, M., McLellan, E., & Connolly, T. (2004). Enhancing student performance in online learning and traditional face-to-face class delivery. *Journal of Information Technology Education, 3,* 173–188.

Stephenson, J. (Ed.). (2001). *Teaching and learning online: Pedagogies for new technologies.* London: Kogan Page.

Stiggins, R. J. (1987). Design and development of performance assessments [Electronic version]. *Educational Measurement: Issues and Practice, 6*(3), 33–42.

Strain, J. (1987). The role of the faculty member in distance education [Electronic version]. *American Journal of Distance Education, 1*(2), 61–65.

Strijbos, J. W., Martens, R. L., & Jochems, W. M. G. (2004). Designing for interaction: Six steps to designing computer-supported group-based learning [Electronic version]. *Computers & Education, 42*(4), 403–424.

Strike, K. A. (2004). Community, the missing element of school reform: Why schools should be more like congregations than banks [Electronic version]. *American Journal of Education, 110*(3), 215–232.

Strosnider, K. (1998, January 23). For-profit higher education sees booming enrollments and revenues. *The Chronicle of Higher Education,* A36–A38. Retrieved July 30, 2007, from http://chronicle.com/che-data/articles.dir/art-44.dir/issue-20.dir/20a03601.htm

Suler, J. (2004). The online disinhibition effect [Electronic version]. *CyberPsychology & Behavior, 7*(3), 321–326.

Sutton, L. (2001). The principle of vicarious interaction in computer-mediated communications [Electronic version]. *International Journal of Educational Telecommunications, 7*(3), 223–242.

Tannen, D. (2001). *You just don't understand: Women and men in conversation.* New York: Harper.

Taylor, E. W. (1998). *The theory and practice of transformative learning: A critical review.* Information Series No. 374. Columbus: OH: ERIC Clearinghouse on Adult, Career, and Vocational Education, Center on Education and Training for Employment, College of Education, Ohio State University.

Taylor, C. S., & Nolen, S. B. (2008). *Classroom assessment: Supporting teaching and learning in real classrooms.* Upper Saddle River, NJ: Pearson.

Technology, Education and Copyright Harmonization Act, Report of the House Committee on the Judiciary, HR Rep. 107-687, 107th Cong., 2nd Sess. (2002).

Thompson, L. F., & Lynch, B. J. (2003). Web-based instruction: Who is inclined to resist it and why? *Journal of Educational Computing Research, 29*(3), 375–385.

Tinto, V. (1987). *Leaving college: Rethinking the causes and cures of student attrition.* Chicago: University of Chicago Press.

Tisdell, E. J. (2000). Feminist pedagogues. In E. Hayes & D. D. Flannery (Eds.), *Women as learners: The significance of gender in adult learning* (pp. 155–184). San Francisco: Jossey-Bass.

Tough, A. (1982). The other 80 percent of learning. In R. Gross (Ed.), *Invitation to lifelong learning* (pp. 153–157). Chicago: Follett.

Trentin, G. (2002). From distance education to virtual communities of practice: The wide range of possibilities for using the Internet in continuous education and training. *International Journal on E-Learning, 1*(1), 55–66.

Triandis, H. C., Chen, X. P., & Chan, D. K. (1998). Scenarios for the measurement of collectivism and individualism. *Journal of Cross-Cultural Psychology, 54*(2), 323–338.

Twigg, C. A. (2001). *Innovations in online learning: Moving beyond no significant difference.* Paper preseneted at the Pew Symposia in Learning and Technology (4th, Phoenix, AZ, December 8–9, 2000). Retrieved December 12, 2007, from http ://www. eric .ed.gov/ERICDocs/data/ericdocs2sql/content_storage_01/0000019b/80/1a /88/cl .pdf

U.S. Department of Commerce. (2000). *Falling through the net: Toward digital inclusion.* Washington, DC: U.S. Government Printing Office.

U.S. Department of Education. (2000). *1999–2000 national postsecondary student aid study* (NPSAS 2000). Washington, DC: National Center for Education Statistics.

U.S. Department of Education, Office of Postsecondary Education. (2006). *Evidence of quality in distance education programs drawn from interviews with the accreditation community.* Washington, DC: Author.

U.S. Department of Education. (2007). *Accreditation in the U.S.* Washington, DC: Author. Retrieved July 30, 2007, from http://www.ed.gov/admins/finaid/accred/accreditation_ pg2.html

Van Dusen, G. C. (2000). *Digital dilemma: Issues of access, cost, and quality in media-enhanced and distance education.* San Francisco: Jossey-Bass.

Vavrus, M. (2002). *Transforming the multicultural education of teachers: Theory, research and practice.* New York: Teachers College Press.

Villegas, A. M., & Lucas, T. (2002). Preparing culturally responsive teachers: Rethinking the curriculum. *Journal of Teacher Education, 53*(13), 20–32.

von Prümmer, C., & Rossié, U. (2001). Gender-sensitive evaluation research. In E. Burge & M. Haughey (Eds.), *Using learning technologies: International perspectives on practice* (pp. 135–144). New York: RoutledgeFalmer.

Wegerif, R. (1998). The social dimension of asynchronous learning networks [Electronic version]. *Journal of Asynchronous Learning Networks, 2*(1), 34–49.

Wenger, E. (1998). *Communities of practice: Learning, meaning and identity.* New York: Cambridge University Press.

Wholey, J. S. (1979). *Evaluation: Promise and performance.* Washington, DC: The Urban Institute.

Wholey, J. S. (1994). Assessing the feasibility and likely usefulness of evaluation. In K. E. Newcomer, H. P. Hatry, & J. S. Wholey (Eds.), *Handbook of practical program evaluation* (pp. 15–39). San Francisco: Jossey-Bass.

Wilkes, C. W., & Burnham, B. R. (1991). Adult learner motivations and electronic distance education [Electronic version]. *American Journal of Distance Education, 5*(1), 43–50.

Williams, K., Goldstein, D., & Goldstein, J. (2002). Improving the study habits of minority students through Web-based courses. *TechTrends, 46*(2), 21–28.

Willis, B. (1993). *Instructional development for distance education.* Syracuse, NY: Syracuse University.

Witkin, H. A., & Goodenough, D. R. (1981). *Cognitive styles, essence and origins: Field dependence and field independence.* New York: International Universities.

Wolfe, J. L. (1999). Why do women feel ignored? Gender differences in computer-mediated classroom interaction. *Computers and Composition, 16*(1), 153–166.

Wright, T. (2002). Cost, access, and quality in online nursing and allied health professions. *Journal of Asynchronous Learning Networks, 6*(2). Retrieved July 30, 2007, from http://www.aln.org/publications/jaln/v6n2/pdf/v6n2_wright.pdf

Young, J. R. (1998, March 13). For students with disabilities, the Web can be like a classroom without a ramp. *The Chronicle of Higher Education, 44*(27), A31. Retrieved August 10, 2007, from http://chronicle.com/che-data/articles.dir/art-44.dir/issue-27.dir/27a03101.htm

Zemsky, R., Wegner, G. R., & Massy, W. F. (2005). *Remaking the American university: Market-smart and mission-centered.* Piscataway, NJ: Rutgers University Press.

Zimmerman, B. J., Bonner, S., & Kovach, R. (1996). *Developing self-regulated learners: Beyond achievement to self-efficacy.* Washington, DC: American Psychological Association.

Index

About the Authors

Alfred P. (Fred) Rovai, a native of San Jose, California, received MS (education) and PhD (urban services with a concentration in academic leadership) degrees from Old Dominion University, an MA (public administration) degree from the University of Northern Colorado, and a BA (mathematics) degree from San Jose State University. He also completed postgraduate work in systems management at the University of Southern California, and possesses a postgraduate professional license in mathematics from the Commonwealth of Virginia. Professor Rovai presently teaches online courses in statistics, strategic planning, and program evaluation in blended EdD and PhD programs at the School of Education, Regent University, Virginia Beach, Virginia.

He has presented at national and international conferences on the topics of instructional technology and distance education, has authored more than 50 publications in scholarly journals, and has served on editorial review boards, including *Educational Technology Research and Development, Internet and Higher Education, International Review of Research in Open and Distance Learning,* and *Journal of Computing in Higher Education.* Additionally, he is co-editor of *Closing the African American Achievement Gap in Higher Education* (2007).

Michael K. Ponton is professor of education at Regent University, teaching primarily research-related courses in EdD and PhD programs. He has published extensively in the field of self-directed learning, where his research interests include adult learning, personal initiative, autonomous learning, and social cognitive theory. He serves on the editorial boards for the *International Journal of Self-Directed Learning* and *New Horizons in Adult Education and Human Resource Development.* Before coming to Regent University, he was associate professor of higher education at the University of Mississippi. Prior to entering academe full-time, he was an aerospace engineer for the National Aeronautics and Space Administration at the Langley Research Center.

Ponton holds an EdD degree in higher education administration and an MS degree in engineering, both from the George Washington University, and a BS degree in physics from Old Dominion University.

Jason D. Baker is an associate professor of education at Regent University, where he serves as the distance education advisor in the blended EdD program. He earned a BS degree in electrical engineering from Bucknell University, an MA degree in education from the George Washington University, and a PhD in communication from Regent University. Baker has authored or edited five Internet-related books and numerous publications and presentations related to online learning, and currently serves on four editorial review boards for academic journals interested in education and technology. Additionally, he has consulted with various organizations regarding the effective use of educational technology and the development and management of online learning programs.

DATE DUE

MAY 0 6 2011			